FOREIGN AFFAIRS

Volume 102, Number 3

The Nonaligned World

Cover illustration by Ed Johnson

Essays

Reviews and Responses

"Foreign Affairs . . . *will tolerate wide differences of opinion. Its articles will not represent any consensus of beliefs. What is demanded of them is that they shall be competent and well informed, representing honest opinions seriously held and convincingly expressed. . . . It does not accept responsibility for the views expressed in any article, signed or unsigned, which appear in its pages. What it does accept is the responsibility for giving them a chance to appear there.*"

Archibald Cary Coolidge, Founding Editor
Volume 1, Number 1 • September 1922

FOREIGN AFFAIRS

MAY/JUNE 2023 · VOLUME 102, NUMBER 3

Published by the Council on Foreign Relations

SUBSCRIPTION SERVICES: ForeignAffairs.com/services | support@ForeignAffairs.com
800-829-5539 U.S./Canada | 845-267-2017 All other countries | P.O. Box 324, Congers, NY 10920

ADVERTISING: Call Michael Pasuit at 212-434-9528 or visit ForeignAffairs.com/advertising

Foreign Affairs is a member of the Alliance for Audited Media and the Association of Magazine Media.
GST Number 127686483RT, Canada Post Customer #4015177 Publication #40035310

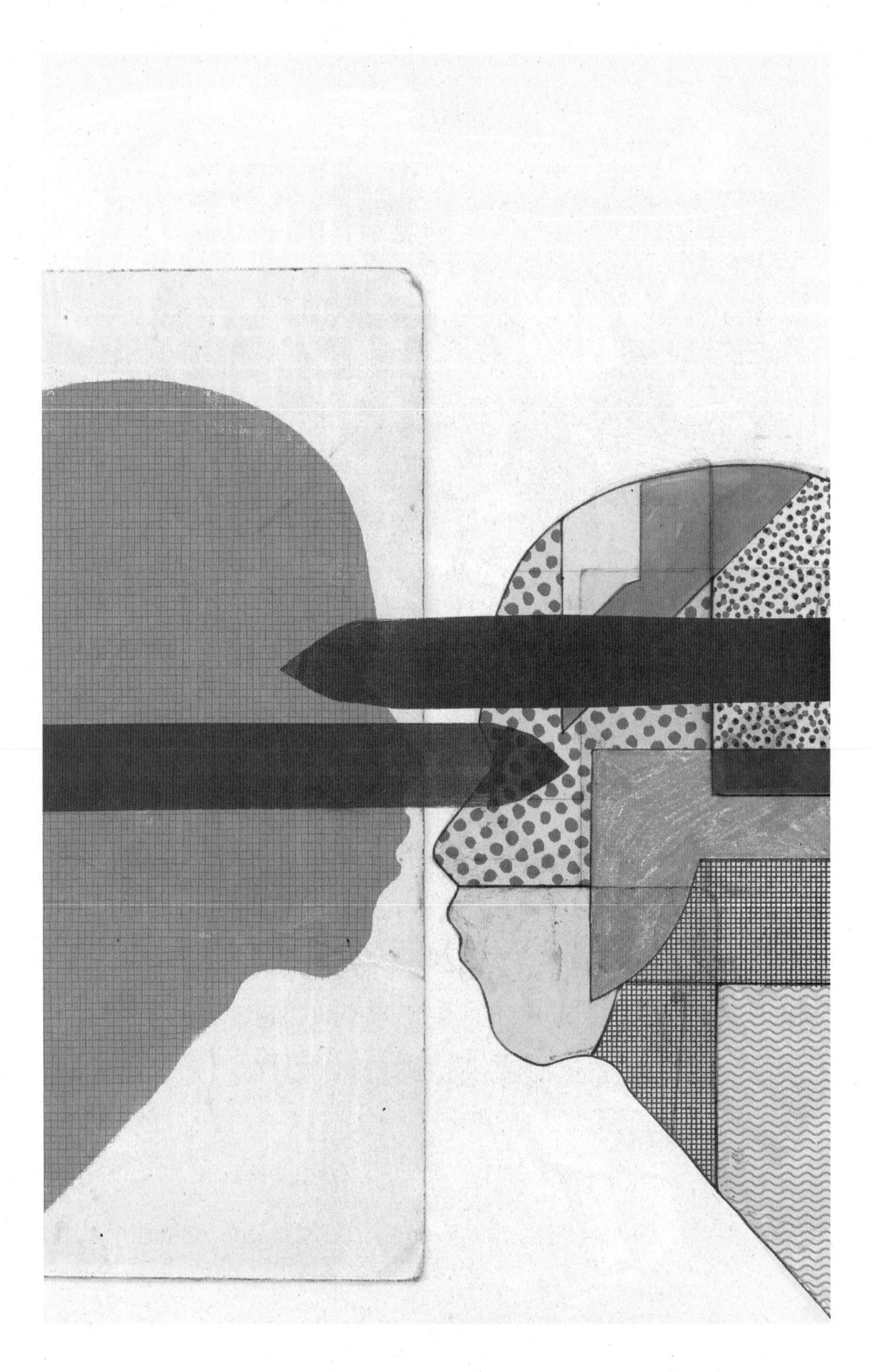

Illustrations by Kumé Pather

INTRODUCTION

The Nonaligned World

It was supposed to be a moment of solidarity, the "free world" standing as one against brutality and aggression. "The democracies of the world are revitalized with purpose and unity found in months that we'd once taken years to accomplish," U.S. President Joe Biden said shortly after the start of Russia's war in Ukraine. The months since have in many ways vindicated such proclamations: the United States and its allies in East Asia and Europe have demonstrated remarkably deep resolve and minimal dissension in their support of Kyiv.

But elsewhere, it's another story. The unity among Washington's closest partners has made clear just how differently much of the rest of the world sees not only the war in Ukraine but also the broader global landscape. Governments and populations across much of the developing world have met gauzy "free world" rhetoric with a series of increasingly vehement objections: about Western double standards and hypocrisy, about decades of neglect of the issues most important to them, about the mounting costs of the war and of sharpening geopolitical tensions.

In the essays that follow, policymakers and scholars from Africa, Latin America, and South and Southeast Asia explore the dangers, as well as the new opportunities, that the war and the broader return of great-power conflict present for their countries and regions. Whatever the merits of the individual arguments—on Ukraine, on geopolitics, on the international system—leaders cannot afford to disregard the resentments and interests animating them. If unaddressed, they will become a source of even greater challenge and disorder in the years ahead, no matter what happens on the ground in Ukraine.

In Defense of the Fence Sitters

What the West Gets Wrong About Hedging

MATIAS SPEKTOR

As countries in the global South refuse to take a side in the war in Ukraine, many in the West are struggling to understand why. Some speculate that these countries have opted for neutrality out of economic interest. Others see ideological alignments with Moscow and Beijing behind their unwillingness to take a stand—or even a lack of morals. But the behavior of large developing countries can be explained by something much simpler: the desire to avoid being trampled in a brawl among China, Russia, and the United States.

Across the globe, from India to Indonesia, Brazil to Turkey, Nigeria to South Africa, developing countries are increasingly seeking to avoid costly entanglements with the major powers, trying to keep all their options open for maximum flexibility. These countries are pursuing a strategy of hedging because they see the future distribution of global power as uncertain and wish to avoid commitments that will be hard to discharge. With limited resources with which to influence global politics, developing countries want to be able to quickly adapt their foreign policies to unpredictable circumstances.

In the context of the war in Ukraine, hedgers reason that it is too early to dismiss Russia's staying power. By invading its neighbor, Russia may have made a mistake that will accelerate its long-term decline, but the country will remain a major force to reckon with in the foreseeable future and a necessary player in negotiating an end to the war. Most countries in the global South also see a total Russian defeat as undesirable, contending that a broken Russia would open a power vacuum wide enough to destabilize countries far beyond Europe.

Western countries have been too quick to dismiss this rationale for neutrality, viewing it as an implicit defense of Russia or as an excuse to normalize aggression. In Washington and various European capitals, the global South's response to the war in Ukraine is seen as making an already difficult problem harder. But such frustrations with

---

MATIAS SPEKTOR is Professor of International Relations at Fundação Getulio Vargas in São Paulo, a Nonresident Scholar at the Carnegie Endowment for International Peace, and a Visiting Scholar at Princeton University.

hedgers are misguided—the West is ignoring the opportunity created by large developing countries' growing disillusionment with the policies of Beijing and Moscow. As long as these countries feel a need to hedge their bets, the West will have an opportunity to court them. But to improve relations with developing countries and manage the evolving global order, the West must take the concerns of the global South—on climate change, trade, and much else—seriously.

ONE FOOT IN

Hedging is not a new strategy. Secondary powers have long used it to manage risks. But in recent years, a growing number of influential states from the postcolonial world have embraced this approach. Indian Prime Minister Narendra Modi, for example, has developed strong diplomatic and commercial ties with China, Russia, and the United States simultaneously. For Modi, hedging acts as an insurance policy. Should conflict erupt among the major powers, India could profit by aligning with the most powerful side or joining a coalition of weaker states to deter the strongest one.

As a strategy for managing a multipolar world, hedging entails keeping the channels of communication open with all the players. This is easier said than done. Under President Luiz Inácio Lula da Silva, for example, Brazil has condemned Russia's unlawful invasion of Ukraine but has also declined European requests to send military equipment to Kyiv. Lula reasoned that refusing to criticize Moscow would impede dialogue with U.S. President Joe Biden, and selling weapons to the Western coalition would undermine his ability to talk to Russian President Vladimir Putin. As a result, Brazilian officials have made boilerplate calls for an end to the fighting without doing anything that might trigger a backlash from either Washington or Moscow.

Hedging can be difficult to sustain over time, and a state's ability to do so often depends on its domestic politics. Political constituencies can jeopardize hedging strategies when their economic interests are at stake. In 2019, for example, Lula's predecessor, Jair Bolsonaro, sought to counterbalance Brazil's growing dependence on China by courting support from U.S. President Donald Trump. In response, the powerful farming caucus in the Brazilian Congress stopped Bolsonaro in his tracks, anticipating that farmers would lose market access in China if the president pressed ahead with his pivot.

Hedging also inevitably involves disappointing allies when national interests are at stake. For instance, Turkish President Recep Tayyip Erdogan has publicly affirmed support for Ukraine's territorial integrity and sent Kyiv humanitarian aid. But his government has avoided being drawn into the conflict, despite Turkey being a NATO member with strong and valuable ties to the United States and the EU. Erdogan recognizes that Turkey cannot afford to alienate Russia because Moscow wields influence over areas of major interest to Ankara, including the Caucasus, Nagorno-Karabakh, and Syria.

Hedgers are wary of economic interdependence because it weakens their sovereignty. As a result, they

seek to strengthen domestic markets and national self-reliance, promoting industrialization and building up vital sectors such as transportation, energy, and defense. This has been the approach taken by Southeast Asia's largest economy. Indonesia under President Joko Widodo has courted Chinese and Western investment to reverse two decades of deindustrialization. Because taking sides in the war in Ukraine could jeopardize these plans, he has studiously sought to stand above the fray. In 2022, he was one of only a few world leaders to have met with Biden, Putin, Chinese President Xi Jinping, and Ukrainian President Volodymyr Zelensky.

Since hedgers value freedom of action, they may form partnerships of convenience to pursue specific foreign policy objectives, but they are unlikely to forge general alliances. This differentiates today's hedgers from nonaligned countries during the Cold War. Amid the bipolar competition of that era, nonaligned developing states rallied around a shared identity to demand greater economic justice, racial equality, and the end of colonial rule. To that end, they formed enduring coalitions in multilateral institutions. By contrast, hedging today is about avoiding the pressure to choose between China, Russia, and the United States. It is a response to the rise of a new, multipolar world.

DO AS I SAY, NOT AS I DO

For countries in the global South, hedging is not just a way to extract material concessions. The strategy is informed by these countries' histories with the great powers and their conviction that the United States, in particular, has been hypocritical in its dealings with the developing world. Consider the reaction of many in the global South to a speech by U.S. Vice President Kamala Harris at the Munich Security Conference in February. Harris told an audience of Western leaders that Russia's atrocities were "an attack on our common humanity." She described the horrors of war and the forced deportation of hundreds of thousands of Ukrainians, some of whom were separated from their children. "No nation is safe in a world where . . . a country with imperialist ambitions can go unchecked," she added. Ukraine, Harris declared, should be seen as a test for the "international rules-based order."

Across the global South, leaders know that Russia's behavior in Ukraine has been barbaric and inhumane. Yet from their vantage point, Harris's speech only underscored Western hypocrisy. As the Chilean diplomat Jorge Heine pointed out, the United States cannot expect other countries to sanction Russia for its brutality in Ukraine when Washington is supplying weapons to Saudi Arabia for its proxy war against Iran in Yemen, which has resulted in the unlawful killing of thousands of civilians, the destruction of a rich cultural heritage, and the displacement of millions of people. The moral high ground requires consistency between values and actions.

Furthermore, most countries in the global South find it difficult to accept Western claims of a "rules-based order" when the United States and its allies frequently violate the rules—committing atrocities in their various wars,

mistreating migrants, dodging internationally binding rules to curb carbon emissions, and undermining decades of multilateral efforts to promote trade and reduce protectionism, for instance. Western calls for developing nations to be "responsible stakeholders" ring hollow in much of the global South.

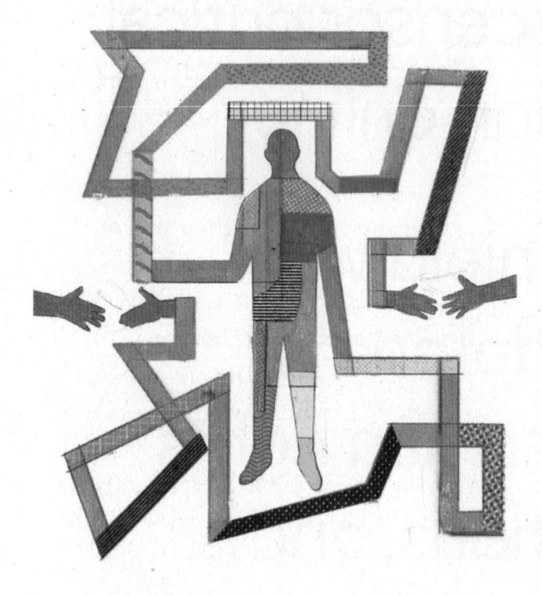

The developing world also sees hypocrisy in Washington's framing of its competition with Beijing and Moscow as a battle between democracy and autocracy. After all, the United States continues to selectively back authoritarian governments when it serves U.S. interests. Of the 50 countries that Freedom House counts as "dictatorships," 35 received military aid from the U.S. government in 2021. It should be no surprise, then, that many in the global South view the West's pro-democracy rhetoric as motivated by self-interest rather than a genuine commitment to liberal values.

As frustrating as it is to countries in the global South, Western hypocrisy has an upside: it gives developing countries a lever they can pull to effect change. Because the United States and its European allies appeal to moral principles to justify many of their decisions, third parties can publicly criticize them and demand reparation when those principles are inconsistently applied. Developing countries have no such leverage over China and Russia since neither couches its foreign policy preferences in terms of universal moral values.

THE MORE, THE MERRIER?

Many in the West associate a multipolar world order with conflict and instability, preferring a dominant United States, as was the case after the collapse of the Soviet Union. Not so among countries in the global South, where the prevailing view is that multipolarity could serve as a stable foundation for international order in the twenty-first century.

Part of this reasoning is informed by recent memory. People in developing countries remember the post–Cold War unipolar moment as a violent time—with wars in Afghanistan, the Balkans, and Iraq. Unipolarity also coincided with the unsettling influx of global capital into eastern Europe, Latin America, and Southeast Asia. As the scholar Nuno Monteiro warned, when U.S. hegemony is unchecked, Washington becomes capricious, picking fights against recalcitrant states or letting peripheral regional conflicts fester.

Memories of bipolarity in the global South are no better. From the perspective of many developing countries, the Cold War was cold only in that it did not lead to an earth-extinguishing confrontation between two nuclear-armed superpowers. Outside Europe and North America, the second half of the twentieth century was red hot, with political violence spreading across and within many countries. Bipolarity was not marked by stable competition along the Iron Curtain but by bloody superpower interventions in the peripheries of the globe.

Yet hedgers from the global South are optimistic about multipolarity for reasons beyond history. One prevalent belief is that a diffusion of power will give developing countries more breathing space since intense security competition among the great powers will make it harder for the strong to impose their will on weaker states. Another common view is that rivalries among the great powers will make them more responsive to appeals for justice and equality from smaller states, since the strong must win the global South's favor to compete with their rivals. A third view is that diffuse power will open opportunities for small states to voice their opinions in international institutions, such as the United Nations and the World Trade Organization. When they do, global institutions will begin to reflect a wider range of perspectives, increasing the overall legitimacy of these international bodies.

But such optimism about the prospects of a multipolar order may be unwarranted. Security competition in multipolar systems may push the great powers to create stricter hierarchies around them, limiting chances for smaller states to express their preferences. For example, the United States has cajoled many countries into pushing back against Chinese influence, shrinking their freedom of action. Furthermore, the great powers might act in concert to repress calls for justice and equality from smaller countries, as the so-called Holy Alliance among Austria, Prussia, and Russia did in the nineteenth century, when it quashed nationalist and liberal grassroots movements across Europe. In the past, great powers have maintained their authority by excluding and imposing their will on others. The victors of World War II, for example, appointed themselves as the five permanent members of the UN Security Council, cementing their power within multilateral institutions. It is far from obvious that developing countries will fare better under multipolarity than they did under previous global orders.

RISE OF THE MIDDLEMEN

The prevalence of hedging among the major countries of the global South presents both a challenge and an opportunity for the United States. The challenge is that hedging could magnify security competition among Beijing, Moscow, and Washington, as developing countries play the three great powers off one another. As a result, the United States may need to offer more concessions than it has in the past to persuade developing countries to cooperate and strike bargains.

The opportunity for Washington is that hedgers are unlikely to permanently join forces with Beijing or Moscow. Across the global South, moreover, people are increasingly open to engagement with the West. The populations of most developing countries are young, energetic, and impatient, striving to create a world order in which they can thrive. Among the global South's cultural and economic elites and grassroots movements, influential voices are pushing for progressive reforms that could provide a foundation for cooperation with the West.

To win friends in a multipolar world, the United States should start taking the concerns of the global South more seriously. Adopting a condescending stance or, worse, shutting these countries out of the conversation entirely is a recipe for trouble. Major developing countries are not only indispensable partners in tackling climate change and preventing global economic turmoil but also in managing China's rise and Russia's reassertion of power.

Engaging these countries will take humility and empathy on the part of U.S. policymakers, who are not used to either. Crucially, the United States should pay close attention to the global South's grievances with China. Rather than pressuring countries to sever ties with Beijing, Washington should quietly encourage them to test the limits of Chinese friendship for themselves. Developing countries increasingly recognize that China can be just as much of a bully as established Western powers.

The United States must also drop the expectation that the global South will automatically follow the West. Large and influential developing countries can never be true insiders in the liberal international order. They will, therefore, seek to pursue their own interests and values within international institutions and contest Western understandings of legitimacy and fairness.

But the West and the global South can still cooperate. History provides a guide. For the better part of the twentieth century, postcolonial countries challenged the West on a number of issues, pushing for decolonization, racial equality, and economic justice. Relations were tense. Yet a commitment to diplomacy ensured that the West and the developing world could jointly benefit from international norms and institutions governing topics as varied as trade, human rights, navigation of the seas, and the environment. Today, the West and the global South do not need to aim for total consensus, but they should work together to reach mutually beneficial outcomes.

One promising area for cooperation is adaptation to and mitigation of climate change. The United States and EU countries have made rapid progress within their own borders, opening a window of opportunity for engaging large developing states. Another area ripe for partnership between the West and the global South is international trade, an arena in which more balanced relationships are possible.

The countries of the global South are poised to hedge their way into the mid-twenty-first century. They hedge not only to gain material concessions but also to raise their status, and they embrace multipolarity as an opportunity to move up in the international order. If it wants to remain first among the great powers in a multipolar world, the United States must meet the global South on its own terms.

The Upside of Rivalry

India's Great-Power Opportunity

NIRUPAMA RAO

For China, Russia, and the West, the last year has been one of fear and conflict. Russia's invasion of Ukraine has killed tens of thousands, perhaps even hundreds of thousands, of people. It has prompted the United States and Europe to rearm and has pushed Moscow and Washington back into Cold War–style competition. In the Pacific, China and the United States are eyeing each other with increasing hostility and suspicion, and some U.S. analysts believe that the countries could wind up at war over Taiwan. These dangers prompted U.S. President Joe Biden to declare that the world is at risk of annihilation for the first time since the Cuban missile crisis. In a speech from Moscow, Russian President Vladimir Putin said the 2020s are "the most dangerous decade" since the end of World War II.

But thousands of miles away, in the world's second-largest country, the global outlook is very different. As India prepares to hold the G-20's 18th summit, the government has put up signs and posters across the country that speak about international harmony. In announcing India's G-20 vision, Indian Prime Minister Narendra Modi wrote that his country would catalyze a new mindset within humanity, help the world move beyond greed and confrontation, and cultivate a "universal sense of one-ness." The theme, Modi said, was "One Earth, One Family, One Future." Rather than war and rivalry, the prime minister declared, the greatest challenges humanity faces today are climate change, terrorism, and pandemics—issues that "can be solved not by fighting each other, but only by acting together."

To Western officials, these hymns to cooperation and shared challenges surely sound off-key. But India has limited patience for U.S. and European narratives, which are both myopic and hypocritical. The divisions of the Cold War have not been revived; instead, today's world is a complex network of interconnections where trade, technology, migration, and the Internet are bringing humans together as never before. Europe and Washington may be right that Russia is violating human rights in Ukraine, but

---

NIRUPAMA RAO was India's Foreign Secretary from 2009 to 2011. She also served as India's Ambassador to China and the United States. She is the author of *The Fractured Himalaya: India, Tibet, China, 1949–1962*.

Western powers have carried out similarly violent, unjust, and undemocratic interventions—from Vietnam to Iraq. New Delhi is therefore uninterested in Western calls for Russia's isolation. To strengthen itself and address the world's shared challenges, India has the right to work with everyone.

This perspective isn't unique to New Delhi. Much of the global South is wary of being dragged into siding with the United States against China or Russia. Developing countries are understandably more concerned about their climate vulnerability, their access to advanced technology and capital, and their need for better infrastructure, health care, and education systems. They see increasing global instability—political and financial alike—as a threat to tackling such challenges. And they have watched rich and powerful states disregard these views and preferences in pursuit of their geopolitical interests. For example, the aggressive economic sanctions imposed by wealthy countries on Russia have generated costs, including higher food prices, for people who are far removed from the war in Ukraine. India wants to make sure the voices of these poorer states are heard in international debates, so it is positioning itself as a heartland of the global South—a bridging presence that stands for multilateralism.

For New Delhi, fostering cooperation will not be easy. The invasion of Ukraine may not have fractured the world, but the longer the conflict lasts, the harder it will be for India to work with both Moscow and Washington. India has also come under criticism from some international politicians for what they believe is democratic backsliding. These politicians have protested, in particular, New Delhi's 2019 decision to revoke Kashmir's special status under the Indian constitution, the government's arrest of journalists and civil society activists, and anti-Muslim violence in parts of the country. And India is feuding with—and primed to fight—China over where the two countries' Himalayan border lies.

But if New Delhi can successfully navigate this complex moment and collaborate with China, Russia, and the West, the benefits will be enormous—both for India and for the developing states it champions. India is home to more than 1.4 billion people and a rapidly growing economy. It trades with and has managed to maintain good relations with almost every country. That means India has the potential to spread growth and foster dialogue across the world, even when global tensions are running high.

GO YOUR OWN WAY

To New Delhi, neutrality is nothing new. "We are not pro-Russian, nor for that matter are we pro-American," said Jawaharlal Nehru, India's first prime minister. "We are pro-Indian." Setting the tone for many future Indian foreign policy statements, he continued, "I am on my own side and nobody else's." Nehru made good on these words. During his 17 years in power, he helped craft an explicit policy of nonalignment, one that many other postcolonial states adopted. For India, at least, the strategy worked. New Delhi steered a course through the Cold War that kept it from becoming entrapped in the proxy wars that plagued so many other countries.

Today, the country is experiencing a nationalistic upsurge that marks the India of Modi. The median age of India's population is around 28 years, one of the youngest on the planet. The Indian economy has expanded steadily over the last three decades, even during the pandemic. Among large economies, it now ranks as the world's fastest growing.

Given all these advantages, it is little surprise that India has become an independent pole of global power and a leader among developing countries. It has used this position to emphasize a different set of priorities from those of the West. Speaking at the Voice of the Global South virtual summit convened by India in January, Modi said that all developing states had encountered similar challenges in the last three years, such as rising prices for fuel, fertilizer, and food as well as increasing geopolitical tensions that have affected their economies. "Developing countries desire a globalization that does not create climate crisis or debt crisis" or an "unequal distribution of vaccines or over-concentrated global supply chains," Modi declared. He called for fundamental reforms to major international organizations, including the UN Security Council and international financial institutions such as the International Monetary Fund, so that they will better represent the global South. New Delhi has also promised to provide its digital, nuclear, and space technology—such as its highly successful countrywide electronic payments interface—to other developing states.

India is the third-largest producer of pharmaceuticals in the world, and its Vaccine Maitri (or Vaccine Friendship) program has distributed over 235 million doses of COVID-19 vaccines to 98 lower-income countries. It is a founding member of the International Solar Alliance and is working to transport solar energy across borders. India has also generally expanded its grant assistance, lines of credit, technical consulting, disaster relief, humanitarian aid, educational scholarships, and other programs for global South countries. The biggest recipients include Bangladesh, Bhutan, the Maldives, Nepal, and Sri Lanka, in line with India's Neighborhood First policy. But there are also recipients in Africa, Central and Southeast Asia, Latin America, and Oceania. Indeed, India has extended $12.35 billion in credit to African countries alone.

New Delhi's efforts have not been received as warmly in the global North. Russia's invasion of Ukraine has tested the rules-based international order, and India's carefully orchestrated neutrality has frustrated the United States and European countries. Its refusal to speak up in Kyiv's favor has brought it under intense scrutiny and questioning by friends and partners in the West.

But India, rightfully, sees these critiques as hypocritical. The West routinely cut deals with violent autocracies to advance its own interests. The United States, for instance, is improving ties with Venezuela to get more oil. Europe is signing energy contracts with repressive Arab Gulf regimes. Remarkably, the West nonetheless claims that its foreign policy is guided by human rights and democracy. India, at least, lays no claim to being the conscience-keeper of the world. Like any other state, it acts in accordance with its interests—and severing its partnership with Russia would harm them.

India's relationship with Russia has deep roots stretching back to the Cold War, and both countries refer to their ties as "special and privileged." New Delhi relies on Moscow for roughly 60 percent of its defense equipment, and over the years, Russia has offered India advanced weapons technologies (for which India pays top dollar). Moscow has also become an important source of cheap energy for India, which is importing oil from Russia at heavy discounts.

India has other, less technical reasons not to join the fight against Moscow. The country wants Russia to maintain some distance from China, and it worries that isolating Moscow would just push it closer to Beijing. Despite the battlefield setbacks, Russia is still a global power of consequence—with a military footprint that extends across continents and a United Nations Security Council veto—that can help prevent a cold war between China and the United States. And although the West may like to think that Russia's invasion was entirely unprovoked, India understands that the war is not purely an imperial project. NATO was founded as an anti-Moscow alliance, and over the last 30 years, it has expanded right up to Russia's borders. Over the last ten, Western leaders have slapped all kinds of sanctions on Moscow. The Kremlin was right to think that Washington and Europe wanted to weaken Russia.

New Delhi's refusal to condemn Moscow does not mean that India supports Russia's invasion. The Kremlin has clearly contravened the principles of sovereignty and territorial integrity, international humanitarian law, and the precept of noninterference in other countries' internal affairs. But Russia is not the only state to violate these rules: the United States has also displayed a questionable commitment to sovereignty and noninterference. And India did not respond to Washington's past abuses with sanctions or acrimony. New Delhi instead continued doing business with the United States—even if it opposed the country's invasions—because doing so helped India and made it easier for the world to address shared challenges. New Delhi has every right to take the same approach with Moscow, no matter what the West says.

HAVE YOUR CAKE AND EAT IT, TOO

Indian public opinion is extremely sensitive to any badgering by Western governments, legislators, and media about New Delhi's sovereign decisions. But India still wants to have a solid relationship with Western countries, especially the United States—and for good reason. New Delhi wants to strengthen itself, and Washington is providing invaluable backing.

Consider, for example, the two countries' economic links. The United States is India's largest export destination and largest trading partner. The two countries' bilateral trade in goods surpassed $131 billion in 2022, and estimates suggest that their trade in goods and services crossed $190 billion last year. They are close technological partners, especially in cutting-edge industries such as semiconductors and nanotechnologies. American and Indian workers are together developing tools for space research and travel, speech recognition, and digital translation that will prove immeasurably useful when dealing with cross-border threats, insurgencies, and other security challenges.

This technological partnership is poised to deepen. In May 2022, Modi and Biden announced the creation of the U.S.-India initiative on Critical and Emerging Technology, which will bring together New Delhi, Washington, and both countries' private sectors to strengthen quantum communications, build a semiconductor ecosystem in India, explore commercial space opportunities, and collaborate on high-performance computers. In January 2023, the two governments' national security advisers agreed to a Defense Industrial Cooperation Roadmap to help produce better jet engines, munitions systems, maritime security tools, and intelligence, surveillance, and reconnaissance systems.

Some of this collaboration is driven by a sense of democratic affinity and economic opportunity. But a shared concern with China's rising power has created a special synergy between New Delhi and Washington. Over the last several years, India has found itself in repeated standoffs with Chinese forces along the border in the Himalayas, where both states claim thousands of square miles across their disputed frontier. China has also begun making increasingly bold incursions into what is unambiguously Indian territory, leading to multiple skirmishes. One of those fights, which took place in Ladakh in 2020, resulted in the death of 20 Indian soldiers.

Because China is more powerful than India, a good part of New Delhi's strategy for dealing with a belligerent Beijing runs through Washington. In the wake of the confrontation in

Ladakh, India has kept in close touch with the United States over the border situation. The two countries have exchanged intelligence, and Indian and U.S. troops have participated in high-altitude training exercises close to India's border, sending a clear signal to Beijing. Between 2008 and 2020, sales of defense supplies from the United States to India amounted to over $20 billion.

This security partnership is perhaps best illustrated by the two countries' participation in the Quadrilateral Security Dialogue, popularly known as the Quad. India has moved purposefully to revitalize its membership in the group, which also includes Australia and Japan and which Modi has termed "a force for good." New Delhi has eagerly embraced summit-level engagements within the Quad, where the top leadership of the four countries meet in person, as well as military-level meetings and joint exercises in the Indo-Pacific region. The Quad has also become a venue for a variety of other initiatives, including ones that improve cybersecurity, conduct disaster response, and advance infrastructural development.

India, of course, benefits from being a part of this organization. But its partnership is not a one-way street. India's geographic position, intelligence assets about Chinese activities in the neighborhood, and naval coverage of the area bring significant assets to the group. Its strong business and commercial networks are also beneficial for the United States and the Quad as a whole because they can help counter Chinese commercial interests in Africa and the Indian Ocean region. As U.S. Defense Secretary Lloyd Austin said in April 2022, India's cooperation in the pact creates a favorable balance of power in the Indo-Pacific. Indeed, it is a testament to India's sway and importance in the area that the Biden administration has largely accepted New Delhi's autonomous foreign policy even as it sporadically complains about its behavior regarding Russia's invasion of Ukraine.

But U.S. policymakers should not mistake India's Quad involvement for an alliance; New Delhi will not act as a balancer for Washington against Beijing. Instead, India is playing both sides in the U.S.-Chinese rivalry. India is a part of the Washington-led Quad but also the Beijing-led Shanghai Cooperation Organization. It routinely attends trilateral meetings with both China and Russia. It continues to actively participate in the multilateral forum known as BRICS, which stands for Brazil, Russia, India, China, and South Africa. India severed ambassadorial relations with China after the two states fought a war in 1962, but today, it keeps communication channels open with Beijing and with Chinese military commanders at the border. The two states regularly confer at the diplomatic and ministerial levels. India will host the G-20 this year, when its officials will frequently interact with their Chinese counterparts at meetings. Chinese President Xi Jinping is even expected to attend the summit in September.

Perhaps no issue better illustrates India's ability to both compete and cooperate with Beijing than trade. Washington is pushing hard for states to reduce their economic ties to China, and in sensitive sectors, India has worked to reduce its dependence on Chinese imports and investments. For instance, India has prevented Chinese companies such as Huawei and ZTE from providing equipment for 5G services in the country. And after a border clash in June 2020, India canceled railway and power project tenders that Chinese companies had effectively secured, and it barred the use of Chinese apps, including TikTok, on national security grounds. But China remains India's largest trading partner in goods, and India's business and trade relations with Beijing have been difficult to curtail. Last year, for example, the two countries traded $136 billion in goods alone, up 8.4 percent from 2021.

India's relationship with Taiwan also remains ambiguous. After Nancy Pelosi, then the U.S. House Speaker, visited the island in August 2022, New Delhi urged restraint and the avoidance of unilateral changes to the status quo in the region—sentiments that could be a critique of Pelosi's inflammatory trip but also of China's subsequent, provocative military maneuvers. India's business, investment, and trade ties with the island are flourishing. But New Delhi has steered clear of the kind of critical rhetoric or official visits to the island that have raised tensions between Beijing and Washington.

HIGH WIRE

So far, India has done an impressive job of maintaining its balancing act. Whether it can continue to do so in the years ahead is an open question. Beijing has become increasingly belligerent, and it may eventually decide it will not deal with India if New Delhi strengthens its security ties to Washington. China could similarly put more intense pressure on India on the Himalayan border, forcing New Delhi to adopt harsher anti-Chinese measures. As the war in Ukraine drags on, Russia may rely more on China, reducing Moscow's capacity to stop Beijing from pressuring New Delhi. Russia will also be increasingly constrained in its ability to sell defense equipment to the Indian armed forces. And a prolonged invasion could lead India to tussle more with Washington as the United States pushes harder for neutral states to come off the sidelines.

India could face other headwinds, as well. The country's economy is not free of regulatory bottlenecks, and its growth rate could decline—especially because of the slowing global economy and rising interest rates. A slowdown in exports or a decrease in consumer demand could also undermine India's economy. Transnational threats such as climate change may trigger developmental challenges and degrade human security, especially among economically vulnerable parts of India's population. New Delhi's historical struggle with Pakistan could flare up, diverting India's security resources away from China and back toward its western border. And Western concerns about what certain policymakers see as democratic backsliding in India could result in some U.S.-Indian estrangement.

But Indians have little patience for being hectored about their democracy, especially from a country where insurrectionists recently breached the capitol and where racial inequalities run deep. They do not have much tolerance for European critiques, either, given the continent's own harsh immigration policies and sordid colonial history. In fact, the government will not allow any outside powers to browbeat the country, especially when it is finding its sweet spot. Much as in during Nehru's time, India's self-interested foreign policy has earned it many partners and very few enemies despite worldwide turmoil. It is learning to punch above its weight and displaying a newfound confidence. It will not be stopped from asserting its international interests.

Order of Oppression

Africa's Quest for a New International System

TIM MURITHI

Following Russia's invasion of Ukraine last year, many African countries declined to take a strong stand against Moscow. Seventeen African states refused to vote for a UN resolution condemning Russia, and most countries on the continent have maintained economic and trade ties with Moscow despite Western sanctions. In response, the United States and other Western countries have berated African leaders for failing to defend the "rules based" international order, framing African neutrality in the Ukrainian conflict as a betrayal of liberal principles. During a trip to Cameroon in July 2022, French President Emmanuel Macron bemoaned the "hypocrisy" of African leaders and criticized them for refusing "to call a war a war and say who started it."

But the truth is that the rules-based international order has not served Africa's interests. On the contrary, it has preserved a status quo in which major world powers—be they Western or Eastern—have maintained their positions of dominance over the global South. Through the UN Security Council, in particular, China, France, Russia, the United Kingdom, and the United States have exerted outsize influence over African nations and relegated African governments to little more than bystanders in their own affairs. The British-, French-, and U.S.-led bombardment of Libya in 2011, justified by a contested interpretation of a UN Security Council resolution authorizing a no-fly zone, stands out as a case in point. Before NATO intervened, the African Union was pursuing a diplomatic strategy to de-escalate the crisis in Libya. But once the military operation began, the AU effort was rendered moot, and Libya was plunged into a cycle of violence and instability from which it has yet to escape.

For decades, African countries have called for the UN Security Council to be reformed and the broader international system to be reconfigured on more equitable terms. And for decades, their appeals have been ignored. The current global order, dominated by a few powerful countries that define peace and security as the imposition of their will on others, is now at an inflection point. More and more countries in Africa and elsewhere in the global South are refusing to align with either the West or the

---

TIM MURITHI is Head of Peacebuilding Interventions at the Institute for Justice and Reconciliation and Professor of African Studies at the University of Cape Town and Stellenbosch University in South Africa.

Please rush!

NO POSTAGE
NECESSARY
IF MAILED
IN THE
UNITED STATES

BUSINESS REPLY MAIL
FIRST-CLASS MAIL PERMIT NO. 354 CONGERS, NY

POSTAGE WILL BE PAID BY ADDRESSEE

FOREIGN
AFFAIRS

PO BOX 324
CONGERS NY 10920-9935

East, declining to defend the so-called liberal order but also refusing to seek to upend it as Russia and China have done. If the West wants Africa to stand up for the international order, then it must allow that order to be remade so that it is based on more than the idea that might makes right.

WHOSE ORDER?

For most of the last 500 years, the international order was explicitly designed to exploit Africa. The transatlantic slave trade saw more than ten million Africans kidnapped and shipped to the Americas, where their forced labor made elites in Europe and the United States exceptionally wealthy. European colonialism and apartheid rule were likewise brutal, extractive, and dehumanizing for Africans, and the legacies of these systems are still felt across the continent. The CFA franc, a relic of the colonial past that still gives France tremendous sway over the economies of 14 West African and central African countries, offers a daily reminder of this historical subjugation, as does the persistence of white economic power in South Africa. Both reinforce the perception that today's international order still treats Africans as global second-class citizens.

Many Western pundits are quick to demand that Africa "get over" these injustices and stop harping on the past. But African societies do not see the past as past. They see it as present, still looming large over the pan-African landscape. Moreover, the tormentors of yesteryear have not changed their mindsets and attitudes—just their rhetoric and methods. Instead of taking what they want with brute force, as they did in the past, major powers now rely on preferential trade deals and skewed financing arrangements to drain the continent of its resources, often with the collusion of corrupt African elites.

And of course, major powers still use force. Despite claiming to uphold an international system based on rules, these powers and their allies have frequently imposed their will on other countries, from the NATO bombardments of Yugoslavia and Libya to the U.S.-led invasions of Afghanistan and Iraq to the Russian invasions of Georgia and Ukraine. In 2014, the United States, the United Kingdom, and France led a military intervention in Syria in support of rebel forces, which was followed, in 2015, by a Russian military intervention in support of the Syrian government. Russia's 2022 invasion of Ukraine is not a departure from this pattern but a continuation of the reign of the powerful over the less powerful.

Major-power interventions have steadily eroded the pretense of a rules-based order and made the world much less stable. For instance, the illegal invasions of Iraq and Syria stoked violent extremist movements, including al Qaeda and the Islamic State (also known as ISIS), which have since spread like a virus across Africa. Thanks in part to the chaos spawned by NATO's intervention in Libya, Islamist terrorism has taken root across the Sahel region, affecting Burkina Faso, Chad, Mali, Mauritania, and Niger. Similarly, in East Africa, religious extremism imported from the Middle East is undermining stability in Kenya, Mozambique, Somalia, and Tanzania, all of which are terrorized by an extremist group known as al Shabab. These threats are not acutely felt in

Washington, London, Paris, Brussels, Moscow, or Beijing. Rather, they are faced by Africans who had little say in the interventions that ignited them.

The major powers have created a curious juxtaposition: on one hand, illegal interventions that have sowed terror across the global South, and on the other, international failures to intervene in humanitarian crises—in Rwanda in 1994, Srebrenica in 1995, Sri Lanka in 2009, and now in China, where more than a million Uyghurs have been imprisoned in camps. This discrepancy exposes the lie at the heart of today's international system. Those who continue to call for the protection of an illusionary rules-based order have evidently not been on the receiving end of an unsanctioned military incursion. Many Africans see these voices as part of the problem rather than part of the solution.

The myth of a functioning system of international norms that constrains the whims of nations must now be discarded. World powers must acknowledge what African countries have known for decades: that the dysfunctional international order poses a clear and present danger to many developing countries. The United Nations' system of collective security is slowly dying, suffocated by the egregious actions of some of its most powerful members. Not only does this system exclude a majority of the world's population from international decision-making, but it also often leaves them at the mercy of hostile powers and forces. It is past time to rethink and remake the global order. That does not necessarily mean throwing the UN baby out with the bath water, but it does mean reimagining multilateralism and redesigning international institutions to create a more effective global system of collective security.

A PAN-AFRICAN VISION

An African vision for global order would be based on the principle of equality and the need to redress historical wrongs. Africa's political and intellectual tradition draws on its experience as a freedom-seeking continent, deriving insights from the anticolonial and antiapartheid struggles. This emphasis on self-determination is evident in the work of many African governments to advance economic development, which is the ultimate form of empowerment. Solidarity among African states and societies helped sustain the campaigns against colonialism and apartheid in the twentieth century. Today, that sentiment underpins the AU and its Agenda 2063, a development plan that seeks to transform the continent into an economic powerhouse. And although the pan-African project remains a work in progress—and more must be done to consolidate democratic governance across the continent—it has much to teach the world.

Africa is constantly struggling for a more equitable global order. As targets of historical injustice, Africans are leading voices for justice—defined as fairness, equality, accountability, and redress for past harms. African societies have also shown the world how to promote reconciliation between warring groups and communities, most notably in South Africa. Africans are "reconciliactors," as they proved at independence. When the former colonial powers withdrew from Africa, Africans did not immediately retaliate against Europeans for the brutal and exploitative system that they imposed on the people of the continent.

This long record of pursuing peace and reconciliation gives Africans the moral authority to demand a reconfiguration of the global order. Indeed, segments of the African foreign-policy-making community are clamoring to reform the multilateral system, replacing an order based on might makes right with one grounded in the pursuit of self-determination, global solidarity, justice, and reconciliation. In particular, they are pushing to transform the UN system into something fairer and more consonant with Africa's own historical experiences.

THE NEW MULTILATERALISM

No institution epitomizes the paternalistic exclusion of Africa more than the UN Security Council. According to the nonprofit International Peace Institute, more than half of Security Council meetings and 70 percent of Security Council resolutions with Chapter 7 mandates—those authorizing peacekeepers to use force—concern African security issues. Yet there are no African countries among the Security Council's five permanent members, who are empowered to veto any resolution. The continent must make do with two or three rotating member seats that lack veto powers. It is a travesty of justice that African countries can only participate in deliberations and negotiations about their own futures on such unequal terms.

Africa has made the case for reform of the UN system before. In March 2005, the AU issued a proposal for reforming the world body that noted that "in 1945, when the UN was being formed, most of Africa was not represented and that in 1963, when the first reform took place, Africa was represented but was not in a particularly strong position." The AU went on to state that "Africa is now in a position to influence the proposed UN reforms by maintaining her unity of purpose," adding that "Africa's goal is to be fully represented in all the decision-making organs of the UN, particularly in the Security Council." But for almost 20 years, this appeal has been rebuffed by the permanent members of the Security Council, many of which are now scrambling to enlist African countries in their struggle over Ukraine.

Instead of attempting to resuscitate the 2005 AU proposal, which has largely been overtaken by events, African nations should go back to the drawing board and begin a new process for reforming the multilateral system. The founders of the UN recognized that the world body would not be able to survive indefinitely in its original form. As a result, they included a provision to review and amend its charter. Article 109 of the UN Charter enables a special "charter review conference" to be convened by a two-thirds majority of the UN General Assembly and a vote from any nine of the members of the Security Council. Such a vote cannot be vetoed by the permanent members, which in the past have sabotaged attempts to reform the council. Theoretically, therefore, there are no major obstacles to convening a charter review conference, apart from securing a two-thirds majority in the General Assembly. A coalition of African countries and other progressive states could immediately begin drafting a General Assembly resolution to put a charter review conference on the agenda.

Such a review conference would have the power to substantially alter the UN Charter and introduce new provisions that would transform the multilateral system. Unlike the current system, which privileges the interests of a few powerful states, the conference would be relatively democratic, since Article 109 states that "each member of the United Nations shall have one vote" and that provisions shall be approved by a two-thirds majority. Its recommendations would therefore hold a high degree of moral legitimacy, and the conference could further buttress its standing by conducting broad-based consultations with governments, civil society, businesses, trade unions, and academics.

The specifics of a revised multilateral system would be hashed out in the review conference, but the new order should be more democratic and better able to address the needs of the downtrodden—those who are displaced, affected by war, or simply impoverished. In practical terms, a new multilateral system should not be two tiered, as the current one is, since history has repeatedly shown that more powerful countries will abuse their privileged positions. No country should enjoy veto power over collective decision-making, and authority should be split between nation-states and supranational actors, including the AU, the EU, the Association of Southeast Asian Nations, and the Organization of American States. A world parliament akin to the current UN General Assembly, except with expanded democratic powers, might be reinforced by a global court of justice, both of which would have their own sources of funding—for instance, from taxes on international capital flows.

A SYSTEM REBORN

It would be naive to think that the beneficiaries of the current system, notably the five permanent members of the Security Council, would allow a review of the UN Charter simply because African countries have demanded one. Consequently, Africa will have to build a coalition of the willing, rallying the rest of the global South and whatever developed countries can be persuaded behind its bid to remake the multilateral system. But an institutional overhaul on this scale is not without precedent: other international organizations have transformed themselves in the past, notably the European Economic Community, which became the EU, and the Organization of African Unity, which became the AU.

African countries have an important role to play in reforming a multilateral system that is failing a majority of the world's population. But until their interests and concerns are taken seriously, African governments will continue to pursue a strategy of nonalignment and intentional ambiguity in their dealings with major powers. Attempts to cajole or strong-arm them into picking a side in the latest might-makes-right contest in Ukraine are bound to fail, since no one in Africa believes that the international order is based on rules. It doesn't have to be that way, however. Africa is showing the world how to build a fairer and more just global order.

THE NONALIGNED WORLD

How to Survive a Great-Power Competition

Southeast Asia's Precarious Balancing Act

HUONG LE THU

As relations between China and the United States grow more antagonistic, the rest of the world is watching with unease. Washington has repeatedly accused Beijing of spying on Americans and trying to steal its secrets, most recently by sending a balloon over the United States. Beijing has alleged that Washington is working to cut it off from international markets. The two sides are engaged in an ongoing trade war, and they continue to increase their military expenditures. A violent showdown over Taiwan looks increasingly possible.

This alarming competition has created headaches for many countries, but it is arguably most challenging for developing ones. Washington is pressing partners and allies to support its efforts to penalize its adversary, as is Beijing—even though good relations with both China and the United States have helped lift hundreds of millions of people from poverty. A confrontation between Beijing and Washington, even a nonviolent one, would weaken the trading system that has allowed the global South to flourish. And if the two powers did go to war, smaller and weaker states could get dragged into the conflict.

Few places have come under more intense pressure from the U.S.-Chinese

HUONG LE THU is Principal Fellow at the Perth U.S. Asia Center at the University of Western Australia and a Nonresident Fellow at the Center for Strategic and International Studies.

rivalry, or have more to lose from it, than Southeast Asia. The region, home to nearly 700 million people, is often seen as a testing ground for China's attempts to expand its power. Beijing often refers to the area as its "periphery," and it is building a strong military presence in the region's waters while rolling out a variety of Southeast Asian infrastructure projects under its Belt and Road Initiative. Washington, for its part, has campaigned hard to stop Southeast Asian countries from agreeing to Chinese-led programs. It wants partners and allies to support its ban on various Chinese technologies, even though Beijing's systems help foster economic growth on the cheap.

For Southeast Asia, these demands feel all too familiar. During the Cold War, the region was an epicenter of great-power rivalry as the Soviet Union and the United States (and later China) vied for supremacy. The contest led to violence that killed millions—in traditional wars, civil wars, and systematic state repression. The region's people do not remember this period fondly, and they do not want to repeat it.

But for Southeast Asia, this new era of great-power conflict is unlikely to resemble the last one. Despite China's economic power, the region's countries have been able to resist its attempts at domination, and they have done so without consistently relying on Washington's containment initiatives. Instead, Southeast Asia has strengthened and established multilateral institutions, anchored in the Association of Southeast Asian Nations (ASEAN), that have made the region an independent force. When the area's countries have fostered ties with China and the United States, they have done so on their own terms. They have learned how to use U.S.-Chinese competition to their advantage, playing the two powers against each other for their own economic benefit. Southeast Asia has even become a diplomatic behemoth, one able to bring great powers together.

Whether the region can maintain its position is an open question. If tensions between Beijing and Washington lead to a military conflict, the area's countries could find themselves under intense pressure to pick sides. Southeast Asia is far from a monolith: its countries have different foreign policies and aims, some of which are at odds with one another. But the region's rapid growth and expanding economy suggest that its countries will become more powerful over time and, with it, quite possibly more able to prevent external interference. Southeast Asia may have once been defined by great-power conflict, but today, it can become a model for how to manage great-power competition.

THEN AND NOW

Throughout the Cold War, Southeast Asia was internally divided. Many countries in the region, such as Indonesia, were led by anti-Soviet regimes that violently suppressed communist movements. Others, such as Cambodia, were ruled by Marxist-Leninists. As a result, the area was fraught with tension. In 1967, for instance, noncommunist states founded ASEAN to check the expansion of Marxism-Leninism. Communists in Laos and Vietnam, meanwhile, fought and won bloody civil wars.

But as the Cold War ended, Southeast Asia worked hard to move beyond this acrimonious past. Vietnam, for example, overcame diplomatic isolation and turned into one of the region's most proactive and outgoing countries. ASEAN extended membership to its former adversaries, transforming itself from an anticommunist group into one with a broad political and economic agenda. It also became

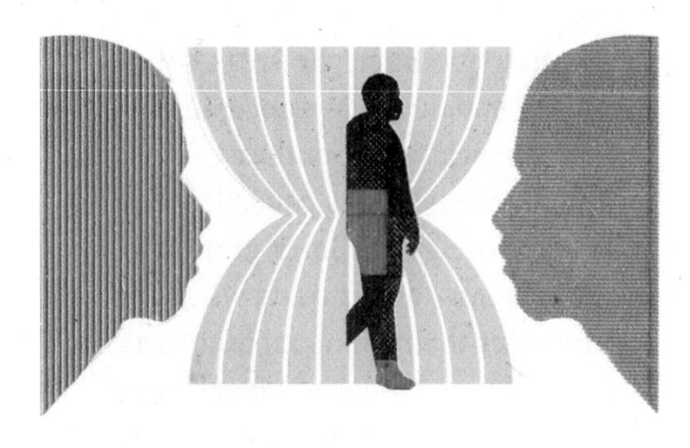

a security forum that frequently brings the region's diplomatic and defense leaders together to work on trust building and conflict prevention.

Southeast Asians have benefited greatly from this peace dividend. The relatively stable international system fostered global integration, allowing the region's states to become manufacturing hubs and the recipients of substantial investment. They signed various free-trade agreements, bolstering connectivity and economic growth. In 1990, only two of the world's 40 largest economies were in Southeast Asia. By 2020, that number had increased to six.

But competition between China and the United States threatens these gains—and in ways that feel disconcertingly familiar. Washington, for example, has justified its competition against China by arguing that it is promoting democracy, the same explanation it gave for the war in Vietnam decades ago. It is an excuse that will win the United States few friends in Southeast Asia. The region is home to many different political systems, and its states proudly work across ideological lines to advance their interests. Even Vietnam has moved past its ideologically driven foreign policy, instead striking up friendships with any government that can offer support. Today, that includes Washington.

The United States' emphasis on ideology under the Indo-Pacific Strategy is not the only way it is antagonizing Southeast Asians. Washington's push to get countries to decouple from China has also proved deeply irritating, even to longtime friends such as Singapore. The push also means that the United States is adopting a trait of its adversary: typically, it has been China that demands that governments make binary choices. (In 2017, for example, Beijing disinvited Singaporean Prime Minister Lee Hsien Loong from a Belt and Road forum after he defended an international court's ruling about maritime claims that went against China and in favor of the Philippines.) But ever since U.S. President Donald Trump announced his "free and open Indo-Pacific" strategy alongside a volley of trade actions against China, Washington has come across as the great power demanding that countries pick a side.

Beijing, of course, has also undermined its own aims in Southeast Asia. China's economic weight is attractive to the region, but its economic deals come with strings attached. The country's loans, for example, often foist unsustainable debt on recipients that Beijing can wield against them. Laos now owes China some $12 billion, which is nearly 65 percent of Laos's GDP. Indonesia's external debt to China at the end of June 2021 stood at $21 billion, nearly five times what it was at the end of 2011. (Nongovernment studies suggest the figure may be even higher.) Cambodia now owes China a different kind of tribute: Beijing's investments in the country appear to have won it access to the Ream Naval Base, a military facility that will give the Chinese military easier access to the South China Sea.

China's growth-killing "zero COVID" policy now casts doubt on the country's actual economic strength. And its extensive claims to Southeast Asia's waters and construction on the region's reefs are a constant reminder of Beijing's belligerence. This assertiveness, combined with the United States' hawkish behavior, has led many Southeast Asian states to worry that the two great powers could soon come to blows. Such a conflict would be dangerous for the entire world, but it could be especially catastrophic for this region. A U.S.-Chinese war over Taiwan, for example, would almost certainly result in a heavily militarized South China Sea, making it difficult for ships to travel freely to and from Southeast Asia. It would also significantly impede regional communications as the warring parties moved to cut or take control of the area's undersea Internet cables. In a worst-case scenario, a conflict might even lead to attacks on the fleets of various Southeast Asian militaries. Either way, regional trade and supply chains could be harmed, stranding the area's economy.

CHOOSING NOT TO CHOOSE

Virtually every country in Southeast Asia recognizes that an open conflict between China and the United States is undesirable. They also know that it would be bad, for politics and business, if either state dominated the region. Neutrality may be one of the few positions on which this heterogeneous group of states can agree. The question is how they can best achieve it.

So far, different countries have taken different approaches. Some have maintained their policies from the past three decades, when China and the United States got along well enough that the region was rarely pushed or pulled into one particular camp. Malaysia and Thailand, by contrast, have moved away from their past, proactive approach to diplomacy as domestic instability has absorbed each government's attention.

Stasis and inaction might seem like a safe bet: why change course or speak out if it risks antagonizing either Beijing or Washington? But doing nothing is a losing strategy. If ASEAN states don't act, they could become bystanders in their own region as major powers conduct military exercises, and possibly even fight, across the surrounding seas. Passivity could cost this group of smaller and medium-sized countries the agency they fought hard to obtain. If the region wants to stay neutral and succeed, it must do so in a way that is careful and considered.

Overall, however, the region has carefully navigated the rising tensions. In 2019, as a collective response to the United States' aggressive Indo-Pacific strategy, ASEAN issued a white paper, "Outlook on the Indo-Pacific," that explicitly rejected zero-sum regional competition and regional dominance by any single power. Instead, it positioned ASEAN at the heart of the area's dynamics. ASEAN then made good on this self-elevation. Over the last several decades, the group has gotten outside states to invest in and trade with the region. It has brought other countries to its diplomatic conclaves, becoming the host—rather than just the subject—of discussions about regional politics. The ASEAN Defense Ministers Meetings–Plus, for example, gathers defense ministers from the ten ASEAN states and a variety of other countries, including China, Russia, and the United States, to discuss matters of regional and global concern. The group's inclusive multilateralism may not sit well with many Americans, who mentally divide the world between friends and competitors (particularly after the outbreak of the war in Ukraine). But cooperating with everyone is a great way to avoid making enemies with anyone.

Southeast Asia has worked hard to maintain and expand this diplomatic and security outreach. Along with the ASEAN-led multilateral security architecture, the region has established many plurilateral and bilateral arrangements with external states. They include ad hoc groups, such as the joint patrols in the Mekong River by China, Laos, Myanmar, and Thailand. They also include institutionalized agreements, such as Singapore and Malaysia's 50-year-old Five-Power Defense Arrangement with Australia, New Zealand, and the United Kingdom. As the geopolitical environment becomes more tense, the already high number of these partnerships is likely to increase. The complex and often overlapping arrangements are critical to Southeast Asia's efforts to engage with all but make exclusive commitments to none.

Southeast Asian states are also becoming more active in groups that include participants outside their neighborhood. Last year, for example, Cambodia hosted the high-profile East Asia Summit, Thailand held the Asia-Pacific Economic Cooperation forum, and Indonesia chaired the G-20. Indonesia's chairmanship proved particularly successful. In November 2022, at the sidelines of the G-20 meeting in Bali, Indonesia hosted a summit that helped break the ice between China and the United States by bringing U.S. President Joe Biden and Chinese President Xi Jinping face to face for the first time since Biden assumed office. Australian Prime Minister Anthony Albanese also spoke with Xi at the proceedings, ending years of silence between Australia's and China's heads of state. Both meetings would have been impossible were it not for Indonesia's neutral stance, and they helped reinforce Southeast Asia's belief that multilateralism remains invaluable even in a disorderly world.

Individually, some Southeast Asian governments have learned that there are benefits to U.S.-Chinese competition. Beijing and Washington's clash may frighten the region's politicians, but it has led both governments to try to win the hearts and minds of nonaligned countries. This has helped Southeast Asian countries—home to young populations and cheap labor—extract all kinds of economic benefits. Vietnam, for example, has profited tremendously from the United States' decoupling from China as U.S. companies have moved production to Vietnamese factories. Indonesia has also received a boost in investment from U.S. companies, including Amazon, Microsoft, and Tesla. The region is becoming increasingly critical to global supply chains.

EVERYBODY, EVERYWHERE

There is no guarantee that Southeast Asia's balancing act will work forever. As U.S.-Chinese competition heats up, many analysts expect that the region's states will, one day, have to take sides. Even Lee, the Singaporean leader, who is no fan of Beijing and Washington's rivalry, said at the 2018 ASEAN Summit that ASEAN may eventually have to choose.

But unlike in the Cold War, when Southeast Asia was mostly poor, newly independent, and weak, today's ASEAN states are largely middle income and can be influential—as the region's diplomacy illustrates. In the years to come, these countries' economies will continue to grow, as should their populations. Both increases will give the region dividends that Beijing and Washington lack: China's population is contracting, and the United States is struggling with domestic political polarization that could hamper its growth and leadership capacities. The two competitors may therefore find that their relative power will decline in the decades ahead—a trend that will narrow the power disparity between these two states and the ASEAN countries.

In fact, the coming decades could give Southeast Asia distinct global advantages. The International Monetary Fund has projected that the region will have some of the highest levels of economic expansion in the world over the next several years. If there is a global recession, Southeast Asia could become the growth engine for the broader Asia-Pacific region. Indonesia and Vietnam, Southeast Asia's biggest and third-biggest states by population, respectively, are on pace to become high-income countries in the next two decades. Southeast Asia, then, could soon have substantial international influence.

For most of ASEAN's members, the additional sway may not always be welcome. International governance requires time and resources that many Southeast Asians would prefer to spend on their own development. But the region's flexibility and adaptiveness will help its countries thrive and exert influence, even in turbulent times. It will help them handle a more fragmented world and make deals with parties that do not get along. Their proactive approach to neutrality is certainly a better model than the passive nonalignment that defined the Cold War's Non-Aligned Movement. Southeast Asia's extensive network of diplomatic connections advances its political agency, bargaining power, and economic growth. Aligning with many states is more fruitful than aligning with none.

Indeed, it may be better to think of Southeast Asia's approach not as nonalignment but as multi-alignment. The region wants as many ties and choices as it can muster. In addition to China and the United States, it has welcomed Australia, India, Japan, and European states to be actively engaged with the region—to trade, invest, and participate in its international dialogues. Creating all these ties may take time and effort. But as Southeast Asia has illustrated, it is an effective and affordable way for developing countries to both avoid great-power conflict and become players themselves.

The World Beyond Ukraine

The Survival of the West and the Demands of the Rest

DAVID MILIBAND

"Ukraine has united the world," declared Ukrainian President Volodymyr Zelensky in a speech on the first anniversary of the start of the war with Russia. If only that were true. The war has certainly united the West, but it has left the world divided. And that rift will only widen if Western countries fail to address its root causes.

The traditional transatlantic alliance of European and North American countries has mobilized in unprecedented fashion for a protracted conflict in Ukraine. It has offered extensive humanitarian support for people inside Ukraine and for Ukrainian refugees. And it is preparing for what will be a massive rebuilding job after the war. But outside Europe and North America, the defense of Ukraine is not front of mind. Few governments endorse the brazen Russian invasion, yet many remain unpersuaded by the West's insistence that the struggle for freedom and democracy in Ukraine is also theirs. As French President Emmanuel Macron said at the Munich Security Conference in February, "I am struck by how we have lost the trust of the global South." He is right. Western conviction about the war and its importance is matched elsewhere by skepticism at best and outright disdain at worst.

The gap between the West and the rest goes beyond the rights and wrongs of the war. Instead, it is the product of deep frustration—anger, in truth—about the Western-led mismanagement of globalization since the end of the Cold War. From this perspective, the concerted Western response to the Russian invasion of Ukraine has thrown into sharp relief the occasions when the West violated its own rules or when it was conspicuously missing in action in tackling global problems. Such arguments can seem beside the point in light of the daily brutality meted out by Russian forces in Ukraine. But Western leaders should address them, not dismiss them. The gulf in perspectives is dangerous for a world facing enormous global risks. And it threatens the renewal of a rules-based order that reflects a new, multipolar balance of power in the world.

DAVID MILIBAND is President and CEO of the International Rescue Committee. From 2007 to 2010, he served as Secretary of State for Foreign and Commonwealth Affairs of the United Kingdom.

THE WEST APART FROM THE REST

The Russian invasion has produced remarkable unity and action from the liberal democratic world. Western countries have coordinated an extensive slate of economic sanctions targeting Russia. European states have increasingly aligned their climate policies on decarbonization with national security-related commitments to end their dependence on Russian oil and gas. Western governments have rallied to support Ukraine with enormous shipments of military aid. Finland and Sweden aim to be soon admitted to NATO. And Europe has adopted a welcoming policy toward the eight million Ukrainian refugees within its borders. All these efforts have been advocated by a U.S. administration that has been sure-footed in partnering with European allies and others. The squabbles over Afghanistan and the AUKUS security partnership (a 2021 deal struck by Australia, the United Kingdom, and the United States that irked France) seem a long time ago.

Many in the West have been surprised at this turn of events. Clearly, so was the Kremlin, which imagined that its invasion would not provoke a strong and determined Western response. The West's unity and commitment are not matched elsewhere, however. At the beginning of the war, the UN General Assembly voted 141 to 5, with 47 absences or abstentions, to condemn the Russian invasion. But that result flattered to deceive. As the team of analysts at the International Crisis Group have noted: "Most non-European countries that voted to deplore Russia's aggression last March did not follow up with sanctions. Doing the right thing at the UN can be an alibi for not doing much about the war in the real world."

In a series of UN votes since the war started, around 40 countries representing nearly 50 percent of the world's population have regularly abstained or voted against motions condemning the Russian invasion. Fifty-eight countries abstained from a vote, in April 2022, to expel Russia from the UN Human Rights Council. According to the Economist Intelligence Unit, two-thirds of the world's population live in countries that are officially neutral or supportive of Russia. These countries do not form some kind of axis of autocracy; they include several notable democracies, such as Brazil, India, Indonesia, and South Africa.

Much of the fence-sitting is not driven by disagreements over the conflict in Ukraine but is instead a symptom of a wider syndrome: anger at perceived Western double standards and frustration at stalled reform efforts in the international system. The distinguished Indian diplomat Shivshankar Menon put the point sharply in *Foreign Affairs* earlier this year when he wrote, "Alienated and resentful, many developing countries see the war in Ukraine and the West's rivalry with China as distracting from urgent issues such as debt, climate change, and the effects of the pandemic."

ON THE FENCE

Realpolitik has played its part in determining the positions of certain countries on the Ukraine conflict. India has traditionally been dependent on Russia for military supplies. The Wagner paramilitary company—the Russian mercenary organization now active in

Ukraine—has worked with governments in western and central Africa to support their security and survival. And China, which is one of Russia's principal sources of support, is the largest trading partner of more than 120 countries around the world and has proved unforgiving of diplomatic slights.

But there are also other factors. Some countries contest the Western narrative about the causes of the war. For example, although Brazilian President Luis Inácio Lula da Silva has described the invasion as a "mistake," he has also given credence to the argument that Russia has been wronged. "Zelensky is as responsible as Putin for the war," Lula claimed last summer in a statement that highlighted global ambivalence about the conflict.

Many observers outside the West also perceive that impunity is, in general, the province of all strong countries, not just Russia. The United States is in an especially weak position to defend global norms after the presidency of Donald Trump, which saw contempt for global rules and practices in areas as diverse as the climate, human rights, and nuclear nonproliferation. Critics point to the U.S.-led wars in Afghanistan and Iraq to claim that hypocrisy, not principle, is driving the West. And U.S. support for the Saudi-led coalition's war in Yemen, which spawned a humanitarian crisis in that country, is adduced as evidence of doublespeak when it comes to concern for civilians. It is also argued that the West has shown far more compassion for the victims of war in Ukraine than for the victims of wars elsewhere. The UN appeal for humanitarian aid for Ukraine has been 80 to 90 percent funded. Meanwhile, the UN's 2022 appeals for people caught in crises in Ethiopia, Syria, and Yemen have been barely half funded.

On their own, some of these reasons for sitting on the sidelines might seem petty to Ukrainians fighting on the frontlines. But the wariness of supporting Ukraine must not obscure a bigger problem. The West has failed since the financial crisis of 2008 to show that it is willing or able to drive forward a more equal and sustainable global economic bargain or to develop the political institutions appropriate to manage a multipolar world. This failure is now coming home to roost. Even before the COVID-19 pandemic, for example, the world was massively off track in achieving the UN's Sustainable Development Goals, which member states set with great fanfare in 2015. In 2018, four out of five fragile and conflict-ridden states were failing on SDG measures. World Bank figures for 2020 show that people born in those places were ten times more likely to end up poor as those born in stable countries, and the gap was growing.

Since then, as a result of protracted conflicts, the climate crisis, and the pandemic, the guardrails have come off altogether. More than 100 million people are currently fleeing for their lives from warfare or disaster. The UN reports that 350 million people today are in humanitarian need, compared with 81 million people ten years ago. More than 600 million Africans lack access to electricity. The UN Development Program reports that 25 developing countries are spending over 20 percent of government revenues on debt servicing, with 54 countries suffering from severe debt problems. And the unequal access to vaccines to combat the pandemic—a gulf especially glaring during the early phases of the vaccine rollout in 2021—has become a poster child for empty promises.

Western governments have also failed to fulfill their commitments in other arenas. The UN's climate Adaptation Fund, established in 2001 to protect poor countries from the consequences of carbon emissions from rich countries, has not yet met its inaugural funding commitment of raising $100 billion a year and is seen as a symbol of Western bad faith: all talk, no walk. The lengthy delays in putting it together have fueled the demand for a new fund to cover "loss and damage" arising from the climate crisis. This new fund was inaugurated last year, but it is not yet funded. Yet another underfunded global initiative will only deepen the deficit of trust between rich countries and poor ones.

HOLLOW SOLIDARITY

If the next two decades are like the last two, marked by the West's confused priorities and failed promises, multipolarity in the global system will come to mean more than greater economic competition. It will mean strengthened ideological challenges to the principles of Western countries and weakened incentives for non-Western countries to associate or cooperate with the West. Instead, liberal democratic countries that support a rules-based global system need to think and act with long-term strategic purpose as they engage with the rest of the world. China has been doing so since 1990.

Hard power in terms of military partnerships and trade cooperation will be critical in determining the West's relations with the rest of the world. But Western governments also need to attend to a number of soft-power issues, notably in three areas: to offer commitments to solidarity and equity in managing global risks, to embrace reforms that widen the range of voices at the table in international affairs, and to develop a winning narrative in an era when democracy is in retreat. These actions would not only help sustain the global position of the West; they are also the right thing to do.

The call for more solidarity and equity in managing global risks is fundamental to the current moment. Great-power competition is exacerbating global challenges to the extreme detriment of the poorest countries. The food crisis arising from the war in Ukraine, and the inadequate global response to it, is but one example. This trend makes the efforts of the Center for Global Development to apply a "global public goods" lens to international development especially important. Such goods include programs to lower the risk of pandemics, mitigate climate change, address antimicrobial resistance, and combat nonstate terrorism and cybercrime. Investment in staving off these looming threats, however, suffers from a market failure: because all people benefit, not just those who pay, no one pays. According to the CGD, around six percent of the total U.S. State Department budget over the past decade went to development-relevant global public goods, and that proportion does not seem to have increased over time.

Pandemics are a good example. In 2022, the Independent Panel for Pandemic Preparedness and Response, which the World Health Assembly asked the World Health Organization (WHO) to establish and on which

I served, published a comprehensive review of the global actions that would be required to prevent and mitigate future pandemics. The report estimated that the financial cost of pandemic prevention would be $15 billion per year, less than half what Americans spend on pizza every year.

The most shocking revelation was that 11 high-level panels and commissions in 16 reports over the preceding 20 years had made sensible recommendations about how to prepare for, detect, and contain pandemics, but most of the recommendations had not been implemented. The Independent Panel's conclusion was that this problem could be overcome only by encouraging leaders to mobilize a sustained whole-of-government commitment to pandemic preparedness. We suggested the creation of a Global Health Threats Council separate from the WHO (because pandemics are not just a health issue) with a mission to ensure that governments sufficiently prepare for pandemics, whether through effective surveillance systems or the timely sounding of alarms on outbreaks. This proposal should not be allowed to gather dust.

Support for refugees presents a further example of how global costs are shared unequally. Although many Western countries bemoan the influx of refugees, poor and lower middle-income countries host over 80 percent of them. Bangladesh, Ethiopia, Jordan, Kenya, Lebanon, Pakistan, Turkey, and Uganda all take in large numbers of refugees. Poland, currently hosting over 1.6 million Ukrainians, and Germany, with 1.5 million Syrians, are outliers among rich countries. Poor and lower middle-income countries receive limited recompense from richer countries for the responsibilities they bear and therefore have limited incentive to enact policies that promote the inclusion of refugees in work, education, and health systems.

Two World Bank initiatives reflect a willingness to address the concerns of developing countries hosting large numbers of refugees, but they need to be scaled up significantly. The Window for Host Communities and Refugees program promises to support meaningful medium- to long-term interventions that support low-income countries hosting refugees. Seventy-seven percent of WHR funds have been committed to African countries. But the program needs to be better resourced; expanded to include other multilateral development banks, such as the African Development Bank and the Islamic Development Bank; and made more effective through coordination with bilateral sources of aid. Another World

Bank initiative, the Global Concessional Financing Facility, does include other multilateral development banks and supports middle-income countries hosting refugees (for instance, the World Bank has allocated Colombia $1.6 billion to help its efforts with Venezuelan refugees). But contributions to the fund are ad hoc and cannot meet the needs of host countries.

The climate crisis is the global risk that looms largest and presents the greatest test of the sincerity of Western countries' solidarity with the rest of the world. Wealthy countries need to spend trillions of dollars to decarbonize their economies, but they also need to support low-carbon development in poor countries and pay for the inevitable costs of adaptation to climate change already foreshadowed by current levels of global warming.

The appointment of a new managing director of the World Bank at the 2023 spring meetings is, therefore, of the highest importance. As former U.S. Treasury Secretary Larry Summers has written, "There is an urgent need for the U.S. and its allies to regain the trust of the developing world. There is no better means of regaining trust than through the collective provision of large-scale support for countries' highest priorities. And there is no more rapid and effective way of mobilizing support than through the World Bank."

The new leadership of the World Bank will need to make up for lost time. According to the analyst Charles Kenny, the bank's contributions as a proportion of the gross national income of borrowing countries fell from 4.0 percent in 1987 to 0.7 percent in 2020. The World Bank can and should do more. Its far too conservative approach to risk, its too limited range of partners (nongovernmental and governmental), and its culture and modus operandi need to be the focus of reform, alongside the proposals for new financing in Barbadian Prime Minister Mia Mottley's Bridgetown Agenda, which calls for a major new mobilization of funds through international financial institutions for countries grappling with climate change and poverty. The new managing director needs to not only raise more funds but also develop delivery systems that recognize that fragile and conflict-ridden states need to be treated differently from their more stable counterparts.

A SEAT AT THE TABLE

In addition to crafting a more equitable way to address global risks, Western countries need to embrace demands from developing countries for a greater say in the international arena. Many countries resent the unbalanced nature of global power in today's international institutions. One recent example occurred during the pandemic. The WHO's Access to COVID-19 Tools Accelerator was an important initiative intended to drive global access to vaccines, treatments, and diagnostics. But representatives of low-income and middle-income countries were not meaningfully included in the governance of the program. This lack of representation hampered efforts to achieve the fair distribution of vaccines and the effective delivery of other health services.

The case of the UN Security Council veto, at the apex of the international system, provides a useful lens for thinking about how all international institutions need to rebalance the way they work to recognize the realities of modern power. Currently, the five permanent members of the Security Council—China, France, Russia, the United Kingdom, and the United States—have the right to veto any resolution, in effect sidelining the other ten members, many of which are low-income and middle-income countries.

Fundamental reform that would change the number of veto-holding states on the council seems unlikely. But the ongoing conflicts in Ethiopia, Syria, Ukraine, and Yemen provide telling examples of how impunity reigns when the Security Council is paralyzed by the veto or the threat to use it. A sign of the frustration regarding this issue is the "veto initiative" passed by the UN General Assembly in 2022, which requires that when a country uses a veto in the Security Council, the General Assembly is automatically convened to discuss the matter at hand. In addition, more than 100 countries have signed on to a French and Mexican proposal, which I support, that calls for the permanent members of the Security Council to agree to refrain from using their veto in cases of mass atrocities. Some permanent members are already exercising restraint. The United Kingdom has not used its veto on any issue since 1989.

The proposal envisions that the UN secretary-general would identify cases that merit the suspension of the veto, based on a clear definition of "mass atrocities." Such a reform would immediately open the decision-making process in the council to more equitably include the views of the ten elected members in addition to the five permanent ones. The United States has said it is worried about the potential politicization of the process for identifying atrocities. Although U.S. officials are understandably concerned about the consequences of giving up the veto (albeit in limited circumstances), Moscow's repeated vetoes of resolutions on Ukraine in the past year should give Washington pause as to whether it has more to gain or to lose by refusing to consider limits on the veto.

A LOOK IN THE MIRROR

In the battle for global opinion, narrative matters. The preferred Western framing of the war in Ukraine—as a contest between democracy and autocracy—has not resonated well outside Europe and North America. Although it is true that Ukrainians are fighting for their democracy as well as their sovereignty, for the rest of the world the invasion primarily represents a fundamental transgression of international law. So, too, do Russia's military attacks, which have targeted Ukrainian civilians and civilian infrastructure.

There is a better alternative. Western governments should frame the conflict as one between the rule of law and impunity or between law and anarchy rather than one that pits democracy against autocracy. Such an approach has many advantages. It correctly locates democracy among a range of methods for the promotion of accountability and the curbing of the abuse of power. It broadens the potential coalition of support. It tests China at its weakest point because China claims to support a rules-based international system. It also sounds less self-regarding, which is important given the obvious problems plaguing many liberal democracies. A coalition built around the need for international rules is far more likely to be broader than one based on calls for democracy.

To defend the rule of law, however, Western countries must abide by it and subscribe to it. The U.S. condemnation of Chinese breaches of the UN Convention on the Law of the Sea—with respect to China's military installations on islands in the South China Sea, for example—would be far more persuasive if the United States ratified the convention. And although U.S. Vice President Kamala Harris made a powerful call at the recent Munich Security Conference for the prosecution of war crimes in Ukraine, it would have been much more effective had the United States ratified the Rome Statute that created the International Criminal Court in 1998. Critics and adversaries of Western powers relentlessly cite these double standards. And it is not hard to see why.

It is worth asking whether it really matters how the rest of the world lines up on Ukraine. Russian President Vladimir Putin, for one, said in a speech in June 2022 that he believes it does, arguing that in the wake of the war, "new powerful centers have formed on the planet," a reference to the rise of powers such as Brazil, China, and South Africa. These changes, Putin claims, are "fundamental and pivotal." Meanwhile, China has launched a series of global projects under the rubric of its "Community of Common Destiny Future for Mankind," including the vast infrastructure investment program known as the Belt and Road Initiative, that reflect the changing global order.

Yet U.S. President Joe Biden spent less than three minutes discussing the wider world beyond Ukraine in his State of the Union address in February, which was more than an hour long. It was a striking lacuna given his administration's creditable record: over 90 percent of humanitarian aid going to Somalia, for example, currently comes from the United States. An agenda focused on courting the rest of the world has little domestic traction, of course; that is not where the votes are. But other countries also have votes—not in U.S. elections but in how American interests are perceived and advanced around the world. In the case of Ukraine, Russia's economy has been sustained despite Western sanctions by expanded trade with the non-Western world, new energy alliances, and new sources of weapons supplies. These ties matter.

As a geopolitical entity, the West remains a powerful and influential actor, more so with its newfound unity. To be sure, the relative shares of global income among Western countries will be lower in the twenty-first century than they were in the twentieth. But income per capita in Western countries remains high by global standards. The West's military and diplomatic strength is real. The alternative systems to democracy are repressive and unattractive.

At the same time, the demands from a variety of countries for a new deal at the international level are in many cases reasonable. Addressing them with urgency and in good faith is essential to building a global order that is satisfactory to liberal democratic states and their citizens. The war in Ukraine has allowed the West to rediscover its strength and sense of purpose. But the conflict should also help Western governments confront their weaknesses and missteps.

Blundering on the Brink

The Secret History and Unlearned Lessons of the Cuban Missile Crisis

SERGEY RADCHENKO AND VLADISLAV ZUBOK

There aren't enough palm trees, the Soviet general thought to himself. It was July 1962, and Igor Statsenko, the 43-year-old Ukrainian-born commander of the Red Army's missile division, found himself inside a helicopter, flying over central and western Cuba. Below him lay a rugged landscape, with few roads and little forest. Seven weeks earlier, his superior—Sergei Biryuzov, the commander of the Soviet Strategic Missile Forces—had traveled to Cuba disguised as an agricultural expert. Biryuzov had met with the country's prime minister, Fidel Castro, and shared with him an extraordinary proposal from the Soviet Union's leader, Nikita Khrushchev, to station ballistic nuclear missiles on Cuban soil. Biryuzov, an artilleryman by training

---

SERGEY RADCHENKO is the Wilson E. Schmidt Distinguished Professor at the Johns Hopkins School of Advanced International Studies and the author of the forthcoming book *To Run the World: The Kremlin's Cold War Bid for Global Power*.

VLADISLAV ZUBOK is Professor of International History at the London School of Economics and the author of *Collapse: The Fall of the Soviet Union*.

who knew little about missiles, returned to the Soviet Union to tell Khrushchev that the missiles could be safely hidden under the foliage of the island's plentiful palm trees.

But when Statsenko, a no-nonsense professional, surveyed the Cuban sites from the air, he realized the idea was hogwash. He and the other Soviet military officers on the reconnaissance team immediately raised the problem with their superiors. In the areas where the missile bases were supposed to go, they pointed out, the palm trees stood 40 to 50 feet apart and covered only one-sixteenth of the ground. There would be no way to hide the weapons from the superpower 90 miles to the north.

But the news apparently never reached Khrushchev, who moved forward with his scheme in the belief that the operation would remain secret until the missiles were in place. It was a fateful delusion. In October, an American high-altitude U-2 reconnaissance plane spotted the launch sites, and what became known as "the Cuban missile crisis" began. For a week, U.S. President John F. Kennedy and his advisers debated in secret about how to respond. Ultimately, Kennedy chose not to launch a preemptive attack to destroy the Soviet sites and instead declared a naval blockade of Cuba to give Moscow a chance to back off. Over the course of 13 frightening days, the world stood on the brink of nuclear war, with Kennedy and Khrushchev facing off "eyeball to eyeball," in the memorable words of Secretary of State Dean Rusk. The crisis ended when Khrushchev capitulated and withdrew missiles from Cuba in return for Kennedy's public promise to not invade the island and a secret agreement to withdraw American nuclear-tipped missiles from Turkey.

The details of the palm tree fiasco are just some of the revelations in the hundreds of pages of newly released top-secret documents about Soviet decision-making and military planning. Some come from the archives of the Soviet Communist Party and were declassified before the war in Ukraine; others were quietly declassified by the Russian Ministry of Defense in May 2022, in the run-up to the sixtieth anniversary of the Cuban missile crisis. The decision to release these documents, without redaction, is just one of many paradoxes of President Vladimir Putin's Russia, where state archives continue to release vast troves of evidence about the Soviet past even as the regime cracks down on free inquiry and spreads ahistorical propaganda. We were fortunate to obtain these documents when we did; the ongoing tightening of screws in Russia will likely reverse recent strides in declassification.

The documents shed new light on the most hair-raising of Cold War crises, challenging many assumptions about what motivated the Soviets' massive operation in Cuba and why it failed so spectacularly. At a time of escalating tensions with another brash leader in the Kremlin, the story of the crisis offers a chilling message about the risks of brinkmanship. It also illustrates the degree to which the difference between catastrophe and peace often comes down not to considered strategies but to pure chance.

The evidence shows that Khrushchev's idea to send missiles to Cuba was a remarkably poorly thought-through gamble whose success depended on improbably good luck. Far from being a bold chess move motivated by cold-blooded realpolitik, the Soviet operation was a consequence of Khrushchev's resentment of U.S. assertiveness in Europe and his fear that Kennedy would order an invasion of Cuba, overthrowing Castro and humiliating Moscow in the process. And far from being an impressive display of Soviet cunning and power, the operation was plagued by a profound lack of understanding of on-the-ground conditions in Cuba. The palm tree fiasco was just one of many blunders the Soviets made throughout the summer and fall of 1962.

The revelations have special resonance at a time when, once again, a leader in the Kremlin is engaged in a risky foreign gambit, confronting the West as the specter of nuclear war lurks in the background. Now, as then, Russian decision-making is driven by hubris and a sense of humiliation. Now, as then, the military brass in Moscow is staying silent about the massive gap between the operation the leader had in mind and the reality of its implementation.

At a question-and-answer session he held in October, Putin was asked about parallels between the current crisis and the one Moscow faced 60 years earlier. He responded cryptically. "I cannot imagine myself in the role of Khrushchev," he said. "No way." But if Putin cannot see the similarities between Khrushchev's predicament and the one he now faces, then he truly is an amateur historian. Russia, it seems, still has not learned the lesson of the Cuban missile crisis: that the whims of an autocratic ruler can lead his country into a geopolitical cul-de-sac—and the world to the edge of calamity.

In 1962, Khrushchev reversed course and found a way out. Putin has yet to do the same.

A MODEST PROPOSAL

"Our whole operation was to deter the USA so they don't attack Cuba," Khrushchev told his top political and military leaders on October 22, 1962, after learning from the Soviet embassy in Washington that Kennedy was about to address the American people. Khrushchev's words are preserved in the detailed minutes of the meeting, recently declassified in the Soviet Communist Party archives. The United States had nuclear missiles in Turkey and Italy. Why couldn't the Soviet Union have them in Cuba? He went on: "In their time, the USA did the same thing, having encircled our country with missile bases. This deterred us." Khrushchev expected the United States to simply put up with Soviet deterrence, just as he had put up with U.S. deterrence.

"Our whole operation was to deter the USA," Khrushchev said.

Khrushchev had gotten the idea to send missiles to Cuba months earlier, in May, when he concluded that the CIA's failed Bay of Pigs invasion in April 1961 had been just a trial run. An American takeover of Cuba, he recognized, would deal a serious blow to the Soviet leader's credibility and expose him to charges of ineptitude in Moscow. But as the minutes of the October 22 meeting make clear, there was more to Khrushchev's decision-making than concerns about Cuba. Khrushchev deeply resented what he perceived as unequal treatment by the United States. And contrary to the conventional story, he was equally worried about China, which he feared would exploit a defeat in Cuba to challenge his claim to leadership of the global communist movement.

Khrushchev entrusted the implementation of his daring idea to three top military commanders—Biryuzov, Rodion Malinovsky (the defense minister), and Matvei Zakharov (the head of the general staff)—and the whole operation was planned by a handful of officers in the general staff working in utmost secrecy. One of the key newly released documents is a formal proposal for the operation prepared by the military and signed by Malinovsky and Zakharov. It is dated May 24, 1962—just three days after Khrushchev broached his idea of putting missiles in Cuba at the Defense Council, the supreme military-political body he chaired.

According to the proposal, the Soviet army would send to Cuba the 51st Missile Division, consisting of five regiments: all of the group's officers and soldiers, about 8,000 men, would leave their base in western Ukraine and be permanently stationed in Cuba. They would bring with them 60 ballistic missiles: 36 medium-range R-12s and 24 intermediate-range R-14s. The R-14s were a particular challenge: at 80 feet long and 86 metric tons, the missiles required a host of construction engineers and technicians, as well as dozens of tracks, cranes, bulldozers, excavators, and cement mixers to install them on launching pads in Cuba. The troops of the missile division would be joined by many other soldiers and equipment in Cuba: two antiaircraft divisions, one regiment of IL-28 bombers, one air force squadron of MiG fighters, three regiments with helicopters and cruise missiles, four infantry regiments with tanks, and support and logistics troops. The list of these units filled five pages of the proposal on May 24: 44,000 men in uniform, plus 1,800 construction and engineering specialists.

Soviet generals had never before deployed a full missile division and so many troops by sea, and now they had to send them to another hemisphere. Unfazed, the military planners christened the operation with the code name "Anadyr," after the Arctic river, across the Bering Sea from Alaska—geographical misdirection designed to confuse U.S. intelligence.

At the top of the proposal, Khrushchev wrote the word "agree" and signed his name. Some distance below are the signatures of 15 other senior leaders. If the operation failed, Khrushchev wanted to make sure no other members of the leadership could distance themselves from it. He had successfully browbeaten his colleagues into literally signing on to his hare-brained scheme. A strikingly similar scene would repeat itself 60 years later, when, days before the invasion of Ukraine, Putin forced members of his security council, one by one, to speak out loud and endorse his "special military operation" at a televised meeting.

OPERATION ANADYR

On May 29, 1962, Biryuzov arrived in Cuba with a Soviet delegation and posed as an agricultural engineer by the name of Petrov. When he conveyed Khrushchev's proposal to Castro, the Cuban leader's eyes lit up. Castro embraced Soviet missiles as a service to the entire socialist camp, a Cuban contribution to the struggle against American imperialism. It was during this trip that Biryuzov also reached his pivotal conclusion that palm trees could camouflage the missiles.

In June, when Khrushchev met with the military again, Aleksei Dementyev, a Soviet military adviser in Cuba who was summoned to Moscow, emerged as a lonely voice of caution. As he began to say that it was impossible to hide the missiles from the American U-2s, Malinovsky kicked his subordinate under the table to make him shut up. The operation had already been decided; it was too late to challenge it, much less to Khrushchev's face. By now, there was no stopping Anadyr. In late June, Castro sent his brother Raúl, the defense minister, to Moscow to discuss a mutual defense agreement that would legitimize Soviet military deployments in Cuba. With Raúl, Khrushchev was full of bombast, even promising to send a military flotilla to Cuba to demonstrate Soviet resolve in the United States' backyard. Kennedy, he boasted, would do nothing. Yet behind the usual bluster lay fear. Khrushchev wanted to keep Anadyr secret for as long as possible, lest the U.S. intervene and upend his ambitious plans. And so the Soviet-Cuban military agreement was never published.

Top Soviet commanders also wanted to conceal the true purpose of Operation Anadyr—even from much of the rest of the Soviet military. The official documents, part of the recently declassified trove, referred to the operation as an "exercise." Thus, the greatest gamble in nuclear history was presented to the rest of the military as routine training. In a striking parallel, Putin's misadventure in Ukraine was also billed as an "exercise," with unit-level commanders being left in the dark until the last moment.

Operation Anadyr began in earnest in July. On the 7th, Malinovsky reported to Khrushchev that all the missiles and personnel were ready to leave for Cuba. The expedition was named the Group of Soviet Forces in Cuba, and its commander was Issa Pliev, a grizzled, 59-year-old cavalry general, a veteran of both the Russian Civil War and World War II. The same day, Khrushchev met with him, Statsenko, and 60 other generals, senior officers, and commanders of units as they prepared to depart. Their mission was to fly to Cuba for reconnaissance to prepare everything for the arrival of the armada with missiles and troops in the following months. On July 12, the group arrived in Cuba aboard an Aeroflot passenger plane. A week later, a hundred additional officers arrived on two more flights.

The hasty journey was rife with mishaps. The rest of Soviet officialdom botched the cover story for the reconnaissance group: in newspapers, the passengers on the Aeroflot planes were called "specialists in

CRISTIANA COUCEIRO

civil aviation," even though in Cuba, they had been billed as "specialists in agriculture." When one flight landed in Havana, no one greeted the passengers, so the officers poked around the airport for three hours before finally being whisked away. Another flight ran into storms and had to divert to Nassau, the Bahamas, where curious American tourists snapped pictures of the Soviet plane and its passengers.

Statsenko arrived on July 12. From July 21 to 25, he and other Soviet officers crisscrossed the island, wearing Cuban army uniforms and accompanied by Castro's personal bodyguards. They inspected the sites that had been selected for the deployment of five missile regiments, all in western and central Cuba in keeping with Biryuzov's optimistic report. Statsenko wasn't just disturbed by the sparsity of palm trees. As he later complained in a report—another recently released document—the Soviet team lacked even basic knowledge of the conditions in Cuba. No one provided them with briefing materials on the geography, climate, and economic conditions of the tropical island. They didn't even have maps; those were scheduled to arrive later by ship. Heat and humidity hit the team hard. Castro sent a few of his staff officers to help with the inspections, but there were no interpreters, so the reconnaissance team had to take a crash course in elementary Spanish. What little Spanish the officers had picked up in a few days did not get them far.

With the initial missile sites hopelessly exposed, Pliev, the man in charge, ordered the reconnaissance teams to find better locations, in remote areas protected by hills and forests. (According to Castro's instructions, they also had to find sites that would not require the large-scale resettlement of peasants.) Twice, Pliev asked the general staff back in Moscow if he could move some missile locations to more suitable areas. Each time, Moscow rejected the initiative. Some new areas were rejected because they "were in the area of international flights"—a sensible precaution to avoid the possibility of Soviet surface-to-air missiles accidentally shooting down civilian aircraft. But other locations were rejected because they "did not correspond to the directive of the general staff"—in other words, the planners in Moscow did not want to change what their superiors had already approved. In the end, the missiles were assigned to exposed areas.

The reconnaissance team had to take a crash course in elementary Spanish.

Apart from the unexpected difficulties siting the missiles, the Soviets encountered other surprises in Cuba. Pliev and other generals planned to dig underground shelters for the troops, but Cuban soil proved too rocky. Soviet electrical equipment, meanwhile, was incompatible with the Cuban electricity supply, which operated on the North American standard of 120 volts and 60 hertz. The Soviet planners had also forgotten to consider the weather: hurricane season in Cuba runs from June through November, precisely when the missiles and troops had to be deployed, and the unceasing rains impeded transportation and construction. Soviet electronics and engines, designed for the cold and temperate climates of Europe, quickly corroded in the sweltering humidity. Only in September, well after the operation began, did the general staff send instructions for operating and maintaining weaponry in tropical conditions.

"All this should have been known before the reconnaissance work started," Statsenko told his superiors two months after the crisis ended, his memo dripping with irritation. He took planners to task for knowing so little about Cuba. "The whole operation should have been preceded at least by a minimal acquaintance and study—by those who were supposed to carry out the task—of the economic capabilities of the state, the local geographic conditions, and the military and political situation in the country." He did not dare mention Biryuzov by name, but at any rate, it was clear to all that the real culprit was Khrushchev, who had left his military no time to prepare.

PRECIOUS CARGO

For all the fumbles, Anadyr was a considerable logistical accomplishment. The scale of the shipments was enormous, as the newly declassified documents detail. Hundreds of trains brought troops and missiles to eight Soviet ports of departure, among them Sevastopol in Crimea, Baltiysk in Kaliningrad, and Liepaja in Latvia. Nikolayev—today, the Ukrainian city of Mykolayiv—on the Black Sea served as the main shipping hub for the missiles because of its giant port facilities and railroad connections. Since the port's cranes were too small to load the bigger rockets, a floating 100-ton crane was brought in to do the job. The loading proceeded at night and usually took two or three days per missile. Everything was done for the first time, and Soviet engineers had to solve countless problems on the fly. They figured out how to strap missiles inside ships that were normally used to transport grain or cement and how to store liquid rocket fuel safely inside the hold. Two hundred and fifty-six railroad cars delivered 3,810 metric tons of munitions. Some 8,000 trucks and cars, 500 trailers, and 100 tractors were sent, along with 31,000 metric tons of fuel for cars, aircraft, ships, and, of course, missiles. The military dispatched 24,500 metric tons of food. The Soviets planned to stay in Cuba for a long time.

From July to October, the armada of 85 ships ferried men and supplies from the Black Sea, through the Mediterranean, and across the Atlantic Ocean. The ships' crews could see that their vessels were not going unnoticed. As declassified reports from captains, military officers, and KGB officers reveal, planes—some from NATO countries, others unidentified—flew over the ships more than 50 times. According to a declassified Soviet report, one of the planes even crashed into the sea. Some of the ships were followed by the U.S. Navy. Each Soviet vessel was armed with two double-barreled heavy machine guns. Secret instructions from Moscow allowed the troops on board to fire if their ship was about to be boarded; if it was on the verge of being seized, they were to move all men to rafts, destroy all documents, and sink the ship with its cargo. But a potential emergency was just one of many worries. Some troops traveled by passenger ship, in relative comfort, but most sailed on merchant ships that the Soviets had assigned to the operation. These troops faced an ordeal: they huddled in cramped cargo holds that they shared with equipment, metal parts, and lumber. Often, they fell sick. Some of the men died en route and were buried at sea.

But the ships got lucky and reached Cuba without incident. On September 9, the first six R-12 missiles, stowed inside the cargo ship *Omsk*, arrived in the port of Casilda, on Cuba's southern coast. Others arrived later in Mariel, just west of Havana. The missiles were offloaded secretly at night, between 12 and 5 AM. The construction workers who were supposed to build pads for the heavier R-14 missiles had not yet arrived, so the soldiers on hand had to do all the work. Soviet military boats and scuba divers secured the nautical zone. Everyone changed into Cuban uniforms. Speaking Russian, according to the instructions of the general staff, was "categorically forbidden."

Three hundred Cuban soldiers and even some "specially tested and selected fishermen" were charged with protecting the ports where the missiles were to be brought in. The Cuban army and police cordoned the roads and even staged fake car accidents along the route from the port to the missile sites to keep the local population away. A spot west of Havana that would serve as a launch site for R-14 missiles was impossible to conceal, so it was presented to the Cuban public as "the construction site for a Cuban military training center." Very few Cubans knew about the missiles. In fact, only 14 Cuban officials had a complete view of the operation: Fidel, Raúl, the Argentine revolutionary Che Guevara (then one of Fidel's top advisers), Pedro Luis Rodríguez (the head of Cuban military intelligence), and ten other senior military officers.

There were now about 42,000 Soviet military personnel on Cuban soil. Those from Statsenko's missile division focused on constructing launching pads for R-12 missiles. Others manned the bombers, surface-to-air missiles, fighter jets, and other weaponry that Moscow had sent to the island. Once again, however, tropical conditions slowed progress. Rain, humidity, and mosquitoes descended on the arriving regiments. Soldiers slept in soaked tents. Temperatures exceeded 100 Fahrenheit. The camouflage remained an unsolvable problem: among the sparse palm trees, the tents, like the missiles, were impossible to conceal. Commanders draped the equipment in camouflage nets, the new documents reveal, but the color of the nets matched the green foliage of Russia and stood out sharply against the sun-scorched Cuban landscape.

The Soviet general staff wanted the R-12 launch pads completed by November 1. From September through the first half of October, the crews worked overtime to meet this deadline, but again they were delayed by snafus. The construction crews that were supposed to install R-14 missiles, for example, spent a whole month in Cuba waiting for their equipment to arrive. Some of the parts for the R-12 launchers were weeks late. By mid-October, none of the missile sites was ready. The one that was closest to completion—the R-12 site near Calabazar de Sagua, in central Cuba—was plagued by communications problems, with no reliable radio link between it and the headquarters in Havana. And then came October 14.

CAUGHT RED-HANDED

That morning, an American U-2 spy plane, flying at 72,500 feet and equipped with a large-format camera, passed over some of the construction sites. Two days later, the photographs were on Kennedy's desk.

In retrospect, it is remarkable that it took so long for the Americans to discover the missiles, given the extent of Soviet blunders in Cuba. Luck played a large role. The storms that hindered the Soviet troops also protected them from American snooping since the dense cloud cover prevented aerial photography. And as it happened, the CIA made a blunder of its own. Although the agency had detected the arrival of Soviet antiaircraft weaponry in late August, it failed to draw the obvious conclusion as to what the Soviet forces were so keen to protect, concluding instead that the weapons were merely for Cuba's conventional defense, despite the suspicions of CIA Director John McCone.

For several days, Kennedy deliberated with his top advisers about how to respond to what he viewed as a blatant act of provocation. Many in the group, known as EXCOMM, favored an all-out attack on Cuba to obliterate the Soviet bases. Kennedy instead opted for a more cautious response: a naval blockade, or "quarantine," of Cuba. His caution was warranted, for no one could guarantee that all the missiles would be wiped out.

This caution stemmed partly from another source of uncertainty: whether any of the missiles were ready. In fact, as the newly declassified documents reveal, only on October 20 did the first site—one with eight R-12 launchers—become operational. By October 25, two more sites were readied, although again in less-than-ideal circumstances: the rockets had to share fueling equipment, and the Soviets had to cannibalize personnel from regiments originally intended to operate the R-14s. By nightfall of October 27, all 24 launchers for the R-12s, eight per regiment, were ready.

Or rather, almost ready. The storage facility for the R-12 nuclear warheads was located at a considerable distance from the missile sites: 70 miles from one regiment, 90 miles from another, and 300 miles from another. If Moscow gave an order to fire the missiles at U.S. targets, the Soviet commanders in Cuba would need between 14 and 24 hours to truck the warheads across miles of often treacherous terrain. Recognizing that this was too long a lead time, Statsenko, on October 27, ordered some of the warheads moved closer to the farthest regiment, shrinking the lead time to ten hours. Kennedy knew nothing about these logistical challenges. But their existence suggests yet again the role of luck. Had EXCOMM learned of these difficulties, the hawks would have had a stronger argument in favor of an all-out strike on Cuba—which would probably have disabled the missiles but could have led to a war with the Soviet Union, whether in Cuba or Europe.

It is now clear that the Soviet troops in Cuba had no predelegated authority to launch nuclear missiles at the United States; any order had to come from Moscow. It is also doubtful that the Soviets in Cuba had the authority to use shorter-range tactical nuclear weapons in the event of a U.S. invasion. Those weapons included nuclear-armed coastal cruise missiles and short-range rockets that had been shipped to Cuba with Statsenko's division. During a long meeting in the Kremlin that began on the evening of October 22 and lasted until the wee hours of October 23, the Soviet leaders debated whether the Americans would invade Cuba and, if so, whether the Soviet troops should use tactical nuclear weapons to repel them. Khrushchev never admitted that the entire operation was folly, but he did speak about grave mistakes. The upshot of this meeting—which coincided with Kennedy's speech announcing the naval blockade—was an order to Pliev to refrain from using either strategic or tactical nuclear weapons except when ordered by Moscow.

There was no American invasion, and the order to fire the missiles never came. If it had, however, it would undoubtedly have been followed to the letter. Statsenko's report noted that he and those under his command "were prepared to give their lives and honorably carry out any order of the Communist Party and the Soviet government."

THE BEST-LAID PLANS

Operation Anadyr's newly declassified documents

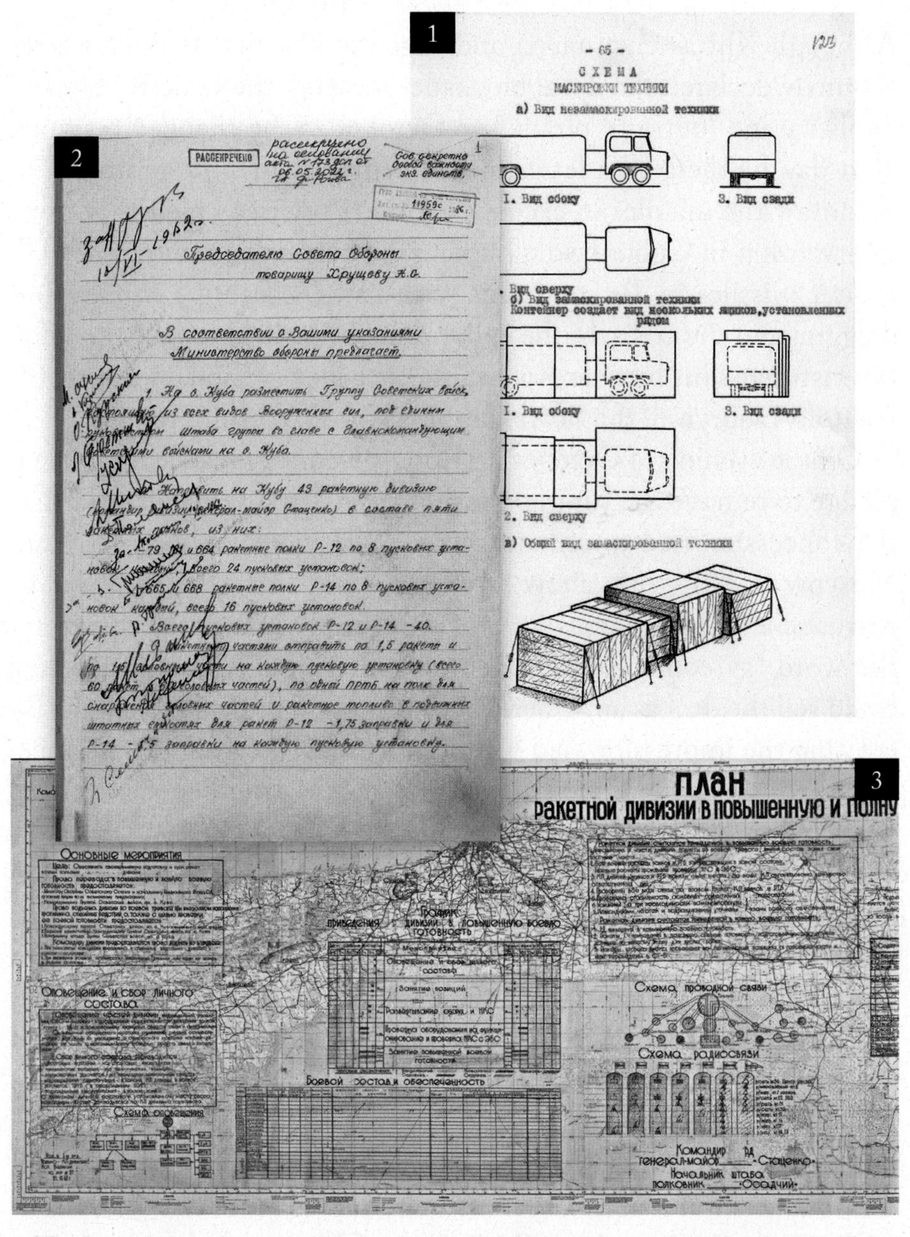

РАССЕКРЕЧЕНО

Сов. секретно
Особой важности
экз. единств.

11959с

Председателю Совета Обороны
товарищу Хрущеву Н.С.

В соответствии с Вашими указаниями
Министерство обороны предлагает.

1. На о. Куба разместить Группу Советских войск, состоящую из всех видов Вооруженных сил, под единым руководством Штаба группы во главе с Главнокомандующим Советскими войсками на о. Куба.

2. Направить на Кубу 43 ракетную дивизию (командир дивизии генерал-майор Стаценко) в составе пяти ракетных полков, из них:

79, 181 и 664 ракетные полки Р-12 по 8 пусковых установок каждый, всего 24 пусковых установок;

665 и 668 ракетные полки Р-14 по 8 пусковых установок каждый, всего 16 пусковых установок.

Всего пусковых установок Р-12 и Р-14 – 40.

С ракетными частями отправить по 1,5 ракеты и по 1,5 головных части на каждую пусковую установку (всего 60 ракет и 60 головных частей), по одной ПРТБ на полк для снаряжения головных частей и ракетное топливо в подвижных штатных емкостях для ракет Р-12 – 1,75 заправки и для Р-14 – 1,5 заправки на каждую пусковую установку.

1. The Soviet military's instructions on how to hide equipment on ships destined for Cuba. **2.** The May 24 proposal to send nuclear missiles to Cuba, signed at the top by Khrushchev and below by 15 other senior leaders. **3.** A map of Cuba annotated with detailed instructions on readying the Soviet missile division in the country.

His words highlight the fallacy that military leaders might act as a check on political leaders bent on starting a nuclear war: military officials in Cuba were never going to countermand political authorities in Moscow.

"THE ABSENCE OF BRAINS"

Although Khrushchev raved and raged in the first two days after Kennedy declared the naval blockade, accusing the United States of duplicity and "outright piracy," on October 25, he changed his tune. That day, he dictated a letter to Kennedy in which he promised to withdraw the missiles in exchange for an American pledge of non-intervention in Cuba. Two days later, he added the removal of U.S. Jupiter missiles in Turkey to his wish list, confusing Kennedy and dragging out the crisis. In the end, Kennedy decided to take the offer. He instructed his brother Robert, the attorney general, to meet with Anatolii Dobrynin, the Soviet ambassador in Washington.

On the evening of October 27, Robert Kennedy made an informal pledge to remove the Jupiter missiles from Turkey but insisted that the concession had to remain secret. Newly available cables from Moscow to Dobrynin show how important this assurance was to Khrushchev. The ambassador was specifically instructed to extract the word "agreement" from Kennedy, presumably so Khrushchev could sell the deal as an American capitulation to his inner circle. By creating the impression that Kennedy was also making concessions, the word "agreement" would help rebrand a surrender as a victory, a Cuba-for-Turkey exchange.

By this point, however, Khrushchev was eager for a deal. He had been spooked by a series of disturbing events. On the morning of the 27th, an American U-2 had been shot down over Cuba by a Soviet-supplied surface-to-air missile on the orders of senior Soviet officers in Cuba. The Soviets in Cuba always assumed that there would be a U.S. invasion, and they blamed the Cubans for failing to detect the American reconnaissance flights before the crisis. Accordingly, as the declassified files reveal, Malinovsky presented the downing of the U-2 to Khrushchev as a necessary measure to prevent the Americans from taking more photographs of Soviet bases. He registered no awareness in his missive to Khrushchev that the shoot-down could have become a prelude for World War III. Nor did Statsenko, when he later reported the shootdown matter-of-factly, likewise portraying it as a routine response that the Soviet military was trained and entitled to do.

In the middle of the day, there had been another incident involving an American U-2: a plane sent to the Arctic to sample the atmosphere for radiation got lost and accidentally flew into Soviet airspace. The Soviet military dutifully mapped its progress on now declassified maps, which also showed the number of hours American planes would need to reach targets in Soviet territory.

The most disturbing development of all, however, was a plea Castro had sent early in the morning of October 27, Havana time, in which he asked Khrushchev to launch a preemptive nuclear strike against the United States if the Americans dared to invade Cuba. Historians have long been aware of this plea, but thanks to the new documents, we now know more about what Khrushchev thought of it. "What is it—a temporary madness or the absence of brains?" he fumed on October 30, according to a declassified dictation taken by his secretary.

Khrushchev was an emotional man, but at the hour of greatest danger, he pulled back from the brink. As he put it to an Indian visitor on October 26, according to the newly released documents, "From the experience of my life, I know that war is like a card game, though I myself never played and never play cards." That final qualification wasn't entirely truthful: to Khrushchev, the whole Cuban operation was one big poker match, which he thought he could win by bluffing. But at least he knew when to fold. On October 28, he announced that he would dismantle the missiles.

LEARNING AND FORGETTING

Since 1962, historians, political scientists, and game theorists have endlessly rehashed the Cuban missile crisis. Volumes of documents have been published, and countless conferences and war games have been held. Graham Allison's classic account of the crisis, *Essence of Decision*, was published in 1971 and updated in 1999 with the help of Philip Zelikow. One of the original book's conclusions, also included in the revised edition, has stood the test of time: the crisis was "the defining event of the nuclear age and the most dangerous moment in recorded history."

But the declassified Soviet documents make some important corrections to the conventional view, highlighting the Achilles' heel of the Kremlin's decision-making process, which persists to this day: a broken feedback mechanism. Soviet military leaders had minimal expertise on Cuba, deceived themselves about their ability to hide their operation, overlooked the dangers of U.S. aerial reconnaissance, and ignored the warnings of experts. A small coterie of high officials who knew nothing about Cuba, acting in extreme secrecy, drew up a sloppy plan for an operation that was doomed to fail and never allowed anyone else to question their assumptions.

Indeed, it was the failure of the feedback mechanism that led to the immediate cause of the crisis, the poorly camouflaged missiles. Allison and Zelikow concluded that this oversight was not the result of incompetence but a consequence of the Soviet military mindlessly following its standard operating procedures, which had been "designed for settings in which camouflage had never been required." In this view, the Soviet forces failed to adequately camouflage the missiles simply because they had never done so before.

The Soviets planned to stay in Cuba for a long time.

The new evidence gives a different answer. The Soviets fully appreciated the importance of hiding the missiles, and Khrushchev's entire strategy was in fact predicated on the flawed assumption that they would be able to do just that. The Soviet military officers in Cuba were also aware of the importance of concealing the missiles. They recognized the danger of U.S. aerial reconnaissance, tried to address it by proposing better sites, and still failed. The core of the problem was the original carelessness and incompetence of Biryuzov. His offhand conclusion that the missiles could be hidden under the palm trees was passed on as an unimpeachable truth. Military experts far below him in the hierarchy noted that the missiles would be exposed to U-2 overflights and duly reported the problem up the chain of command. Yet the planners in the general staff never corrected it, unwilling to bother their superiors or question the idea of the entire operation. Operation Anadyr failed not because the Soviet rocket forces were too wedded to their standard procedures but because the military's hypercentralization prevented the feedback mechanisms from working properly.

In their first reports analyzing the crisis—part of the new trove of documents—Soviet military leaders engaged in a blame game. Ignoring his own culpability, Biryuzov pointed the finger at "the excessive centralization of management" of the operation "at all stages in the hands of the general staff, which chained the initiative below and reduced the quality of decision-making on specific questions" on site in Cuba. He never admitted the lack of camouflage as the main flaw of Anadyr, although his political superiors immediately recognized it as such.

Anastas Mikoyan, a member of the Presidium whom Khrushchev had dispatched to Havana to arrange the withdrawal of missiles, spoke to the Soviet officers in Cuba in November. He tried to turn the lack of camouflage into a joke. "The Soviet rockets stood out like during a parade on the Red Square—but erect," he told Pliev and his comrades. "Our rocket men apparently decided to give Americans a middle finger in this way." Mikoyan even soothed their anguish about the missiles' discovery, saying that it was West German intelligence, not the U-2, that discovered the Soviet missiles. (In fact, the West Germans had picked up some evidence but hardly the smoking gun that the U-2 flight uncovered.) And he alleged that once the Soviet missiles were spotted, they no longer served any purpose of deterrence—a preposterous claim, given that the United States could hardly be deterred by missiles it didn't know about. Despite Mikoyan's best efforts, Soviet commanders and officers took the order to leave Cuba as a humiliating retreat. Many of them had to recover from nervous breakdowns, recuperating at Black Sea resorts not too far from the ports from which they had sailed to Cuba.

Khrushchev was eager to cover his own retreat. He deliberately avoided any criticism of the Soviet military's performance in Cuba. Although the errors in planning were plain to see, the Soviet leader was more interested in depicting the debacle as a victory than in assigning responsibility for the mishaps. In this, his interests overlapped with those of the Soviet supreme command, which wanted to avoid responsibility, and so the secret fumbles of Operation Anadyr were swept under the rug. Documents about the operation were boxed up and sent to gather dust in the archives, where they remained sealed until last year. Biryuzov was promoted to the head of the general staff, and his career remained untarnished until his death in 1964, when he perished in a plane crash five days after Khrushchev was overthrown by his Presidium colleagues.

Soviet military officials viewed operation Anadyr not as a colossal failure but as a shrewd ploy that almost worked. The lessons they learned were simple: had the Soviets done a better job of coping with the enormous logistical challenges, had they tried harder to hide the missiles, or had they shot down U.S. reconnaissance planes earlier, with a little bit of luck, Operation Anadyr could indeed have succeeded. Statsenko, for all his insights, became fixated on U-2s and recommended in his report that the Soviets urgently develop a technology—"invisible rays"—which would allow them to "distort" the images captured by the reconnaissance planes or perhaps just expose the film they carried. Apparently, it never occurred to him that the whole operation was a bad idea from the start. In fact, the entire point of his postmortem was to explore ways to send strategic missiles "to any distance and deploy them on short notice," that is, do the same thing again, but do it better. Perhaps Statsenko deemed it above his pay grade to question the bright ideas sent from on high.

Only in the late 1980s, during the era of Mikhail Gorbachev's "new thinking," did a different view of the crisis emerge within the Soviet Union. Inspired largely by the American literature on the episode, Moscow came to see the crisis as an unacceptably dangerous moment. With the collapse of the Soviet Union, however, fears of a nuclear conflict receded, and for Russia, the Cuban missile crisis lost immediate political relevance and became plain old history. Veterans of the crisis embraced heroic narratives of their exploits. Anatoly Gribkov, a general who helped plan Operation Anadyr, declared in his assessment of the crisis, written in the first decade of this century, that the Soviet military's performance was "an example of the finest military art." Embarrassing failures were mostly forgotten. Castro, who had horrified Khrushchev by proposing to nuke the United States, later strenuously denied having done so. But all agreed that the Cuban missile crisis was never to be repeated.

BACK ON THE BRINK

Until now. Although Russia in theory remains committed to avoiding a nuclear war, Putin seems to be stoking fears of just such a conflict. Like Khrushchev in his time, Putin is rattling the nuclear saber to prove to everyone—and perhaps above all to himself—that Moscow will not be defeated. Also like Khrushchev, Putin is a gambler, and his misadventure in Ukraine suffers from the same feedback failures, excessive secrecy, and hypercentralization that plagued Khrushchev's in Cuba. Just as Khrushchev's lieutenants failed to question his rationale for aiding Cuba, so Putin's top ministers and advisers did not resist his claim that Ukrainians and Russians were one people and therefore Ukraine had to be "returned" to Russia, by force if need be.

Facing no pushback, Putin turned to Sergei Shoigu, his minister of defense, and Valery Gerasimov, the head of the general staff, to carry out his will. They failed even more spectacularly than their predecessors had in 1962, hobbled by the same structural impediments that ruined Operation Anadyr. It is apparent that the general staff has never digested the awkward details of the story of Khrushchev's failure, even with the declassification of this new batch of documents.

As he peered uneasily over the brink of nuclear apocalypse, Khrushchev found time to act as a mediator in the monthlong Sino-Indian War, which broke out during the Cuban missile crisis. "History tells us that in order to stop a conflict, one should begin not by exploring the reasons why it happened but by pursuing a cease-fire," he explained to that Indian visitor on October 26. He added, "What's important is not to cry for the dead or to avenge them, but to save those who might die if the conflict continues." He could well have been referring to his own fears about the events brewing that day in the Caribbean.

To Khrushchev, the whole Cuban operation was one big poker match.

Terrified by those developments, Khrushchev understood at last that his reckless gamble had failed and ordered a retreat. Kennedy, too, opted for a compromise. In the end, neither leader proved willing to test the other's redlines, probably because they did not know where exactly those redlines lay. Khrushchev's hubris and resentment led him to the worst misadventure of his political career. But his—and Kennedy's—caution led to a negotiated solution.

Their prudence holds lessons for today, when so many commentators in Russia and in the West are calling for a resolute victory of one side or the other in Ukraine. Some Americans and Europeans assume that the use of nuclear weapons in the current crisis is completely out of the question and thus that the West can safely push the Kremlin into the corner by obtaining a comprehensive victory for Ukraine. But plenty of people in Russia, especially around Putin and among his propagandists, defiantly say that there would be "no world without Russia," meaning that Moscow should prefer a nuclear Armageddon to defeat.

If such voices had prevailed in 1962, we'd all be dead now.

Postimperial Empire

How the War in Ukraine Is Transforming Europe

TIMOTHY GARTON ASH

History loves unintended consequences. The latest example is particularly ironic: Russian President Vladimir Putin's attempt to restore the Russian empire by recolonizing Ukraine has opened the door to a postimperial Europe. A Europe, that is, that no longer has any empires dominated by a single people or nation, either on land or across the seas—a situation the continent has never seen before.

Paradoxically, however, to secure this postimperial future and stand up to Russian aggression, the EU must itself take on some of the characteristics of an empire. It must have a sufficient degree of unity, central authority, and effective decision-making to defend the shared interests and values of Europeans. If every single member state has a veto over vital decisions, the union will falter, internally and externally.

TIMOTHY GARTON ASH is Professor of European Studies at the University of Oxford and Senior Fellow at the Hoover Institution at Stanford University. This essay draws on the analysis in his new book *Homelands: A Personal History of Europe* (Yale University Press, 2023).

Illustration by Eduardo Morciano

Europeans are unaccustomed to looking at themselves through the lens of empire, but doing so can offer an illuminating and disturbing perspective. In fact, the EU itself has a colonial past. As the Swedish scholars Peo Hansen and Stefan Jonsson have documented, in the 1950s the original architects of what would eventually become the EU regarded member states' African colonies as an integral part of the European project. Even as European countries prosecuted often brutal wars to defend their colonies, officials spoke glowingly of "Eurafrica," treating the overseas possessions of countries such as France as belonging to the new European Economic Community. Portugal fought to retain control of Angola and Mozambique into the early 1970s.

The lens of empire is even more revealing when one peers through it at the large part of Europe that, during the Cold War, was behind the Iron Curtain under Soviet or Yugoslav communist rule. The Soviet Union was a continuation of the Russian empire, even though many of its leaders were not ethnic Russians. During and after World War II, it incorporated countries and territories (including the Baltic states and western Ukraine) that had not been part of the Soviet Union before 1939. At the same time, it extended its effective empire to the very center of Europe, including much of what had historically been known as central Germany, restyled as East Germany.

There was, in other words, an inner and an outer Russian empire. The key to understanding both Eastern Europe and the Soviet Union in the 1980s was to recognize that this was indeed an empire—and an empire in decay. Decolonization of the outer empire followed in uniquely swift and peaceful fashion in 1989 and 1990, but then, even more remarkably, came the disintegration of the inner empire in 1991. This was prompted, as is often the case, by disorder in the imperial center. More unusually, the final blow was delivered by the core imperial nation: Russia. Today, however, Russia is straining to regain control over some of the lands it gave up, thrusting toward the new eastern borders of the West.

GHOSTS OF EMPIRES PAST

Anyone who has studied the history of empires should have known that the collapse of the Soviet Union would not be the end of the story. Empires usually do not give up without a struggle, as the British, French, Portuguese, and "Eurafricanists" demonstrated after 1945. In one small corner, the Russian empire struck back rather quickly. In 1992, General Alexander Lebed used Russia's 14th Armed Guards to end a war between separatists from the region of the newly independent state of Moldova that lies east of the river Dniester and legitimate Moldovan forces. The result was what is still the illegal para-state of Transnistria at the eastern end of Moldova, critically located on the frontier to Ukraine. In the 1990s, Russia also fought two brutal wars to retain control of Chechnya, and it actively supported separatists in the Abkhazia and South Ossetia regions of Georgia.

Yet as Moscow sought to claw back some of its lost colonial territories, the EU was preoccupied with two completions of Europe's characteristic twentieth-century transition from empires to states. The violent disintegration of Yugoslavia and the peaceful divorce of the Czech and Slovak parts of Czechoslovakia drew renewed attention to the legacies of, respectively, the Ottoman and Austro-Hungarian Empires, which had been formally dissolved at the end of World War I. But there was nothing inevitable about the breakup of Czechoslovakia and Yugoslavia. Postimperial multinational states do not have to disintegrate into nation-states, and it is not necessarily the best thing for the people who live there if they do. Yet it is simply an empirical observation that this is the way recent European history has tended to go. Hence today's intricate patchwork of 24 individual states in Europe east of what used to be the Iron Curtain (and north of Greece and Turkey), whereas in 1989, there were just nine.

Russia's larger neocolonial pushback began with Putin declaring a course of confrontation with the West at the Munich Security Conference in 2007, where he denounced the U.S.-led unipolar order. This was followed by his armed seizure of Abkhazia and South Ossetia from Georgia in 2008. It escalated with the annexation of Crimea and the invasion of eastern Ukraine in 2014, beginning a Russo-Ukrainian war that, as Ukrainians frequently remind the West, has been going on for nine years. To adapt a telling phrase of the historian A. J. P. Taylor, 2014 was the turning point at which the West failed to turn. One can never know what might have happened if the West had reacted more forcefully then, by reducing its energy dependence on Russia, stopping the flow of dirty Russian money swilling around the West, supplying more arms to Ukraine, and issuing a more forceful message to Moscow. But there is little doubt that such a course would have put both Ukraine and the West in a different and better position in 2022.

Even as Russia pushed back, the West faltered. The year 2008 marked the beginning of a pause in what had been a remarkable

35-year story of the enlargement of the geopolitical West. In 1972, the European Economic Community, the predecessor of the EU, had just six members, and NATO had only 15. By 2008, however, the EU had 27 member states, and NATO had 26. The territories of both organizations extended deep into central and eastern Europe, including the Baltic states, which had been part of the Soviet-Russian inner empire until 1991. Although Putin had reluctantly accepted this double enlargement of the West, he increasingly feared and resented it.

Europe still ultimately relies for its security on the United States.

At NATO's April 2008 summit in Bucharest, the administration of U.S. President George W. Bush wanted to start serious preparations for Georgia and Ukraine to join NATO, but leading European states, including France and especially Germany, were resolutely opposed. As a compromise, the summit's final communiqué declared that Georgia and Ukraine "will become members of NATO in the future" but without specifying concrete steps to make that happen. This was the worst of both worlds. It increased Putin's sense of a U.S.-led threat to the remains of the Russian empire without guaranteeing the security of Ukraine or Georgia. Putin's tanks rolled into Abkhazia and South Ossetia just four months later. Subsequent NATO enlargements took in the small southeast European countries of Albania, Croatia, Montenegro, and North Macedonia, making today's total of 30 NATO members, but these additions hardly changed the balance of power in eastern Europe.

At the same time, EU expansion stalled, not because of Russian pushback but because of "enlargement fatigue" after new central and eastern European members were admitted in 2004 and 2007, together with the impact of other major challenges to the EU. The global financial crisis of 2008 segued from 2010 onward into a long-running crisis of the eurozone, followed by the refugee crisis of 2015–16, Brexit and the election of U.S. President Donald Trump in 2016, the rise of antiliberal populist movements in such countries as France and Italy, and the COVID-19 pandemic. Croatia slipped into the EU in 2013, but North Macedonia, accepted as a candidate country in 2005, is still waiting today. The EU's approach to the western Balkans over the last two decades recalls nothing so much as the *New Yorker* cartoon of a businessman saying to an obviously unwelcome caller on the telephone, "How about never? Is never good for you?"

EUROPE WHOLE AND FREE

Illustrating once again the truth of Heraclitus's saying that "war is the father of all," the largest war in Europe since 1945 has unblocked both these processes, opening the way to a further, large and consequential eastward enlargement of the West. As late as February 2022, on the eve of Russia's full-scale invasion of Ukraine, French President Emmanuel Macron was still expressing reservations about enlarging the EU to include the western Balkans. German Chancellor Olaf Scholz supported the western Balkan enlargement but wanted to draw the line at that. Then, as Ukraine courageously and unexpectedly resisted Russia's attempt to take over the entire country, Ukrainian President Volodymyr Zelensky put the EU on the spot. Ukrainian opinion had evolved over the last three decades, through the catalytic events of the Orange Revolution in 2004 and the Euromaidan protests in 2014, and his presidency already exhibited a strong European orientation. Accordingly, he repeatedly asked not just for weapons and sanctions but for EU membership, too. It is remarkable that this long-term aspiration should have been among the top three demands from a country facing the imminent prospect of a ruinous Russian occupation.

By June 2022, Macron and Scholz were standing with Zelensky in Kyiv, together with Italian Prime Minister Mario Draghi (who had endorsed the prospect of membership a month earlier and played a notable part in changing his fellow leaders' minds) and Romanian President Klaus Iohannis. All four visitors declared that they supported the EU accepting Ukraine as a candidate for membership. That same month, the EU made this its formal position, also accepting Moldova as a candidate (subject to some preliminary conditions for both countries) and sending an encouraging signal to Georgia that the EU might in the future grant it the same status.

NATO has not made any such formal promise to Ukraine, but given the extent of NATO member states' support for the defense of Ukraine—dramatically symbolized by U.S. President Joe Biden's visit to Kyiv earlier this year—it is now hard to imagine that the war could end without some sort of de facto, if not de jure, security commitments from the United States and other NATO members. Meanwhile, the war has prompted Sweden and Finland to join NATO (although Turkish objections have delayed that process). The war has also brought the EU and NATO into a more clearly articulated partnership as, so to speak, the two strong arms of the West. In the long run, NATO membership for Georgia, Moldova, and Ukraine would be the logical complement to EU membership and those countries' only durable guarantee against renewed Russian revanchism. Speaking at the World Economic Forum's annual meeting this year in Davos, no less a realpolitiker than former U.S. Secretary of State Henry Kissinger endorsed this perspective, noting that the war that Ukraine's non-NATO neutrality was supposed to prevent had already broken out. At the Munich Security Conference in February, several Western leaders explicitly supported NATO membership for Ukraine.

The project of taking the rest of eastern Europe, apart from Russia, in to the two key organizations of the geopolitical West is one that will require many years to implement. The first double eastward enlargement of the West took some 17 years, if one counts from January 1990 to January 2007, when Bulgaria and Romania joined the EU. Among many evident difficulties is that Russian forces currently occupy parts of Georgia, Moldova, and Ukraine. For the EU, there is a precedent for admitting a country that has regions its legitimate government does not control: part of Cyprus, a member state, is effectively controlled by Turkey. But there is no such precedent for NATO. Ideally, future rounds of NATO enlargement would be done in the context of a larger dialogue about European security with Russia, as in fact happened during NATO's 1999 and 2004 rounds of eastward enlargement, with the latter even securing the reluctant agreement of Putin. But that is hard to imagine happening again unless a very different leader is in the Kremlin.

It may take until the 2030s to achieve this double enlargement, but if it does occur, it will represent another giant step toward the goal identified in a 1989 speech by U.S. President George H. W. Bush: Europe whole and free. Europe does not end at any clear lines—although at the North Pole it ends at a point—but merely fades away across Eurasia, across the Mediterranean, and, in some significant sense, even across the Atlantic. (Canada would be a perfect member of the EU.) Yet with the completion of this eastward enlargement, more of geographical, historical, and cultural Europe than ever before would be gathered into a single interlinked set of political, economic, and security communities.

Beyond that, there is the question of a democratic, post-Lukashenko Belarus, if it can free itself from Russia's grip. Another phase, also potentially embracing Armenia, Azerbaijan, and Turkey (a NATO member since 1952 and an accepted candidate for EU membership since 1999), could eventually contribute to a further geostrategic strengthening of the West in an increasingly post-Western world. But the enormous scale of the task the EU has just assumed, combined with political circumstances inside those countries, makes this a prospect that is not on the current agenda of European politics.

THE EU TRANSFORMED

This long-term vision of an enlarged EU, in strategic partnership with NATO, immediately raises two large questions. What about Russia? And how can there be a sustainable European Union of 36, going on 40, member states? It is difficult to address the first question without knowing what a post-Putin Russia will look like, but a significant part of the answer will in any case depend on the external geopolitical environment created to the west and south of Russia. This environment is directly susceptible to shaping by Western policymakers in a way that the internal evolution of a declining but still nuclear-armed Russia is not.

Politically, the most important speech on this subject was delivered by Scholz in Prague last August. Reaffirming his new commitment to a large eastward expansion of the EU—including the western Balkans, Moldova, Ukraine, and, in the longer term, Georgia—he insisted that as with previous rounds of widening, this one would require further deepening of the union. Otherwise, an EU of 36 member states would cease to be a coherent, effective political community. Specifically, Scholz argued for more "qualified majority voting," an EU decision-making procedure that requires the assent of 55 percent of member states, representing at least 65 percent of the bloc's population. This process would ensure that a single member state, such as Viktor Orban's Hungary, could no longer threaten to veto another round of sanctions on Russia or other measures that most member states regard as necessary. In short, the central authority of the EU needs to become stronger to hold together such a large and diverse political community, although always with democratic checks and balances and without a single national hegemon.

Scholz's analysis is evidently correct, and it is doubly important because it comes from the leader of Europe's central power. But is this not itself a version of empire? A new kind of empire, that is, based on voluntary membership and democratic consent. Most Europeans recoil from the term "empire," regarding it as something belonging to a dark past, intrinsically bad, undemocratic, and illiberal. Indeed, one reason Europeans have been talking more about empire recently is the rise of protest movements that call on former European colonial powers to recognize, acknowledge, and make reparation for the evils done by their colonial empires. So Europeans prefer the language of integration, union, or multilevel governance. In *The Road to Unfreedom*, the Yale historian Timothy Snyder characterizes the contest between the EU and Putin's Russia as "integration or empire." But the word "integration" describes a process, not an end state. To counterpose the two concepts is rather like speaking of "rail travel versus city"; the method of transportation does not describe the destination.

Clearly, if one means by "empire" direct control over other people's territory by a single colonial state, the EU is not an empire. But as another Yale historian, Arne Westad, has argued, this is too narrow a definition of the word. If one of the defining features of empire is supranational authority, law, and power, then the EU already has some important characteristics of empire. Indeed, in many policy areas, European law takes precedence over national law, which is what so infuriates British Euroskeptics. On trade, the EU negotiates on behalf of all member states. The legal scholar Anu Bradford has documented the global reach of the EU's "unilateral regulatory power" on everything from product standards, data privacy, and online hate speech to consumer health and safety and environmental protection. Her book is revealingly, if a touch hyperbolically, subtitled *How the European Union Rules the World*.

Moreover, the longest-running empire in European history, the Holy Roman Empire, was itself an example of a complex, multilevel system of governance, with no single nation or state as hegemon. The comparison with the Holy Roman Empire was made already in 2006 by the political scientist Jan Zielonka, who explored a "neo-medieval paradigm" to describe the enlarged EU.

Support for thinking about the EU in this way comes from an especially pertinent source. Dmytro Kuleba, Ukraine's foreign minister, has described the European Union as "the first ever attempt to build a liberal empire," contrasting it with Putin's attempt to restore Russia's colonial empire by military conquest. When he and I spoke in the heavily sandbagged Ukrainian Foreign Ministry in Kyiv in February, he explained that a liberal empire's key characteristic is keeping together very different nations and ethnic groups "not by force but by the rule of law." Seen from Kyiv, a liberal, democratic empire is needed to defeat an illiberal, antidemocratic one.

Several of the obstacles to achieving this goal are also connected with Europe's imperial history. The German political scientist Gwendolyn Sasse has argued that Germany must "decolonize" its view of eastern Europe. This is an unusual version of decolonization. When people speak of the United Kingdom or France needing to decolonize their view of Africa, they mean that these countries should stop seeing it (consciously or unconsciously) through the lens of their own former colonial history. What Sasse suggests is that Germany, with its long historical fascination with Russia, needs to stop seeing countries like Ukraine and Moldova through somebody else's colonial lens: Russia's.

Europe needs to be more conscious of its colonial past.

The imperial legacies and memories of former western European colonial powers also impede European collective action in other ways. The United Kingdom is an obvious example. Its departure from the EU had many causes, but among them was an obsession with strictly legal sovereignty that goes all the way back to a 1532 law that enacted King Henry VIII's break from the Roman Catholic Church, resonantly claiming that "this realm of England is an empire." The word "empire" was here used in an older sense, meaning supreme sovereign authority. The memory of the overseas British Empire "on which the sun never set" also played into a mistaken belief that the United Kingdom would be just fine going it alone. "We used to run the biggest empire the world has ever seen, and with a much smaller domestic population and a relatively tiny civil service," wrote Boris Johnson, the most influential leader of the Leave campaign, in the run-up to the 2016 Brexit referendum. "Are we really unable to do trade deals?" In the French case, memories of past imperial grandeur translate into a different distortion: not rejection of the EU but a tendency to treat Europe as France writ large.

Then there is the perception of Europe in places that were once European colonies or, like China, felt the negative impact of European imperialism. Chinese schoolchildren are taught to contemplate and resent a "century of humiliation" at the hands of Western imperialists. At the same time, President Xi Jinping proudly refers to continuities, from China's own earlier civilizational empires to today's "Chinese dream" of national rejuvenation.

If Europe is to make its case more effectively to major postcolonial countries such as India and South Africa, it needs to be more conscious of this colonial past. (It might also help to point out that a large and growing number of EU member states in eastern Europe were themselves the objects of European colonialism, not its perpetrators.) When European leaders trot around the globe today, presenting the EU as the sublime incarnation of postcolonial values of democracy, human rights, peace, and human dignity, they often seem to have forgotten Europe's long and quite recent colonial history—but the rest of the world has not. That is one reason why postcolonial countries such as India and South Africa have not lined up with the West over the war in Ukraine. Polling conducted in late 2022 and early 2023 in China, India, and Turkey for the European Council on Foreign Relations—in partnership with Oxford University's Europe in a Changing World research project, which I co-direct—shows just how far they are from understanding what is happening in Ukraine as an independence struggle against Russia's war of attempted recolonization.

OVERLAPPING EMPIRES

Beyond this is the fact that, as the war in Ukraine has once again made clear, Europe still ultimately relies for its security on the United States. Macron and Scholz talk often of the need for "European sovereignty," yet when it comes to military support for Ukraine, Scholz has not been ready to send a single class of major weapons (armored fighting vehicles, tanks) unless the United States does so, too. It is a strange version of sovereignty. The war has certainly galvanized European thinking, and action, on defense. Scholz has given the English language a new German word, *Zeitenwende* (roughly, historic turning point), and committed to a sustained increase in German defense spending and military readiness. Germany taking the military dimension of power seriously again would be no small fact in modern European history.

Poland plans to build up the biggest army inside the EU, and a victorious Ukraine would have the largest and most combat-hardened armed forces in Europe outside Russia. The EU has a European Peace Facility, which during the first year of the war in Ukraine spent some $3.8 billion to co-fund member states' arms supplies to Ukraine. European Commission President Ursula von der Leyen is now proposing that the European Peace Facility should directly order ammunition and weapons for Ukraine, comparing this to the EU's procurement of vaccines during the COVID-19 pandemic.

The EU thus also has the very modest beginnings of the military dimension that traditionally belongs to imperial power. If all this happens, the European pillar of the transatlantic alliance should grow significantly stronger, thus also potentially freeing up more U.S. military resources to confront the threat from China in the Indo-Pacific. But Europe is still unlikely to be able to defend itself alone against any major external threat.

Although the United States' own foundational identity is that of an anticolonial power, it has in NATO an "empire by invitation," in the historian Geir Lundestad's phrase. Explaining his use of the word "empire," Lundestad quotes former U.S. National Security Adviser Zbigniew Brzezinski's argument that "empire" can be a descriptive rather than a normative term. This American anti-imperial empire is more hegemonic than the European one but less so than it was in the past. As Turkish President Recep Tayyip Erdogan has repeatedly demonstrated, and Scholz also in his way, the United States can't simply tell other NATO member states what to do. This alliance, therefore, also has a credible claim to be an empire by consent.

One can push the language of empire too far. Comparing the EU and NATO with past empires reveals differences that are as interesting as the similarities. Politically, neither the European Union nor the United States will ever present themselves as an empire, nor would they be well advised to do so. Analytically, however, it is worth reflecting that whereas the twentieth century saw most of Europe transitioning from empires to states, the world of the twenty-first century still has empires—and it needs new kinds of empire to stand up to them. Whether Europe actually manages to create a liberal empire strong enough to defend the interests and values of Europeans will, as always in human history, depend on conjuncture, luck, collective will, and individual leadership.

Here, then, is the surprising prospect that the war in Ukraine reveals: the EU as a postimperial empire, in strategic partnership with an American postimperial empire, to prevent the comeback of a declining Russian empire and constrain a rising Chinese one.

The Myth of Multipolarity

American Power's Staying Power

STEPHEN G. BROOKS AND WILLIAM C. WOHLFORTH

In the 1990s and the early years of this century, the United States' global dominance could scarcely be questioned. No matter which metric of power one looked at, it showed a dramatic American lead. Never since the birth of the modern state system in the mid-seventeenth century had any country been so far ahead in the military, economic, and technological realms simultaneously. Allied with the United States, meanwhile, were the vast majority of the world's richest countries, and they were tied together by a set of international institutions that Washington had played the lead role in constructing. The United States could conduct its foreign policy under fewer external constraints than any leading state in modern history. And as dissatisfied as China, Russia, and other aspiring powers were with their status in the system, they realized they could do nothing to overturn it.

STEPHEN G. BROOKS is a Professor of Government at Dartmouth College and a Guest Professor at Stockholm University.

WILLIAM C. WOHLFORTH is Daniel Webster Professor at Dartmouth College.

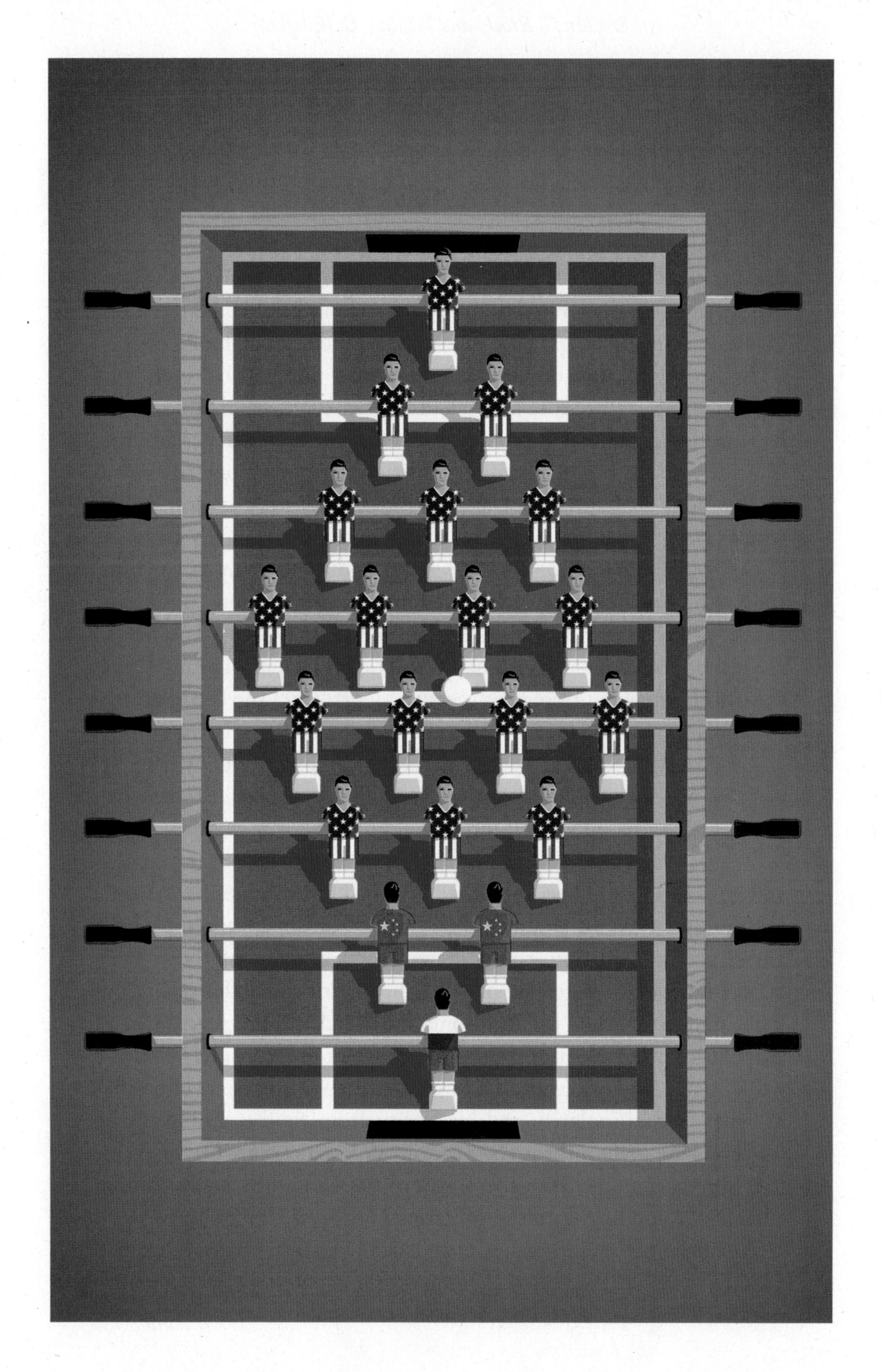

Illustration by Pete Ryan

That was then. Now, American power seems much diminished. In the intervening two decades, the United States has suffered costly, failed interventions in Afghanistan and Iraq, a devastating financial crisis, deepening political polarization, and, in Donald Trump, four years of a president with isolationist impulses. All the while, China continued its remarkable economic ascent and grew more assertive than ever. To many, Russia's 2022 invasion of Ukraine sounded the death knell for U.S. primacy, a sign that the United States could no longer hold back the forces of revisionism and enforce the international order it had built.

According to most observers, the unipolar moment has come to a definitive end. Pointing to the size of China's economy, many analysts have declared the world bipolar. But most go even further, arguing that the world is on the verge of transitioning to multipolarity or has already done so. China, Iran, and Russia all endorse this view, one in which they, the leading anti-American revisionists, finally have the power to shape the system to their liking. India and many other countries in the global South have reached the same conclusion, contending that after decades of superpower dominance, they are at last free to chart their own course. Even many Americans take it for granted that the world is now multipolar. Successive reports from the U.S. National Intelligence Council have proclaimed as much, as have figures on the left and right who favor a more modest U.S. foreign policy. There is perhaps no more widely accepted truth about the world today than the idea that it is no longer unipolar.

But this view is wrong. The world is neither bipolar nor multipolar, and it is not about to become either. Yes, the United States has become less dominant over the past 20 years, but it remains at the top of the global power hierarchy—safely above China and far, far above every other country. No longer can one pick any metric to see this reality, but it becomes clear when the right ones are used. And the persistence of unipolarity becomes even more evident when one considers that the world is still largely devoid of a force that shaped great-power politics in times of multipolarity and bipolarity, from the beginning of the modern state system through the Cold War: balancing. Other countries simply cannot match the power of the United States by joining alliances or building up their militaries.

American power still casts a large shadow across the globe, but it is admittedly smaller than before. Yet this development should be put in perspective. What is at issue is only the nature of unipolarity—not its existence.

MINOR THIRD

During the Cold War, the world was undeniably bipolar, defined above all by the competition between the United States and the Soviet Union. After the collapse of the Soviet Union, the world turned unipolar, with the United States clearly standing alone at the top. Many who proclaim multipolarity seem to think of power as influence—that is, the ability to get others to do what you want. Since the United States could not pacify Afghanistan or Iraq and cannot solve many other global problems, the argument runs, the world must be multipolar. But polarity centers on a different meaning of power, one that is measurable: power as resources, especially military might and economic heft. And indeed, at the root of most multipolarity talk these days is the idea that scholarly pioneers of the concept had in mind: that international politics works differently depending on how resources are distributed among the biggest states.

For the system to be multipolar, however, its workings must be shaped largely by the three or more roughly matched states at the top. The United States and China are undoubtedly the two most powerful countries, but at least one more country must be roughly in their league for multipolarity to exist. This is where claims of multipolarity fall apart. Every country that could plausibly rank third—France, Germany, India, Japan, Russia, the United Kingdom—is in no way a rough peer of the United States or China.

That is true no matter which metric one uses. Polarity is often still measured using the indicators fashionable in the mid-twentieth century, chiefly military outlays and economic output. Even by those crude measures, however, the system is not multipolar, and it is a sure bet that it won't be for many decades. A simple tabulation makes this clear: barring an outright collapse of either the United States or China, the gap between those countries and any of the also-rans will not close anytime soon. All but India are too small in population to ever be in the same league, while India is too poor; it cannot possibly attain this status until much later in this century.

These stark differences between today's material realities and a reasonable understanding of multipolarity point to another problem with any talk of its return: the equally stark contrast between today's international politics and the workings of the multipolar systems in centuries past. Before 1945, multipolarity was the norm. International politics featured constantly shifting alliances among roughly matched

THE GREAT-POWER GAP

Annual GDP of major countries (in current US$trillions)

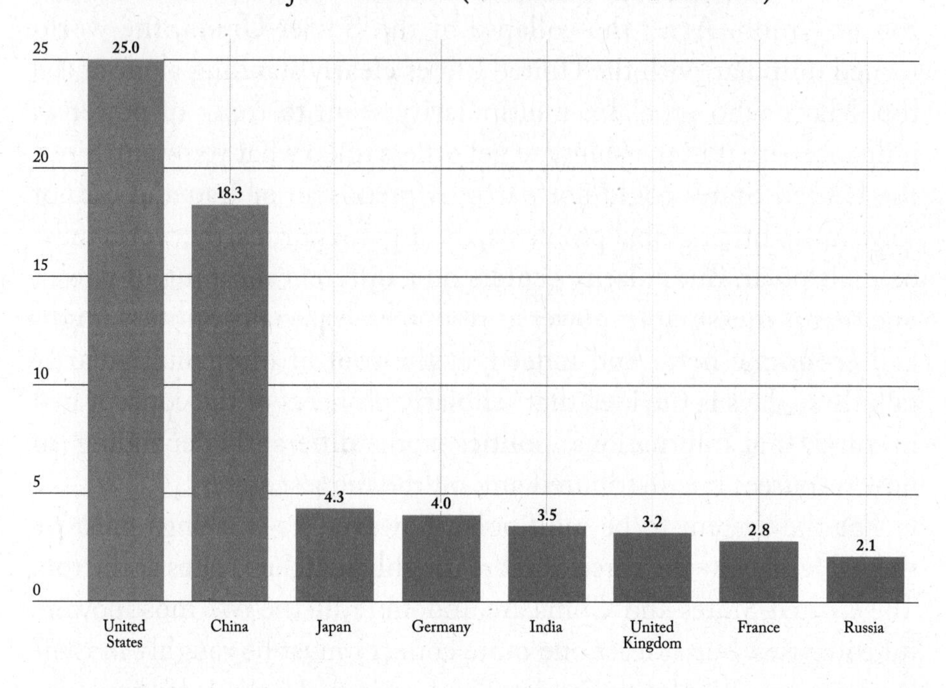

Annual military spending of major countries (in current US$billions)

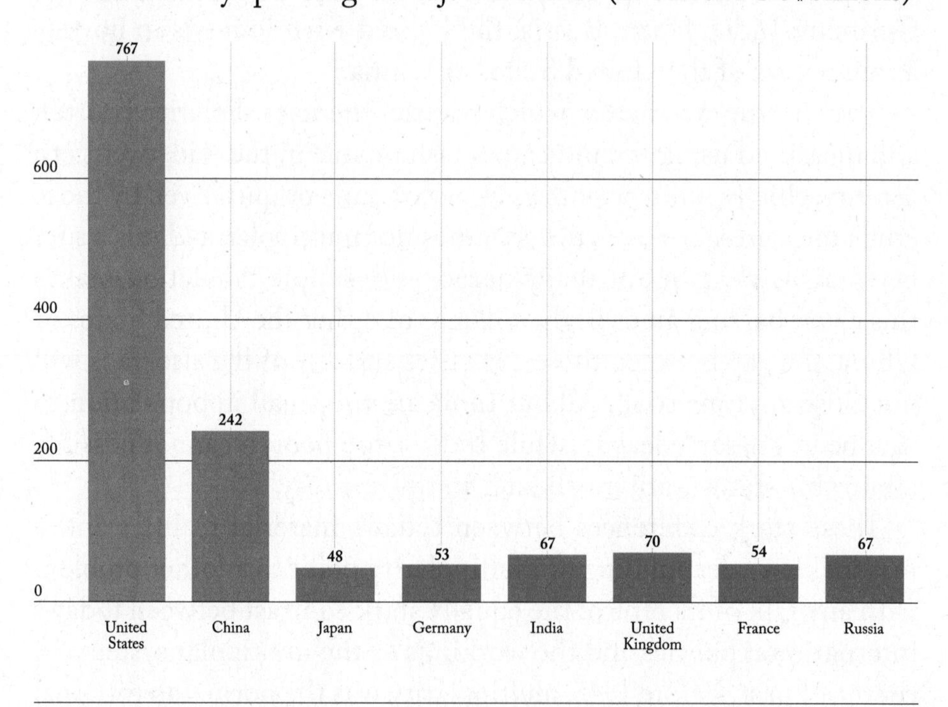

Sources: International Monetary Fund (2022); International Institute for Strategic Studies (2022).

great powers. The alliance game was played mainly among the great powers, not between them and lesser states. Coalition arithmetic was the lodestar of statecraft: shifts in alliances could upset the balance of power overnight, as the gain or loss of a great power in an alliance dwarfed what any one state could do internally to augment its own power in the short run. In 1801, for example, the Russian emperor Paul I seriously contemplated allying with rather than against Napoleon, heightening fears in the United Kingdom about the prospect of French hegemony in Europe—worries that may have, according to some historians, led the British to play a role in Paul's assassination that same year.

Today, almost all the world's real alliances (the ones that entail security guarantees) bind smaller states to Washington, and the main dynamic is the expansion of that alliance system. Because the United States still has the most material power and so many allies, unless it abrogates its own alliances wholesale, the fate of great-power politics does not hinge on any country's choice of partners.

In multipolar eras, the relatively equal distribution of capabilities meant that states were often surpassing one another in power, leading to long periods of transition in which many powers claimed to be number one, and it wasn't clear which deserved the title. Immediately before World War I, for example, the United Kingdom could claim to be number one on the basis of its global navy and massive colonial holdings, yet its economy and army were smaller than those of Germany, which itself had a smaller army than Russia—and all three countries' economies were dwarfed by that of the United States. The easily replicable nature of technology, meanwhile, made it possible for one great power to quickly close the gap with a superior rival by imitating its advantages. Thus, in the early twentieth century, when Germany's leaders sought to take the United Kingdom down a peg, they had little trouble rapidly building a fleet that was technologically competitive with the Royal Navy. The situation today is very different. For one thing, there is one clear leader and one clear aspirant. For another, the nature of military technology and the structure of the global economy slow the process of the aspirant overtaking the leader. The most powerful weapons today are formidably complex, and the United States and its allies control many of the technologies needed to produce them.

The multipolar world was an ugly world. Great-power wars broke out constantly—more than once a decade from 1500 to 1945.

With frightening regularity, all or most of the strongest states would fight one another in horrific, all-consuming conflicts: the Thirty Years' War, the Wars of Louis XIV, the Seven Years' War, the Napoleonic Wars, World War I, and World War II. The shifting, hugely consequential, and decidedly uncertain alliance politics of multipolarity contributed to these conflicts. So did the system's frequent power transitions and the fleeting nature of leading states' grasp on their status. Fraught though the current international environment may be compared with the halcyon days of the 1990s, it lacks these inducements to conflict and so bears no meaningful resemblance to the age of multipolarity.

DON'T BET ON BIPOLARITY

Using GDP and military spending, some analysts might make a plausible case for an emergent bipolarity. But that argument dissolves when one uses metrics that properly account for the profound changes in the sources of state power wrought by multiple technological revolutions. More accurate measures suggest that the United States and China remain in fundamentally different categories and will stay there for a long time, especially in the military and technological realms.

No metric is invoked more frequently by the heralds of a polarity shift than GDP, but analysts in and outside China have long questioned the country's official economic data. Using satellite-collected data about the intensity of lights at night—electricity use correlates with economic activity—the economist Luis Martinez has estimated that Chinese GDP growth in recent decades has been about one-third lower than the officially reported statistics. According to leaked U.S. diplomatic cables, in 2007, Li Keqiang, a provincial official who would go on to become China's premier, told the U.S. ambassador to China that he himself did not trust his country's "man-made" GDP figures. Instead, he relied on proxies, such as electricity use. Since Xi took power, reliable data on the Chinese economy has gotten even harder to come by because the Chinese government has ceased publishing tens of thousands of economic statistics that were once used to estimate China's true GDP.

But some indicators cannot be faked. To evaluate China's economic capacity, for example, consider the proportion of worldwide profits in a given industry that one country's firms account for. Building on the work of the political economist Sean Starrs, research by one of us (Brooks) has found that of the top 2,000 corporations in the world, U.S. firms are ranked first in global profit shares in 74 percent of sectors, whereas Chinese firms are ranked first in just 11 percent of sectors. The data on high-tech sectors is even more telling: U.S. firms now have a 53 percent profit share in these crucial industries, and every other country with a significant high-tech sector has a profit share in the single digits. (Japan comes in second at seven percent, China comes in third at six percent, and Taiwan comes in fourth at five percent.)

The best way to measure technological capacity is to look at payments for the use of intellectual property—technology so valuable that others are willing to spend money on it. This data shows that China's extensive R & D investments over the past decade are bearing fruit, with Chinese patent royalties having grown from less than $1 billion in 2014 to almost $12 billion in 2021. But even now, China still receives less than a tenth of what the United States does each year ($125 billion), and it even lags far behind Germany ($59 billion) and Japan ($47 billion).

Today, almost all the world's real alliances bind smaller states to Washington.

Militarily, meanwhile, most analysts still see China as far from being a global peer of the United States, despite the rapid modernization of Chinese forces. How significant and lasting is the U.S. advantage? Consider the capabilities that give the United States what the political scientist Barry Posen has called "command of the commons"—that is, control over the air, the open sea, and space. Command of the commons is what makes the United States a true global military power. Until China can contest the United States' dominance in this domain, it will remain merely a regional military power. We have counted 13 categories of systems as underlying this ability—everything from nuclear submarines to satellites to aircraft carriers to heavy transport planes—and China is below 20 percent of the U.S. level in all but five of these capabilities, and in only two areas (cruisers and destroyers; military satellites) does China have more than a third of the U.S. capability. The United States remains so far ahead because it has devoted immense resources to developing these systems over many decades; closing these gaps would also require decades of effort. The disparity becomes even greater when one moves beyond a raw count and factors in quality. The United States' 68 nuclear submarines, for example, are too quiet for China to track, whereas China's 12 nuclear submarines remain noisy enough for the U.S. Navy's advanced antisubmarine warfare sensors to track them in deep water.

A comparison with the Soviet Union is instructive. The Red Army was a real peer of the U.S. military during the Cold War in a way that the Chinese military is not. The Soviets enjoyed three advantages that China lacks. First was favorable geography: with the conquest of Eastern Europe in World War II, the Soviets could base massive military force in the heart of Europe, a region that comprised a huge chunk of the world's economic output. Second was a large commitment to guns over butter in a command economy geared toward the production of military power: the percentage of GDP that Moscow devoted to defense remained in the double digits throughout the Cold War, an unprecedented share for a modern great power in peacetime. Third was the relatively uncomplicated nature of military technology: for most of the Cold War, the Soviets could command their comparatively weak economy to swiftly match the United States' nuclear and missile capability and arguably outmatch its conventional forces. Only in the last decade of the Cold War did the Soviets run into the same problem that China faces today: how to produce complex weapons that are competitive with those emerging from a technologically dynamic America with a huge military R & D budget (now $140 billion a year).

Bipolarity arose from unusual circumstances. World War II left the Soviet Union in a position to dominate Eurasia, and with all the other major powers save the United States battered from World War II, only Washington had the wherewithal to assemble a balancing coalition to contain Moscow. Hence the intense rivalry of the Cold War: the arms race, the ceaseless competition in the Third World, the periodic superpower crises around the globe from Berlin to Cuba. Compared with multipolarity, it was a simpler system, with only one pair of states at the top and so only one potential power transition worth worrying about.

With the demise of the Soviet Union and the shift from bipolarity to unipolarity, the system transformed from one historically unprecedented situation to another. Now, there is one dominant power and one dominant alliance system, not two. Unlike the Soviet Union, China has not already conquered key territory crucial to the global balance. Nor has Xi shown the same willingness as Soviet leaders to trade butter for guns (with China long devoting a steady two percent of GDP to military spending). Nor can he command his economy to match U.S. military power in a matter of years, given the complexity of modern weaponry.

PARTIALLY UNIPOLAR

To argue that today's system is not multipolar or bipolar is not to deny that power relations have changed. China has risen, especially in the economic realm, and great-power competition has returned after a post–Cold War lull. Gone are the days when the United States' across-the-board primacy was unambiguous. But the world's largest-ever power gap will take a long time to close, and not all elements of this gap will narrow at the same rate. China has indeed done a lot to shrink the gap in the economic realm, but it has done far less when it comes to military capacity and especially technology.

As a result, the distribution of power today remains closer to unipolarity than to either bipolarity or multipolarity. Because the world has never experienced unipolarity before the current spell, no terminology exists to describe changes to such a world, which is perhaps why many have inappropriately latched on to the concept of multipolarity to convey their sense of a smaller American lead. Narrowed though it is, that lead is still substantial, which is why the distribution of power today is best described as "partial unipolarity," as compared with the "total unipolarity" that existed after the Cold War.

The end of total unipolarity explains why Beijing, Moscow, and other dissatisfied powers are now more willing to act on their dissatisfaction, accepting some risk of attracting the focused enmity of the United States. But their efforts show that the world remains sufficiently unipolar that the prospect of being balanced against is a far stiffer constraint on the United States' rivals than it is on the United States itself.

Ukraine is a case in point. In going to war, Russia showed a willingness to test its revisionist potential. But the very fact that Russian President Vladimir Putin felt the need to invade is itself a sign of weakness. In the 1990s, if you had told his predecessor, Boris Yeltsin, that in 2023, Russia would be fighting a war to sustain its sphere of influence over Ukraine, which Russian officials back then assumed would end up as a reliable ally, he would scarcely have believed that Moscow could sink so low. It is ironic that now, when unipolarity's end is so frequently declared, Russia is struggling to try to get something it thought it already had when U.S. primacy was at its peak. And if you had told Yeltsin that Russia would not be winning that war against a country with an economy one-tenth the size of Russia's, he would have been all the more incredulous. The misadventure in Ukraine, moreover, has greatly undermined Russia's long-term economic prospects, thanks to the massive wave of sanctions the West has unleashed.

But even if Russia had swiftly captured Kyiv and installed a pro-Russian government, as Putin expected, that would have had little bearing on the global distribution of power. There is no denying that the outcome of the war in Ukraine matters greatly for the future of that country's sovereignty and the strength of the global norm against forceful land grabs. But in the narrow, cold-hearted calculus of global material power, Ukraine's small economy—about the same size as that of Kansas—means that it ultimately matters little whether Ukraine is aligned with NATO, Russia, or neither side. Further, Ukraine is not in fact a U.S. ally. Russia would be very unlikely to dare attack one of those. Given how the United States has reacted when Russia attacked a country that is not a U.S. ally—funneling arms, aid, and intelligence to the Ukrainians and imposing stiff sanctions—the Kremlin surely knows that the Americans would do much more to protect an actual ally.

Militarily, China is far from being a peer of the United States.

China's revisionism is backed up by much more overall capability, but as with Russia, its successes are astonishingly modest in the broad sweep of history. So far, China has altered the territorial status quo only in the South China Sea, where it has built some artificial islands. But these small and exposed possessions could easily be rendered inoperative in wartime by the U.S. military. And even if China could secure all the contested portions of the South China Sea for itself, the overall economic significance of the resources there—mainly fish—is tiny. Most of the oil and gas resources in the South China Sea lie in uncontested areas close to various countries' shorelines.

Unless the U.S. Navy withdraws from Asia, China's revisionist ambitions can currently extend no farther than the first island chain—the string of Pacific archipelagoes that includes Japan, the Philippines, and Taiwan. That cannot change anytime soon: it would take decades, not years, for China to develop the full range of capabilities needed to contest the U.S. military's command of the commons. Also, China may not even bother to seek such a capacity. However aggravating Chinese policymakers find their rival's behavior, U.S. foreign policy is unlikely to engender the level of fear that motivated the costly development of Washington's global power-projection capability during the Cold War.

For now, there is effectively only one place where China could scratch its revisionist itch: in Taiwan. China's interest in the island is clearly growing, with Xi having declared in 2022 that "the complete reunification of the motherland must be achieved." The prospect of a Chinese attack on Taiwan is indeed a real change from the heyday of total unipolarity, when China was too weak for anyone to worry about this scenario. But it is important to keep in mind that Beijing's yearnings for Taiwan are a far cry from revisionist challenges of the past, such as those mounted by Japan and Germany in the first half of the twentieth century or the Soviet Union in the second; each of those countries conquered and occupied vast territory across great distances. And if China did manage to put Taiwan in its column, even the strongest proponents of the island's strategic significance do not see it as so valuable that changing its alignment would generate a dramatic swing in the distribution of power of the kind that made multipolarity so dangerous.

What about the flourishing partnership between China and Russia? It definitely matters; it creates problems for Washington and its allies. But it holds no promise of a systemic power shift. When the aim is to balance against a superpower whose leadership and extensive alliances are deeply embedded in the status quo, the counteralliance needs to be similarly significant. On that score, Chinese-Russian relations fail the test. There is a reason the two parties do not call it a formal alliance. Apart from purchasing oil, China did little to help Russia in Ukraine during the first year of the conflict. A truly consequential partnership would involve sustained cooperation across a wide variety of areas, not shallow cooperation largely born of convenience. And even if China and Russia upgraded their relations, each is still merely a regional military power. Putting together two powers capable of regional balancing does not equate to global balancing. Achieving that would require military capabilities that Russia and China individually and collectively do not have—and cannot have anytime soon.

ROUGH TIMES FOR REVISIONISM

All this might seem cold comfort, given that even the limited revisionist quests of China and Russia could still spark a great-power war, with its frightening potential to go nuclear. But it is important to put the system's stability in historical perspective. During the Cold War, each superpower feared that if all of Germany fell to the other, the global balance of power would shift decisively. (And with good reason: in 1970, West Germany's economy was about one-quarter the size of the United States' and two-thirds the size of the Soviet Union's.) Because each superpower was so close to such an economically valuable object, and because the prize was literally split between them, the result was an intense security competition in which each based hundreds of thousands of troops in their half of Germany. The prospect of brinkmanship crises over Germany's fate loomed in the background and occasionally came to the foreground, as in the 1961 crisis over the status of Berlin.

Or compare the present situation to the multipolar 1930s, when, in less than a decade, Germany went from being a disarmed, constrained power to nearly conquering all of Eurasia. But Germany was able to do so thanks to two advantages that do not exist today. First, a great power could build up substantial military projection power in only a few years back then, since the weapons systems of the day were relatively uncomplicated. Second, Germany had a geographically and economically viable option to augment its power by conquering neighboring countries. In 1939, the Nazis first added the economic resources of Czechoslovakia (around ten percent the size of Germany's) and then Poland (17 percent). They used these victories as a springboard for more conquests in 1940, including Belgium (11 percent), the Netherlands (ten percent), and France (51 percent). China doesn't have anything like the same opportunity. For one thing, Taiwan's GDP is less than five percent of China's. For another, the island is separated from the mainland by a formidable expanse of water. As the MIT research scientist Owen Cote has underscored, because China lacks command of the sea surface, it simply "cannot safeguard a properly sized, seaborne invasion force and the follow-on shipping necessary to support it during multiple transits across the 100-plus mile-wide Taiwan Straits." Consider that the English Channel was a fifth of the width but still enough of a barrier to stop the Nazis from conquering the United Kingdom.

Japan and South Korea are the only other large economic prizes nearby, but Beijing is in no position to take a run at them militarily, either. And because Japan, South Korea, and Taiwan have economies that are knowledge-based and highly integrated with the global economy, their wealth cannot be effectively extracted through conquest. The Nazis could, for example, commandeer the Czech arms manufacturer Skoda Works to enhance the German war machine, but China could not so easily exploit the Taiwan Semiconductor Manufacturing Company. Its operation depends on employees with specialized knowledge who could flee in the event of an invasion and on a pipeline of inputs from around the globe that war would cut off.

Today's revisionists face another obstacle: while they are confined to regional balancing, the United States can hit back globally. For instance, the United States is not meeting Russia directly on the battlefield but is instead using its global position to punish the country through a set of devastating economic sanctions and a massive flow of conventional weaponry, intelligence, and other forms of military assistance to Kyiv. The United States could likewise "go global" if China tried to take Taiwan, imposing a comprehensive naval blockade far from China's shores to curtail its access to the global economy. Such a blockade would ravage the country's economy (which relies greatly on technological imports and largely plays an assembly role in global production chains) while harming the U.S. economy far less.

Because the United States has so much influence in the global economy, it can use economic levers to punish other countries without worrying much about what they might do in response. If China tried to conquer Taiwan, and the United States imposed a distant blockade on China, Beijing would certainly try to retaliate economically. But the strongest economic arrow in its quiver wouldn't do much damage. China could, as many have feared, sell some or all of its massive holdings of U.S. Treasury securities in an attempt to raise borrowing costs in the United States. Yet the U.S. Federal Reserve could just purchase all the securities. As the economist Brad Setser has put it, "The U.S. ultimately holds the high cards here: the Fed is the one actor in the world that can buy more than China can ever sell."

Today's international norms also hinder revisionists. That is no accident, since many of these standards of behavior were created by the United States and its allies after World War II. For example, Washington promulgated the proscription against the use of force to alter international boundaries not only to prevent major conflicts but also to lock in place the postwar status quo from which it benefited. Russia has experienced such strong pushback for invading Ukraine in part because it has so blatantly violated this norm. In norms as in other areas, the global landscape is favorable terrain for the United States and rough for revisionists.

AMERICA'S CHOICE

The political scientist Kenneth Waltz distinguished between the truly systemic feature of the distribution of capabilities, on the one hand, and the alliances that states form, on the other. Although countries could not choose how much power they had, he argued, they could pick their team. The U.S.-centric alliance system that defines so much of international politics, now entering its eighth decade, has attained something of a structural character, but Waltz's distinction still holds. The current international order emerged not from power alone but also from choices made by the United States and its allies—to cooperate deeply in the economic and security realms, first to contain the Soviet Union and then to advance a global order that made it easier to trade and cooperate. Their choices still matter. If they make the right ones, then bipolarity or multipolarity will remain a distant eventuality, and the partial unipolar system of today will last for decades to come.

Most consequentially, the United States should not step back from its alliances and security commitments in Europe or Asia. The United States derives significant benefits from its security leadership in these regions. If America came home, a more dangerous, unstable world would emerge. There would also be less cooperation on the global economy and other important issues that Washington cannot solve on its own.

Indeed, in the era of partial unipolarity, alliances are all the more valuable. Revisionism demands punishment, and with fewer unilateral options on the table, there is a greater need for the United States to respond in concert with its allies. Yet Washington still has substantial power to shape such cooperation. Cooperation among self-interested states can emerge without leadership, but it is more likely to do so when Washington guides the process. And American proposals frequently become the focal point around which its partners rally.

Keeping U.S. alliances in Asia and Europe intact hardly means that Washington should sign a blank check: its friends can and should do more to properly defend themselves. Not only will they need to spend more; they will need to spend more wisely, too. U.S. allies in Europe should increase their capacity for territorial defense in areas where the United States can do less while not trying to duplicate areas of U.S. strength. In practice, this means focusing on the simple task of fielding more ground troops. In Asia, U.S. allies would be wise to prioritize defensive systems and strategies, especially with respect to Taiwan. Fortunately, after more than a decade of ignoring calls to prioritize a defensive strategy for securing the island—turning it into a difficult-to-swallow "porcupine"—Taipei appears to have finally awakened to this need, thanks to Ukraine.

In economic policy, Washington should resist the temptation to always drive the hardest bargain with its allies. The best leaders have willing followers, not ones that must be coaxed or coerced. At the heart of today's international order is an implicit pledge that has served the United States well: although the country gains certain unique benefits from its dominance of the system, it doesn't abuse its position to extract undue returns from its allies. Maintaining this arrangement requires policies that are less protectionist than the ones pursued by either the Trump or the Biden administration. When it comes to trade, instead of thinking just about what it wants, Washington should also consider what its allies want. For most, the answer is simple: access to the U.S. market. Accordingly, the United States should put real trade deals on the table for its partners in Asia and Europe that would lower trade barriers. Done properly, market access can be improved in ways that not only please U.S. allies but also create enough benefits for Americans that politicians can overcome political constraints.

The Chinese-Russian partnership holds no promise of a systemic power shift.

The United States must also resist the temptation to use its military to change the status quo. The 20-year nation-building exercise in Afghanistan and the invasion of Iraq were self-inflicted wounds. The lesson should be easy enough to remember: no occupations ever again. Any proposal to use U.S. military force outside Asia and Europe should be deeply interrogated, and the default response should be "no." Preventing China and Russia from changing the status quo in Asia and Europe was once relatively easy, but now it is a full-time job. That is where the U.S. military's focus should lie.

Ultimately, the world in the age of partial unipolarity retains many of the characteristics it exhibited in the age of total unipolarity, just in modified form. International norms and institutions still constrain revisionists, but these states are more willing to challenge them. The United States still has command of the commons and a unique capacity to project military power across the globe, but China has created a fiercely contested zone near its shores. The United States still possesses vast economic leverage, but it has a greater need to act in concert with its allies to make sanctions effective. It still has a unique leadership capacity for promoting cooperation, but its scope for unilateral action is reduced. Yes, America faces limits it did not face right after the Soviet Union's collapse. But the myth of multipolarity obscures just how much power it still has.

The Perils of the New Industrial Policy

How to Stop a Global Race to the Bottom

DAVID KAMIN AND REBECCA KYSAR

In October 2021, the Biden administration achieved a major milestone when it reached an agreement with nearly 140 countries to establish a global minimum tax. That accord, which imposes a minimum tax rate of 15 percent on corporations, promises to end the damaging international tax competition that has gone on for decades. Under the existing system, large multinational firms have been encouraged to shift their profits to low-tax jurisdictions to avoid taxes worldwide, and countries have sought to undercut one another to attract those companies, engaging in what U.S. Treasury Secretary Janet Yellen described as a "global race to the bottom." Over time, however, governments around the world recognized that almost no one was winning this

DAVID KAMIN is Professor of Law at New York University School of Law and served as Deputy Director of the National Economic Council in the White House from 2021 to 2022.

REBECCA KYSAR is Professor of Law at Fordham University School of Law and served as Counselor to the Assistant Secretary for Tax Policy in the U.S. Treasury Department from 2021 to 2022.

race except the corporations themselves and that most countries would be better off if they agreed to end this largely zero-sum game. The new global minimum tax is, in short, a breakthrough in cooperation over competition.

But the Biden administration has also recognized the need for corporate tax incentives to encourage economic activity in certain critical areas. Tax incentives and other kinds of subsidies are now a core part of the U.S. strategy for addressing climate change and the security of supply chains at a time of growing tension with China and Russia. These tools are the primary focus of two landmark bills passed in 2022, the Inflation Reduction Act (IRA) and the CHIPS and Science Act.

The question now is whether this new industrial policy will set off a counterproductive subsidy race against friends and allies or can instead be implemented cooperatively with them, building on the lessons of the global minimum tax. There is real risk of a new race. In the IRA, the electric vehicle tax credit is contingent on where the parts of the EVs are made and, as enacted, could exclude production in the European Union from much of the subsidy, threatening what the United States' European allies see as a key industry. And the CHIPS Act, which justifiably seeks to use subsidies to shift semiconductor production away from China and Taiwan, could threaten production in Japan, South Korea, and Europe, too. Without new forms of cooperation or coordination with allies and friends, these U.S. measures could create a damaging contest. Already, leaders in Europe and elsewhere are responding with their own competing subsidies, and amid growing concerns in the West about supply chain disruptions and great-power rivalry, pressure to adopt more such measures will likely increase in the years to come. Even now, there are calls for Washington to enact similar subsidies and other measures in other sectors, from pharmaceuticals to shipbuilding.

A costly new competition over taxes and subsidies is not inevitable. Significant elements of international cooperation have been built into some of the largest clean energy subsidies in the IRA. From the start, the Biden administration has also rightly focused on the need for global cooperation in trying to implement both the IRA and the CHIPS Act. But Washington will need to employ a variety of tools to ensure that its actions do not instead set off competitive new races among allies and trusted trading partners. And that will likely mean expanding the toolkit beyond subsidies alone.

To build on the Biden administration's success in launching the multilateral global minimum tax, the United States needs a more sustainable, cooperative model for countering the economic threat posed by China and other global rivals. The task is especially challenging, given that China has aggressively subsidized sectors it deems strategic, including semiconductors, EVs, software, and technological hardware. But failure to adopt such a model could have far-reaching consequences for the United States and its allies and friends around the world. Either they can find new ways to cooperate to achieve their common goals of addressing climate change, securing supply chains, and responding to China, or they can each take on these challenges on their own and in competition with each other, risking a new race to the bottom on tax incentives and subsidies that could end up thwarting those goals.

POSITIVE-SUM GAME

In an era of rising great-power rivalry and heightened economic insecurity, the 2021 agreement on a global minimum tax provides a striking example of how cooperation can triumph over competition. The rationale for the global minimum tax is powerful. For decades, governments undercut one another's tax rates to attract corporations and their international capital, diminishing an important and progressive revenue source. Competition from lower-tax jurisdictions encouraged companies that are headquartered in the United States and other major countries to use tax-avoidance strategies to shift their earnings to those jurisdictions—even though they had few or no operations in those havens.

Yet these problems drew comparatively little scrutiny by policymakers until the 2008 financial crisis. During the global recession that followed, widespread job losses and economic suffering brought new attention to income and wealth inequality and pushed governments to find new sources of revenue. Corporate tax avoidance became a large part of that discussion. Beginning in the fall of 2012, public hearings in both the United Kingdom and the United States revealed that many multinational corporations had been aggressively exploiting the differences in the tax regimes of countries. In the United States, for example, a U.S. Senate committee released a memo showing that Microsoft had avoided paying approximately $6.5 billion in U.S. taxes over a three-year period by routing intellectual property rights through Bermuda, Ireland, and Singapore. In the United Kingdom, meanwhile, a Starbucks executive testified in parliament that Starbucks had been quietly shifting some of its British revenues to a subsidiary in the Netherlands, where it had received a favorable tax arrangement, a disclosure that led to public outrage and boycotts. These hearings were followed by leaks from a major accounting firm showing that Luxembourg helped some 340 companies avoid tax by granting them secret tax rulings, with subsequent investigations showing other European governments doing the same. International taxation had become front-page news.

A growing mass of statistics also documented the long-term cost of tax competition. Among countries in the Organization for Economic Cooperation and Development, for example, the average corporate rate was 32 percent in 2000. Twenty years later, it had fallen to just 23 percent. The downward pressure on rates was even more apparent over a longer time horizon: in the 1980s, the OECD average was rarely less than 45 percent—nearly twice the level of 2020. The pressure to lower corporate taxes was particularly costly for the United States. It has been estimated that a cut of just one percent in the corporate rate will, over ten years, reduce federal government revenues by $100 billion. Yet in large part because of global tax competition, the United States reduced its corporate rate from 35 percent to 21 percent in 2017 and only partially paid for that tax cut by broadening the tax base. As the owners of capital profited from their lower taxes, their gains threatened to come at the expense of ordinary workers and others who would have to pay for these corporate tax cuts through either higher taxes or less government investment and fewer government services.

For decades, governments undercut one another's tax rates to attract capital.

These facts drove the Biden administration to revitalize global efforts to end the race to the bottom in corporate taxes. The result was the landmark global minimum tax agreement in 2021, which provides for a floor tax rate of 15 percent on the earnings of large multinational businesses. Countries that had served as tax havens saw that major economies around the world were committed to addressing this problem and signed on to avoid the potential lost revenue and reputational consequences of being left out; even major U.S. rivals such as China saw it in their interest to work multilaterally with the rest of the globe. If fully implemented, the agreement will eliminate the costly effects of the existing situation, increasing global tax revenues on corporate income by approximately $220 billion, or an additional nine percent.

Despite the Biden administration's role in shaping the agreement, however, the United States has not yet changed its own tax code to comply with it. During the drafting of the IRA, Senator Joe Manchin, a Democrat from West Virginia, insisted that measures in the bill that would have implemented the global minimum tax be removed from the final legislation, expressing concerns that by approving the tax before other countries, Washington would be putting U.S. corporations at a disadvantage. Although the United States has failed to act, however, many countries—including all member states of the EU—have taken important steps to implement the global minimum tax by the end of 2023. In fact, the tax is undergirded by a strong enforcement rule that allows countries that implement it to increase taxes on corporations based in countries that have not yet implemented it and are not paying the 15 percent minimum rate in every country in which they're operating. Because of this rule, it truly doesn't pay for a country to stand outside the deal, since its corporations will still pay taxes at the 15 percent rate to countries that implement the agreement.

Nevertheless, the lack of U.S. participation could increase tensions with EU members and other countries over trade and economic policy. Foreign governments, for example, could seek to enforce the deal against U.S. companies, and a future U.S. administration could threaten them with retaliation for doing so. Those tensions can be avoided if Congress takes action. In fact, in 2025, when key elements of the 2017 Trump tax cuts expire, Congress will have the opportunity to bring the U.S. tax code into compliance with the agreement and raise revenue in the process. The question now is whether Congress and the administration in office in 2025 will act to collect revenue that would otherwise be taken by countries implementing the agreement rather than try to fight an agreement that is in Washington's own interest.

MY CHIPS, NOT YOURS

There's some irony that, at a time of historic global cooperation to raise corporate taxes, a vigorous new contest has emerged between countries over corporate subsidies. Much like the old tax regime, these subsidies are aimed at getting corporations to shift their activities to a more favorable jurisdiction. This contest has been heightened by the IRA and the CHIPS Act.

Both pieces of legislation are aimed at addressing critical challenges. The IRA will provide almost $400 billion in government support for clean energy and green technologies over the next decade, with around three-quarters of that in the form of tax credits, and it is the main hope for progress on climate policy in the United States. One analysis found that the package could result in U.S. greenhouse gas emissions falling between 32 and 42 percent below 2005 levels by 2030—seven to 10 percentage points higher than without it. The CHIPS Act provides more than $60 billion in subsidies for companies to build "fabs"—chip manufacturing facilities—in

partners, the government may incur significantly higher costs. This in turn can reduce living standards for workers because they are consumers, too.

FRIEND SCARING

Already, many U.S. allies and partners have perceived Washington's new chips and green energy incentives as a new form of competition that may come at a cost to their own economies. In December 2022, South Korea enacted an initial round of new semiconductor subsidies, and its Finance Ministry almost immediately called for even larger ones, which are now under serious consideration in the South Korean legislature. In February 2023, Japan approved another round of subsidies for its own semiconductor industry. Meanwhile, the EU is considering new subsidies for semiconductor manufacturing in response to the U.S. legislation. And Taiwan has enacted semiconductor tax credits aimed at trying to keep the most advanced semiconductor manufacturing in Taiwan—which, of course, runs exactly counter to the aims of the United States and other governments.

The European reaction to the new U.S. subsidies for clean energy and particularly EVs has been especially heated. "You're hurting my country," French President Emmanuel Macron told Senator Manchin in January 2023. In March, the European Commission announced that it aims to ensure that 40 percent of clean energy technology is made in the EU by 2030 and it has set a similar goal for the critical minerals needed for EV battery production and other industries. When it comes to subsidies, Brussels is waiving its normal state aid rules—which are meant to prevent subsidy races—and allowing countries to adopt "matching aid" to compete with countries outside the EU. The only requirement is that such measures are introduced in response to those other countries' subsidies. Whether these moves will result in a counterproductive subsidy contest with the United States now depends on the actions of the EU countries themselves.

A new race to the bottom over subsidies could undercut the very objectives these tools are designed to achieve. The danger is that rather than helping governments develop green technology and diversify their supply chains, more of the subsidies will be consumed in higher after-tax corporate profits and higher costs of production, with little or no benefit for workers overall. Take semiconductors. Only a few corporations have the necessary know-how and resources to make expensive investments in new fabs, and these require major economies of scale and scope. The largest of these companies can play governments against each other. Japan, South Korea, the United States, and the EU could end up drawing business away not just from China and Taiwan but from one another as well. The winners in this race will be these outsize corporate players, not the competing governments, consumers, or the companies' own workers.

Another consequence of a subsidies race would be to push up costs for the technology in question. For example, some of the subsidies in the IRA do not just reward companies that produce low-carbon technologies but also require that production to be located in the United States or in a few select countries. (For the ten percent bonus on the production and investment tax credits, the domestic content requirements focus on the United States alone. For the EV credit, certain stages of production, such as final assembly, must take place in North America, and critical minerals must be mined and processed in North America or in countries with free trade agreements with the United States—for example, Australia and South Korea but not the EU.) Companies would otherwise tend to allocate their production among a variety of countries in ways that minimize costs. This means that some share of the subsidy will be devoted to offsetting the higher costs of producing technology in the United States alone.

In fact, there is little national security or economic advantage to producing clean energy technology in the United States instead of in allied and partner countries. Although a U.S.-centric approach may increase the number of clean energy jobs in the United States, it comes with associated costs. Those workers would likely come from other productive jobs in the U.S. economy, and the cost of producing clean energy technologies will be higher because the government is subsidizing businesses based on their location in the United States rather than on where those technologies can most efficiently be made. In some cases, it may be significantly more expensive to produce certain kinds of clean energy technologies in the United States than to buy them from allies and friends and then use them to generate energy. The consequence would be both higher energy bills for consumers and less clean energy use overall, undermining two critical objectives. Of course, subsidies should not be entirely neutral with respect to where clean technology is made, and Western governments are right to be concerned about an overreliance on China. But they should keep the subsidies as focused as possible on the real risks to their global supply chains rather than on promoting domestic production over all alternatives, including production in friendly or allied countries that could help lower costs for everyone.

Amid the war on the European continent and growing tensions with China, the potential of U.S. subsidy policies to create economic rifts with close allies and friends also comes with diplomatic costs. Washington relies on its partners to help defend against autocracies and other global menaces, and economic cooperation with the EU and other partners has been essential in standing up to Putin's assault on Ukraine. Cooperative trade in critical technologies such as semiconductors and clean energy can help countries become less vulnerable to Chinese pressure and more amenable to the goals of the United States. By taking a "go it alone" approach, however, Washington will find it harder to maintain that unity and may have to rely more heavily on other tools, such as military power, to try to bring its allies and partners together.

WIN TOGETHER OR LOSE ALONE

To avoid a counterproductive competition with allies and partners, the Biden administration will need to embrace new forms of international cooperation. Fortunately, some of the tools needed for such an approach are already at hand. In March 2023, during a visit by European Commission President Ursula von der Leyen to the White House, the United States and the EU announced the start of negotiations for a free trade agreement for critical minerals needed for EV batteries. If a deal can be reached, it would extend at least half the administration's new EV subsidies to cars with batteries that use minerals sourced from the EU, although final assembly of the cars would still have to happen in North America. That expansion would be a step forward. The announcement also shows the potential for negotiating targeted free trade agreements with other friendly countries.

Yet there are preliminary signs that political opposition in Washington could pose obstacles to such an agreement. Although the administration is pursuing the deal as an executive agreement, which does not require congressional approval, the chair of the Senate Finance Committee, Ron Wyden, a Democrat from Oregon, has asserted the need for the White House to work with Congress on any such deals. And opposition from Congress would make the politics tricky. Manchin, for one, has previously criticized the administration's efforts to extend its clean energy incentives to more U.S. allies, going so far as to vote against Biden's nominee for IRS Commissioner for supporting such efforts.

But the administration has other ways to further cooperation in critical industries. For example, in December 2022, despite European concerns about Biden's U.S.-oriented industrial policies, the United States and the EU announced that they will coordinate their chip subsidies, and the U.S. Commerce Department has said that it intends to engage in such coordination more broadly with allies and partners. It is possible that a coalition of willing governments could agree to not bid against each other where they have discretion—although such efforts will be challenging given that the enacted incentives focus on production in their jurisdictions only. Moreover, the CHIPS Act may not be Washington's last word on semiconductors. Industry observers are already concerned that these subsidies may be insufficient to shift production of the most advanced semiconductors to the United States at the scale the country needs. In addition to working with allies and friends to block technologies from going to China, the United States will need to do more to coordinate its efforts to diversify production away from China and Taiwan without creating an open-ended competition for subsidies.

Coordinated tariffs can help countries become less vulnerable to Chinese pressure.

To achieve these long-term goals, the United States will need to expand its economic toolkit beyond the current subsidies—and in areas that go beyond chips and clean energy. In late March 2023, a report from the Senate Committee on Homeland Security and Governmental Affairs identified U.S. reliance on China and India for the manufacture of critical medicines as a national security and health threat. It cited, for instance, data from the Administration for Strategic Preparedness and Response showing that 90 to 95 percent of the generic sterile injectable drugs that are used for critical acute care in the United States rely on materials from those two countries alone. Health experts such as Ezekiel Emanuel have also called attention to the growing risks of sourcing critical drugs from China. To address this problem, Emanuel has called for a tax subsidy to bring pharmaceutical production back to the United States, and the *Financial Times* has reported that the main pharmaceutical industry lobbying group is making the case for such tax breaks. As with the Biden administration incentives for U.S.-made chips and EVs, however, such subsidies could threaten yet another race to the bottom.

To avoid that scenario, there are several strategies the United States and its partners could pursue. For example, if several leading countries agreed that sourcing pharmaceuticals was a key national security and health priority, they could offer coordinated subsidies for production in any of their countries, provided that domestic regulators can achieve appropriate oversight. In this way, vulnerable supply chains could be secured without creating new competition. Such an approach may be hard to achieve, even if it is attractive in theory, given that it may be difficult to persuade members of Congress that U.S. subsidies should be available for pharmaceuticals produced in Europe or other countries. Alternatively, Washington could pursue coordinated tariffs, which might be more politically palatable. In cooperation, friendly countries and the United States could impose tariffs on critical products whose manufacture relies heavily on China—or any other country that appears to pose a national security concern. With enough lead time, that production could diversify and shift to friendly jurisdictions.

Of course, any of these options would entail risks of their own. Subsidies must be paid for with additional taxes; tariffs will raise prices. But the result would be a stronger, more secure supply chain—giving the U.S. and its partners a cushion against future disruptions and, potentially, a way to avoid a very dangerous outcome if imports from China were suddenly frozen. Still, these kinds of measures should be deployed only in industries where there is a good case for shifting the location of existing production and where the benefits of such a shift would exceed the costs. Although many industries will seek to qualify for such preferential treatment, only a small number of critical sectors will merit it.

Such coordinated actions would be a way to avoid a subsidy race and foster the kind of cooperation that the Biden administration has called for in implementing the IRA and the CHIPS Act—but may not achieve. They could create a strong foundation for what Yellen has labeled "friend shoring," or the pursuit of trade with countries that have shared values rather than trade with the entire world. In essence, this approach involves balancing the immediate economic efficiencies of broader global integration with the long-term benefits of blocking undue influence or leverage from rival states, as well as the future economic costs that that influence could impose. Friend shoring achieves that balance by maintaining global integration but focusing that integration on the economies of allies and friends.

The United States and its allies now face a critical choice. In successfully reaching the global minimum tax agreement, they showed that countries can cooperate to address one of the great challenges of globalization—big corporations playing countries off one another, not in pursuit of greater productivity but simply to maximize profits. The question now is whether Washington can find an analogous solution with its friends and allies to address the location of industries deemed crucial to national security and to the fight against climate change. If it instead helps drive a new race to the bottom over subsidies, the United States and its workers will bear the costs, and the barriers to achieving secure supply chains and a green energy transition will be even higher.

The Age of Energy Insecurity

How the Fight for Resources Is Upending Geopolitics

JASON BORDOFF AND MEGHAN L. O'SULLIVAN

As recently as 18 months ago, many policymakers, academics, and pundits in the United States and Europe were waxing lyrical about the geopolitical benefits of the coming transition to cleaner, greener energy. They understood that the move away from a carbon-intensive energy system that relied on fossil fuels was going to be difficult for some countries. But on the whole, the conventional wisdom held that the shift to new sources of energy would not only aid the fight against climate change but also put an end to the troublesome geopolitics of the old energy order.

JASON BORDOFF is Founding Director of the Center on Global Energy Policy at Columbia University's School of International and Public Affairs and Co-Founding Dean of the Columbia Climate School. During the Obama administration, he served as Special Assistant to the President and Senior Director for Energy and Climate Change on the staff of the National Security Council.

MEGHAN L. O'SULLIVAN is Director-Designate of the Belfer Center for Science and International Affairs and the Jeane Kirkpatrick Professor of the Practice of International Affairs at the Harvard Kennedy School. During the George W. Bush administration, she served as Special Assistant to the President and Deputy National Security Adviser for Iraq and Afghanistan.

Such hopes, however, were based on an illusion. The transition to clean energy was bound to be chaotic in practice, producing new conflicts and risks in the short term. By the fall of 2021, amid an energy crisis in Europe, skyrocketing natural gas prices, and rising oil prices, even the most optimistic evangelist of the new energy order had realized that the transition would be rocky at best. Any remaining romanticism evaporated when Russia invaded Ukraine in February 2022. The war revealed not only the brutal character of Russian President Vladimir Putin's regime and the dangers of an excessive energy dependence on aggressive autocracies but also the risks posed by a jagged, largely uncoordinated scramble to develop new energy sources and to wean the world off old, entrenched ones.

One result of this turmoil has been the revival of a term that had come to seem anachronistic during the past two decades of booming energy supplies and utopian visions of a green future: energy security. To many Americans, that phrase is redolent of the 1970s, conjuring images of boxy sedans and wood-paneled station wagons lined up for miles, waiting to fill their tanks with gasoline at sky-high prices thanks to the Arab oil embargo of 1973 and the Iranian Revolution of 1979. But energy security is hardly a thing of the past: it will be crucial to the future.

Energy security has historically been defined as the availability of sufficient supplies at affordable prices. But that simple definition no longer captures reality; the risks the world now faces are both more numerous and more complicated than in earlier eras. To handle these new challenges, policymakers must redefine the concept of energy security and develop new means of ensuring it. Four broad principles should guide this process: diversification, resilience, integration, and transparency. Although these principles are familiar, the traditional methods of applying them will prove insufficient in this new era; policymakers will need new tools.

There is no reason to despair just yet. After all, the oil crisis of the 1970s sparked a great deal of innovation, including the development of today's wind and solar technologies, greater efficiency in vehicles, and new government and multilateral institutions to make and coordinate energy policy. The policies and technologies that now seem old and outdated were once shiny and new. Today's crisis may likewise lead to novel ideas and techniques, as long as policymakers fully grasp the new realities they face.

THE FUTURE ARRIVED EARLY

The events of the past year and a half have dramatically revealed the many ways in which the energy transition and geopolitics are entangled. Dynamics that were once seen as theoretical or hypothetical are now concrete and evident to even the casual observer.

First, the past 18 months have highlighted the "feast before famine" dynamic facing traditional producers of oil and gas, whose power and influence will increase before it wanes. In 2021, for example, Russia and other oil and gas producers had a banner year in terms of revenue as extreme weather and the world's emergence from pandemic slowdowns boosted demand for natural gas. Such shocks had outsize impacts in a market with a meager cushion. In previous years, poor returns, uncertainty about future demand for energy, and pressure to divest from fossil fuels all contributed to diminished investment in oil and gas, resulting in inadequate supplies. Russia took advantage of these tight energy markets by draining its European gas storage sites and slashing spot gas sales even as it met long-term contractual commitments. Average natural gas prices tripled from the first half to the second half of 2021. Combined with rising oil prices, these developments granted Russia a feast of annual revenues that were 50 percent higher for oil and gas than the Kremlin had expected.

The past year and a half also demonstrated that some oil and gas producers were still prepared to use their energy prowess to ruthlessly advance their political and geostrategic objectives; hopes that the world had moved beyond such behavior were dashed with the brutal Russian invasion of Ukraine in February 2022. In the months that followed, Russia gradually cut its pipeline gas deliveries to Europe by more than three-quarters, triggering a crisis that led European governments to spend a staggering 800 billion euros shielding companies and households from higher energy costs. The world's dependence on Russia for energy initially weakened the global response to the invasion: for many months, Russian oil flows were exempt from European sanctions. To this day, the EU has not sanctioned Russian gas sales; indeed, its members continue to import significant volumes of Russian liquefied natural gas. Tight energy markets allowed Russian oil and gas revenues to soar and gave Moscow a potential means of dividing a newly united Europe.

By last year, the mismatch between declining supplies and rising demand had already tightened the oil market. Prices leaped even further, to a 14-year-high, on market fears that the delivery of millions of barrels per day of Russian oil would be disrupted even as demand surged. At the beginning of the war in Ukraine, the International Energy Agency (IEA) predicted that Russian production would decline by three million barrels per day. Fears of supply shocks drove up oil prices and boosted both the income and the geopolitical heft of major oil producers, particularly Saudi Arabia. The United States had thought its days of begging Saudi Arabia to increase oil output had passed. But in the face of high prices, old patterns reasserted themselves, as Washington pleaded—mostly in vain—for more output from Saudi Arabia, the only country with any meaningful spare oil production capacity.

Energy security is hardly a thing of the past: it will be crucial to the future.

The tremors of the last 18 months also illustrate how the geopolitical environment can affect the pace and scope of the transition to clean energy. Before the Russian invasion of Ukraine, European countries and the United States were committed to transforming their economies to achieve net-zero carbon emissions in the coming decades. The brutality of Russia's actions and the knowledge that those actions were funded by fossil fuel receipts reinforced the determination among many in Europe and the United States to move away from oil, gas, and coal. In Washington, one result was landmark climate legislation in the form of the Inflation Reduction Act. Europe also expedited its green plans, notwithstanding some small near-term increases in coal use.

Many American officials worry, however, that a more accelerated energy transition will necessarily involve greater dependence on China, given its dominance of clean energy supply chains. U.S. Senator Joe Manchin, a Democrat from West Virginia, warned that he did not want to have to wait in line to buy car batteries from China the way he waited in line in the 1970s to buy gasoline made with oil from the Middle East. Such fears led Congress to create incentives for the domestic production, refining, and processing of critical minerals now centralized in China. Rather than praising Washington for finally passing meaningful climate change legislation, however, much of the world resented these moves as acts of U.S. protectionism, stirring talk of climate-provoked trade wars.

Finally, the energy crisis of the last 18 months has widened the rift between rich and poor countries. Many countries in the developing world became more strident in objecting to pressure to diversify away from fossil fuels, noting the rise in food and energy costs emanating from a European war. Developing countries have also denounced what they perceived as the hypocrisy inherent in how the developed world has responded to the crisis: after years of citing climate change as a reason to avoid funding natural gas infrastructure in lower-income countries, for example, European countries were suddenly racing to secure new supplies for themselves and building new infrastructure to accept them. Making matters worse, as Europe bid up the price of gas, demand for coal spiked in Asia and drove prices to record levels, leaving developing and emerging-market countries, such as Pakistan and Bangladesh, struggling to afford energy in any form. These tensions were on full display at the UN climate conference in Egypt in November 2022. Biden arrived to take a victory lap over the passage of a historic domestic climate law but found that poorer countries were unimpressed. Instead, they asked why the United States was not doing more to finance climate-change adaptation and clean energy outside its borders and demanded that their richer counterparts compensate them for the damage that climate change has already caused to their cities, agriculture, and ecosystems.

The energy crisis may have eased in recent months, but it is still far too early for complacency. The vast majority of Europe's reduction in gas demand last year arose from unusually warm weather and the idling of industrial production, as opposed to intentional conservation that can be sustained. Moreover, Europe may not be able to rely on much, if any, Russian gas to refill its storage facilities over the coming year. The flow of piped Russian gas into Europe throughout 2022, albeit in shrinking volumes, has now halted and seems unlikely to resume; the Russian liquefied natural gas still flowing to Europe could come under pressure and be curtailed in the months ahead.

Meanwhile, with growing risks to Russian oil output, global demand is expected to rise nearly twice as much as supply in 2023, according to the IEA. Washington's primary tool for cushioning supply disruptions, the U.S. Strategic Petroleum Reserve, is vastly diminished. If prices begin to soar again, Western countries will have few options but to turn once more to Saudi Arabia and to the United Arab Emirates, which also has some spare capacity. Ironically, by the time the UAE hosts the next major UN climate conference, at the end of 2023, the world may well also be turning to Abu Dhabi not just for climate leadership but for more oil.

SOURCES OF STRESS

Driving the new energy insecurity are three main factors: the return of great-power rivalry in an increasingly multipolar and fragmented international system, the efforts of many countries to diversify their supply chains, and the realities of climate change.

Russia's invasion of Ukraine and its broader confrontation with the West offer a striking example of how the ambitions of a single leader can create energy insecurity for broad swaths of the world's population, and the war serves as a reminder that great-power politics never really went away. The U.S.-Chinese contest, however, may ultimately prove more consequential. The intensifying desire of the United States and China to not rely too much on each other is remaking supply chains and reinvigorating industrial policy to a degree not seen in decades. Even with redoubled efforts to produce more clean energy at home, the United States and others will still depend on China for critical minerals and other clean energy components and technologies for years to come, creating vulnerabilities to Chinese-induced shocks. For instance, in recent months, China has suggested that it may restrict the export of solar energy technologies, materials, and know-how as a response to restrictions that Washington imposed last year on the export of high-end semiconductors and machinery to China. If Beijing were to follow through on this threat or curtail the export of critical minerals or advanced batteries to major economies (just as it cut off rare earth supplies to Japan in the early 2010s), large segments of the clean energy economy could suffer setbacks.

Traditional energy heavyweights are also recalibrating their positions in response to the changing geopolitical landscape in ways that increase energy security risks. Saudi Arabia, for instance, now sees its global stance differently than it did in the decades that followed the famous "oil for security" bargain struck by U.S. President Franklin Roosevelt and Saudi King Abdulaziz ibn Saud on Valentine's Day in 1945. Riyadh is now far less concerned with accommodating Washington's requests, overt or implied, to supply oil markets in ways consistent with U.S. interests. In the face of a perceived or real decrease in U.S. strategic commitment to the Middle East, Riyadh has concluded it must tend to other relationships—especially its links to China, the single largest customer for its oil. The kingdom's acceptance of China as a guarantor of the recent Iranian-Saudi rapprochement bolsters Beijing's role in the region and its global status. Relations with Moscow have also

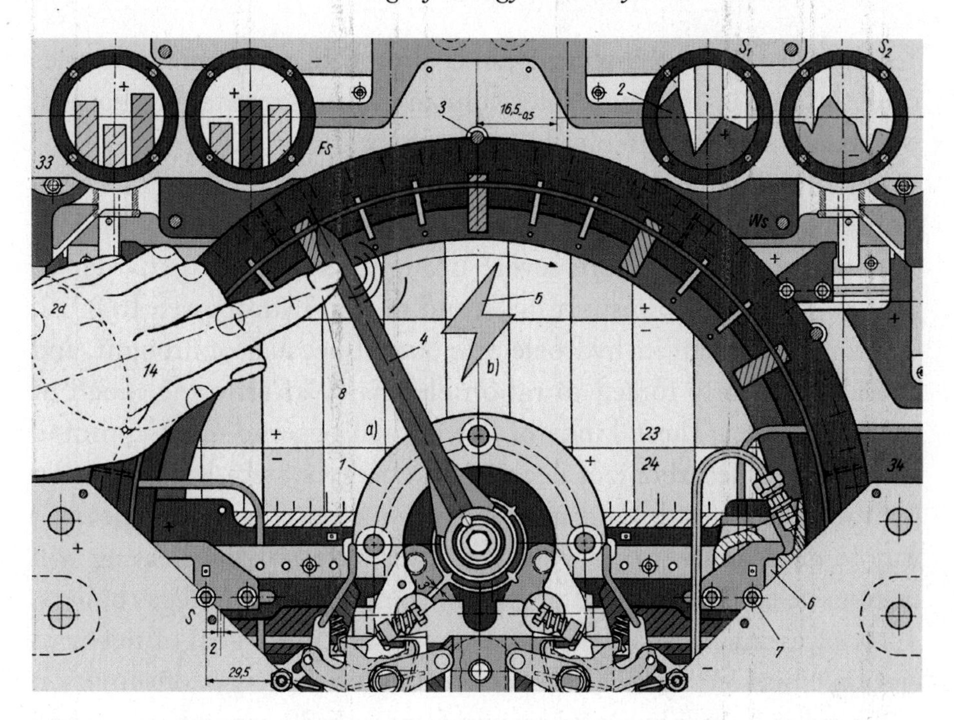

CHRISTIAN GRALINGEN

become particularly important to Saudi Arabia. Regardless of the invasion of Ukraine, the Saudi government believes that Russia remains an essential economic partner and collaborator in managing oil-market volatility. It will therefore be extremely reluctant to take positions that pit the Saudi leadership against Putin.

The new energy insecurity is also shaped by forceful moves many countries have made to domesticate and diversify their supply chains since the invasion of Ukraine and the global pandemic. Such moves are understandable, and even wise, given the now evident risks of excessive dependence on certain countries, notably China, in this new geopolitical era. Yet an interconnected global energy system remains the cornerstone of energy security; markets are still the most efficient way to allocate supplies. Increased self-sufficiency may give countries an increased sense of resilience but could also make them vulnerable; an interconnected global market can ease disruptions caused by extreme weather or political instability. More segmented energy markets will inevitably have fewer options to tap in such circumstances. The U.S. Inflation Reduction Act and Europe's Green Deal industrial plan are intended to accelerate the drive to net-zero emissions, and they reduce energy insecurity in some ways by curbing dependence on globally traded hydrocarbons exposed to geopolitical risks.

Yet they also increase insecurity, since promoting domestic industries runs the risk of stoking protectionism and fragmentation, both of which can make economies less energy secure.

Finally, climate change will be a major threat to energy security in the coming decades, posing risks to infrastructure old and new. Warmer waters and more severe droughts will make it harder to cool power plants, transport fuels, and rely on hydropower. In 2022, California lost half its hydroelectric output because of drought, and Brazil was nearly forced to ration electricity after losing much of its hydropower. These kinds of events will become more common as the world decarbonizes because an energy system less reliant on hydrocarbons will depend more heavily on electricity; the cheapest way to decarbonize sectors such as transportation and heating will be to use electricity instead of gasoline engines or natural gas boilers. The IEA estimates that if the world is to reach the goal of net-zero carbon emissions by 2050, 50 percent of global energy consumption will need to be met by electricity, up from only 20 percent today. And nearly all that electricity will need to be produced from zero-carbon sources, up from only 38 percent today.

Climate change will place much of the infrastructure for this electricity generation, transmission, and distribution at greater risk, since fragile grids and overhead wires are often more vulnerable to extreme weather, wildfires, and other climate-related risks. Climate change can also have a negative impact on renewable sources of electricity, with the UN Intergovernmental Panel on Climate Change projecting that by 2100, average global wind speeds could fall by 10 percent as climate change reduces the differences in atmospheric temperatures that generate wind.

DIVERSIFICATION DILEMMAS

One solution to these problems is to diversify supply. Diversification remains as central to energy security as it was in 1913, when Winston Churchill, then the first lord of the Admiralty, declared that "in variety, and in variety alone" would the United Kingdom find a solution to vulnerabilities created by his decision to shift the British navy from a reliance on Newcastle coal to less secure sources of oil from Persia.

In the long run, the clean energy transition will lead to improved energy security in many cases by diversifying fuel sources and suppliers. For example, transportation, most of which currently runs on oil, will be less vulnerable to fuel supply disruptions in a world where roughly two-thirds of vehicles are electrified, since electricity can be generated from multiple energy sources. And because most electricity is produced close to where it is consumed, a more electrified world will also be less subject to import disruptions caused by disputes among countries.

Yet as the transition progresses and consumers diversify away from fossil fuels, new vulnerabilities and threats to energy security will arise. Even as oil use wanes, geopolitical risks may increase as global production becomes further concentrated in countries that can produce at low cost and with low emissions, many of which are in the Persian Gulf. In the IEA scenario in which the world reaches net-zero carbon emissions by 2050, the share of global oil supply from OPEC producers rises from around one-third today to roughly one-half. The oil giant BP anticipates an even greater global dependence on these producers, estimating that by 2050, they will account for close to two-thirds of global oil supply. In the long run, that will be a large share of a tiny pie, but for decades, oil demand will remain very high and consequential even if annual demand is falling.

The United States thought its days of begging Saudi Arabia to increase oil output had passed.

U.S. policymakers may well ask themselves how comfortable they would feel if global oil production were to be even more heavily concentrated in OPEC countries than it is today. Faced with that outcome, they might consider a number of options, such as extending the increasingly popular concept of "friend shoring" to oil by more actively supporting production at home and in countries such as Norway and Canada, which are perceived as less risky than, say, Iran, Libya, and Venezuela. Some officials might even advocate penalizing less friendly oil sources through import taxes or even sanctions.

Taking such measures to subvert the market and bolster oil production in preferred locations would carry significant risks, however. It would undermine the benefits that come from the ability to reroute oil supplies in case of disruption. It would also risk backlash and retaliation from major global oil producers in OPEC, which can send prices higher by restricting output. Subsidizing domestic supply would also run counter to efforts to encourage consumers to move away from fossil fuels. A better approach would be to embrace global markets but boost defenses against inevitable shocks and volatility with larger, not smaller, strategic oil reserves.

Meanwhile, diversifying the inputs of clean energy will be even more difficult than doing so for fossil fuels. The sources of the requisite technology and components, notably the critical minerals needed for batteries and solar panels, are even more heavily concentrated than oil. The world's largest supplier of lithium (Australia) accounts for around 50 percent of global supply, and the leading suppliers of cobalt (the Democratic Republic of the Congo) and rare earths (China) each account for around 70 percent of those resources. In contrast, the world's largest producers of crude oil—the United States, Saudi Arabia, and Russia—each account for just 10 to 15 percent of global supply. The processing and refining of these minerals are even more concentrated, with China currently performing around 60 to 90 percent of it. Meanwhile, Chinese companies manufacture more than three-quarters of electric vehicle batteries and a similar proportion of the so-called wafers and cells used in solar energy technology.

U.S. policymakers have recently awakened to these vulnerabilities and the fact that they will become more acute as the transition progresses. The Inflation Reduction Act encourages the production of critical minerals in the United States and elsewhere by providing tax credits and loan guarantees for domestic producers, among other measures. The Biden administration recently signed agreements with Congo and Zambia that are intended to increase U.S. imports of their clean-energy minerals. And the U.S. International Development Finance Corporation (DFC) has pursued debt transactions to support the development of solar cell manufacturing outside China. But to get more of the minerals it needs from more of the countries it prefers, Washington will need to strike many more bilateral and multilateral trade agreements and sharpen instruments such as the U.S. Export-Import Bank, which can fund overseas mining operations in friendly countries such as Indonesia. For its part, the U.S. Congress should increase the DFC's authority and expand its ability to make investments.

Another area that badly needs more diversification is enriched uranium, which will become more important as the use of nuclear power increases globally to meet low-carbon electricity needs. Russia's role as a dominant supplier of nuclear fuel services to many countries, including the United States, is a source of great discomfort and vulnerability, given the current geopolitical realities. Boosting uranium production, conversion, and enrichment in the United States and among its Western allies and substantially ramping up their fabrication of the fuel assemblies for Russian-made reactors will be critical to maintaining the existing nuclear fleet and keeping decarbonization goals within reach.

BUILDING RESILIENCE

A secure energy system must be able to withstand and bounce back quickly from unexpected shocks and disruptions. At the most fundamental level, reliable energy infrastructure is the key to that sort of resilience. Governments and private companies have long worked to protect energy infrastructure from dangers of all kinds, from terrorist attacks to hurricanes. As the transition proceeds, they will need to step up such efforts. Moreover, as the clean energy economy becomes more digitized and electrified, it will be exposed to a growing threat of cyberattacks. Private companies and governments will need to coordinate and cooperate to deter and respond to threats such as the 2015 cyberattack that took out large swaths of the grid in western Ukraine.

Resilience also requires flexibility, which in the energy sector is measured by the ability of every part of a system to cope with losses in other parts. Because renewable sources such as solar power and wind are highly variable, the energy they generate needs to be either stored or backed up by other sources, with delivery systems making minute-by-minute adjustments. That is already a difficult task, and it will become even harder in a grid with more intermittent sources of energy and more variable electricity demand. According to the IEA, the global power system's need for flexibility—measured as the amount the rest of the system needs to adjust to handle changes in demand and in solar and wind output—will more than quadruple by 2050 if all countries fulfill their climate pledges. Today, plants that run on coal or gas perform most of these adjustments. But as the transition progresses, the number of such plants—and thus their ability to serve as backstops—will progressively diminish.

To counteract that dynamic, U.S. policymakers should take steps to make sure that the increasing share of renewable energy on the grid is matched by adequate balancing resources and storage capacity. Doing so will require structures such as so-called capacity markets, which pay generators to be available to meet peak demand even if they are idle much of the time. Such mechanisms can help ensure that companies whose resources are needed only infrequently nevertheless stay in business and support a reliable electricity supply even as their utilization rate falls as the grid decarbonizes.

Officials can also make use of new tools to manage demand for energy without massively inconveniencing consumers or creating political headaches. For instance, digital technology can help consumers shift energy-intensive activities to low-demand times of the day (such as running dishwashers and clothes dryers overnight) or prompt them to save energy by lowering thermostats in unoccupied rooms. Artificial intelligence will also play a growing role—for example, by reducing the amount of time that energy systems are down for maintenance, by forecasting demand, and by improving storage. Such tools would have come in handy in December 2022, when grid operators in Texas badly underestimated how much electricity customers would need and the state barely avoided widespread blackouts. Finally, officials should avoid the early retirement of fossil-fired electricity sources that can balance the grid and ensure reliability before alternatives are fully capable of providing the necessary level of service.

Energy security will be advanced not through more autonomy but through more integration.

A resilient system must also be able to weather unexpected shocks and supply disruptions. For decades, policymakers have relied heavily on two types of buffers: the spare capacity of oil-producing countries (especially Saudi Arabia) and strategic stockpiles, which members of the IEA are required to hold as part of an agreement forged after the Arab oil embargo in the 1970s. These historical buffers will still matter as the transition unfolds—even more so if, as seems likely today, declines in energy supply and investment are not synchronized with declines in demand, leading to less slack in the system to handle unexpected shocks and more volatility. Moreover, it is clear that Riyadh has become far less willing to dip into its spare capacity whenever Washington demands it. As coal generation declines in a decarbonizing economy, there will be less opportunity for power generators to toggle between natural gas and coal, as many do now. This new reality could result in more volatility in natural gas prices. And recent turmoil in the refining sector that contributed to skyrocketing gasoline and diesel prices in the United States was a reminder that limited refining investment can bite consumers before vehicle electrification causes fuel use to drop sharply. For those reasons, other strategic stocks of all kinds will become more important—not just those that hold oil but also ones that hold natural gas and oil products such as diesel fuel and gasoline.

The United States will also need strategic stockpiles of the building blocks of clean energy, working with its allies to amass critical minerals such as lithium, graphite, rare earths, and nickel. Such coordination would be enhanced if the IEA had a hand in negotiating agreements, assessing which countries are best positioned to contribute to which stockpiles, and regularly monitoring whether the composition of stockpiles fits current needs. The IEA has played this role admirably for oil and oil products and could do so again with critical minerals if its members chose to expand its mandate.

INTEGRATION AS INSURANCE

A desire for greater security has spurred the decades-long quest for "energy independence" in the United States and elsewhere. And because of the shale revolution, the United States has become energy self-sufficient in net terms. Nevertheless, the country continues to be vulnerable to geopolitical risks because in a global market, supply shocks anywhere affect prices everywhere. Proponents of the transition to a net-zero carbon system have long heralded the greater insulation from geopolitics that would likely result from the end of the fossil-fuel era. But at least for the next few decades, energy security will be advanced not through more autonomy but through more integration—just as it always has been.

Interconnected and well-functioning energy markets increase energy security by allowing supply and demand to respond to price signals so the entire system can better handle unexpected shocks. In 2005, when Hurricanes Katrina and Rita disrupted much of the U.S. Gulf Coast's vast production and refining operations, energy companies were able to avert fuel shortages by quickly importing supplies from the global market. Similarly, after the Fukushima nuclear disaster in 2011, Japan was able to temporarily shut down its nuclear power sector because it could import other sources of fuel from the global market.

But maintaining and cultivating interdependence in today's environment is more difficult than at any time in recent memory, as countries around the world are embracing industrial policies that involve increased state intervention in markets. Although those efforts can deliver benefits, such as minimizing markets' vulnerability to the whims of geopolitical adversaries, many policymakers want to go further, promoting such policies as a means to boost domestic jobs and build political coalitions in support of stronger action on the environment. Indeed, although climate diplomacy has been premised for years on the assumption that progress depends on transnational cooperation, some efforts to advance climate action paradoxically risk undermining cooperation by fueling the forces of fragmentation and protectionism.

The case for energy integration has suffered as a result of Europe's urgent need to decouple from Russian energy during the war in Ukraine. Nevertheless, although shocks may be felt more broadly in an integrated system, they are also felt less intensely. Integration is a form of insurance that spreads the risk of energy supply disruptions among many parties. And even if more autonomy were preferable to more integration, it would not be possible to expand clean energy at the scale and speed needed if each country sought to produce and consume only within its own borders. According to the IEA, the value of global trade in critical minerals will need to triple to achieve net-zero emissions by 2050. Global trade in low-carbon fuels such as hydrogen and ammonia will also need to grow exponentially. For the United States, energy security will require fewer trade barriers and more trade agreements with allies, as well as with other countries that meet certain environmental standards. Washington should also eliminate tariffs on goods and technologies related to clean energy and help finalize the Environmental Goods Agreement, which would reduce tariffs on goods that benefit the environment to lower their costs and increase their trade.

WHAT YOU DON'T KNOW CAN HURT YOU

One of the reasons that the United States, Canada, Japan, and several European countries created the IEA in 1974 was that a lack of accurate, reliable data on prices and supplies had made it hard for governments to craft policies and respond to crises. The lesson was clear: good data allows markets to function, prevents panic, and deters the speculation that exacerbates price spikes, volatility, and shortages. Over the decades, IEA data, along with data assembled by the International Energy Forum, has underpinned decision-making about production levels and guided actions such as coordinated releases of stockpiled oil.

A clean energy economy will need the same kind of transparency. Inadequate data in nascent markets, such as those for green ammonia and hydrogen, can cause supply disruptions, a lack of liquidity, and poor availability of spot price assessments, all leading to pronounced price fluctuations. The energy transition will also depend heavily on the market for critical minerals, such as nickel. But investors were reminded of how market opacity can trigger extreme volatility when the price of nickel on the London Metal Exchange almost quadrupled over just two days in early 2022, owing to massive short-selling caused in part by a lack of price transparency.

Currently, some private companies have good information on prices, but no single entity gathers broad industrywide data and makes it publicly available. The IEA is the clear candidate to fill that role. Ideally, the agency would ask governments to share consumption and production data on minerals and make informed inferences about inventory levels. Such data sharing would be especially important to ensure compliance if governments agreed to create strategic stockpiles, as they do with oil. For such a system to work, however, the IEA would have to bring in countries that are not members of the organization but produce or consume significant amounts of those minerals, which in turn would require a new legal framework for the agency. Meanwhile, to help prevent market manipulation and speculation, national regulators such as the U.S. Commodity Futures Trading Commission should require greater transparency in the pricing and trading of commodities.

SECURITY AND THE CLIMATE

The importance of energy security never diminished; it had simply been taken for granted in a world of abundance and integrated, well-functioning global energy markets. Policymakers now have the opportunity to look at energy security and climate security afresh, to accord appropriate weight to both, and to appreciate that neither can be achieved in the absence of the other.

This effort requires recognizing that energy security is not a static concept but one that has evolved a great deal since the crises of the 1970s. Policymakers must grasp the new risks to energy security and modernize their toolkits to combat them. Doing so is not a distraction from addressing climate change but central to it; without this shift, energy crises might derail the drive to net-zero emissions. In the not-so-distant past, officials and experts thought that excessive fears about energy security might hinder the fight for the climate. Today, the opposite is true: as the transition to a net-zero world proceeds, the bigger danger to the climate will be insufficient attention to energy security.

Israel's One-State Reality

It's Time to Give Up on the Two-State Solution

MICHAEL BARNETT, NATHAN J. BROWN, MARC LYNCH, AND SHIBLEY TELHAMI

Prime Minister Benjamin Netanyahu's return to power in Israel with a narrow, extreme right-wing coalition has shattered even the illusion of a two-state solution. Members of his new government have not been shy about stating their views on what Israel is and what it should be in all the territories it controls: a Greater Israel defined not just as a Jewish state but one in which the law enshrines Jewish supremacy over all Palestinians

---

MICHAEL BARNETT is University Professor of International Affairs and Political Science at the Elliott School of International Affairs at George Washington University.

NATHAN J. BROWN is Professor of Political Science and International Affairs at George Washington University and a Nonresident Senior Fellow at the Carnegie Endowment for International Peace.

MARC LYNCH is Professor of Political Science and International Affairs at George Washington University.

SHIBLEY TELHAMI is Anwar Sadat Professor for Peace and Development at the University of Maryland and a Nonresident Senior Fellow at the Brookings Institution.

They are the editors of *The One State Reality: What Is Israel/Palestine?*

Illustration by Guillem Casasús

who remain there. As a result, it is no longer possible to avoid confronting a one-state reality.

Israel's radical new government did not create this reality but rather made it impossible to deny. The temporary status of "occupation" of the Palestinian territories is now a permanent condition in which one state ruled by one group of people rules over another group of people. The promise of a two-state solution made sense as an alternative future in the years around the 1993 Oslo accords, when there were constituencies for compromise on both the Israeli and the Palestinian sides and when tangible if fleeting progress was made toward building the institutions of a hypothetical Palestinian state. But that period ended long ago. Today, it makes little sense to let fantastical visions for the future obscure deeply embedded existing arrangements.

It is past time to grapple with what a one-state reality means for policy, politics, and analysis. Palestine is not a state in waiting, and Israel is not a democratic state incidentally occupying Palestinian territory. All the territory west of the Jordan River has long constituted a single state under Israeli rule, where the land and the people are subject to radically different legal regimes, and Palestinians are permanently treated as a lower caste. Policymakers and analysts who ignore this one-state reality will be condemned to failure and irrelevance, doing little beyond providing a smokescreen for the entrenchment of the status quo.

Some implications of this one-state reality are clear. The world will not stop caring about Palestinian rights, no matter how fervently many supporters of Israel (and Arab rulers) wish they would. Violence, dispossession, and human rights abuses have escalated over the last year, and the risk of large-scale violent confrontation grows with every day that Palestinians are locked in this ever-expanding system of legalized oppression and Israeli encroachment. But far less clear is how important actors will adjust—if they adjust at all—as the reality of a single state shifts from open secret to undeniable truth.

U.S. President Joe Biden seems fully committed to the status quo, and there is no evidence that his administration has thought about the issue or done much beyond crisis management and mouthing displeasure. A strong sense of wishful thinking permeates Washington, with many U.S. officials still trying to convince themselves that there is a chance of returning to a two-state negotiation after the aberrant Netanyahu government leaves office. But ignoring the new reality will not be an option for much longer. A storm is gathering in Israel and

Palestine that demands an urgent response from the country that has most enabled the emergence of a single state upholding Jewish supremacy. If the United States wants to avoid profound instability in the Middle East and a challenge to its broader global agenda, it must cease exempting Israel from the standards and structures of the liberal international order that Washington hopes to lead.

FROM UNSAYABLE TO UNDENIABLE

A one-state arrangement is not a future possibility; it already exists, no matter what anyone thinks. Between the Mediterranean Sea and the Jordan River, one state controls the entry and exit of people and goods, oversees security, and has the capacity to impose its decisions, laws, and policies on millions of people without their consent.

A one-state reality could, in principle, be based on democratic rule and equal citizenship. But such an arrangement is not on offer at the moment. Forced to choose between Israel's Jewish identity and liberal democracy, Israel has chosen the former. It has locked in a system of Jewish supremacy, wherein non-Jews are structurally discriminated against or excluded in a tiered scheme: some non-Jews have most of, but not all, the rights that Jews have, while most non-Jews live under severe segregation, separation, and domination.

A peace process in the closing years of the twentieth century offered the tantalizing possibility of something different. But since the 2000 Camp David summit, where U.S.-led negotiations failed to achieve a two-state agreement, the phrase "peace process" has served mostly to distract from the realities on the ground and to offer an excuse for not acknowledging them. The second Intifada, which erupted soon after the disappointment at Camp David, and Israel's subsequent intrusions into the West Bank transformed the Palestinian Authority into little more than a security subcontractor for Israel. They also accelerated the rightward drift of Israeli politics, the population shifts brought about by Israeli citizens moving into the West Bank, and the geographical fragmentation of Palestinian society. The cumulative effect of these changes became evident during the 2021 crisis over the appropriation of Palestinian homes in East Jerusalem, which pitted not just Israeli settlers and Palestinians but also Jewish and Palestinian citizens of Israel against each other in a conflict that split cities and neighborhoods.

Netanyahu's new government, composed of a coalition of right-wing religious and nationalist extremists, epitomizes these trends.

Its members boast of their mission to create a new Israel in their image: less liberal, more religious, and more willing to own discrimination against non-Jews. Netanyahu has written that "Israel is not a state of all its citizens" but rather "of the Jewish people—and only it." The man he appointed as minister of national security, Itamar Ben-Gvir, has declared that Gaza should be "ours" and that "the Palestinians can go to . . . Saudi Arabia or other places, like Iraq or Iran." This extremist vision has long been shared by at least a minority of Israelis and has strong grounding in Zionist thought and practice. It began gaining adherents soon after Israel occupied the Palestinian territories in the 1967 war. And although it is not yet a hegemonic view, it can plausibly claim a majority of Israeli society and can no longer be termed a fringe position.

The fact of a one-state reality has long been obvious to those who live in Israel and the territories it controls and to anyone who has paid attention to the inexorable shifts on the ground. But in the past few years, something has changed. Until recently, the one-state reality was rarely acknowledged by important actors, and those who spoke the truth out loud were ignored or punished for doing so. With remarkable speed, however, the unsayable has become close to conventional wisdom.

DEMOCRACY FOR SOME

To see the reality of a single state, many observers will need to put on new glasses. These are people who are used to seeing a distinction between the occupied territories and Israel proper—that is, the state as it existed before 1967, when Israel captured the West Bank and Gaza—and think Israel's sovereignty is limited to the territory it controlled before 1967. But the state and sovereignty are not the same. The state is defined by what it controls, whereas sovereignty depends on other states' recognizing the legality of that control.

These new glasses would disaggregate the concepts of state, sovereignty, nation, and citizenship, making it easier to see a one-state reality that is ineluctably based on relations of superiority and inferiority between Jews and non-Jews across all the territories under Israel's differentiated but unchallenged control. Consider Israel through the lens of a state. It has control over a territory that stretches from the river to the sea, has a near monopoly on the use of force, and uses this power to sustain a draconian blockade of Gaza and control the West Bank with a system of checkpoints, policing, and relentlessly expanding settlements. Even after it withdrew forces from Gaza in 2005, the Israeli government retained control over the territory's entry and exit points. Like parts of the West Bank, Gaza enjoys a degree of autonomy, and since the brief Palestinian civil war of 2007, the territory has been administered internally by the Islamist organization Hamas, which brooks little dissent. But Hamas does not control the territory's coastline, airspace, or boundaries. In other words, by any reasonable definition, the Israeli state encompasses all lands from its border with Jordan to the Mediterranean Sea.

It has been possible to overlook that reality because Israel has not made formal claims of sovereignty over all these areas. It has annexed some of the occupied territories, including East Jerusalem and the Golan Heights. But it has not yet declared sovereignty over the rest of the land that it controls, and only a handful of states would be likely to recognize such claims if Israel were to make them.

Israel no longer even pretends to maintain liberal aspirations.

Controlling territory and consolidating institutional domination without formalizing sovereignty enables Israel to maintain a one-state reality on its terms. It can deny responsibility for (and rights to) most Palestinians because they are residents of its territory but not citizens of the state, cynically justifying this discrimination on the grounds that it keeps alive the possibility of a two-state solution. By not formalizing sovereignty, Israel can be democratic for its citizens but unaccountable to millions of its residents. This arrangement has allowed many of Israel's supporters abroad to continue to pretend that all this is temporary—that Israel remains a liberal democracy and that, someday, Palestinians will exercise their right to self-determination.

But even within its pre-1967 borders, Israel's democracy has limits, which become apparent when viewed through the lens of citizenship. Israel's Jewish identity and its one-state reality have produced an intricate series of legal categories that distribute differentiated rights, responsibilities, and protections. Its 2018 "nation-state" law defines Israel as "the nation-state of the Jewish People" and holds that "the exercise of the right to national self-determination in the State of Israel is unique to the Jewish People"; it makes no mention of democracy or equality for non-Jewish citizens.

According to this hierarchy of membership, the fullest class of citizenship is reserved for Israeli Jews (at least those whose Jewishness meets rabbinical standards); they are citizens without conditions. Palestinians who have Israeli citizenship and reside in pre-1967 Israel have political and civil rights but confront other limits—both legal and extrajudicial—on their rights, responsibilities, and protections. Palestinian residents of Jerusalem theoretically have the option of becoming Israeli citizens, but most reject it because doing so would be an act of disloyalty. Palestinians who reside in the territories are the lowest class of all. Their rights and responsibilities depend on where they live, with those in Gaza at the bottom of the hierarchy—a position that has only deteriorated since Hamas took control. Asking a Palestinian to describe his or her legal status can elicit an answer that lasts for several minutes—and is still full of ambiguities.

As long as hope existed for a two-state solution that would see Palestinians' rights recognized, it was possible to view the situation within Israel's 1967 boundaries as one of de jure equality combined with de facto discrimination against some citizens—an unfortunate but common reality in much of the world. But when one acknowledges the one-state reality, something more pernicious is revealed. In that one state, there are some whose movement, travel, civil status, economic activities, property rights, and access to public services are severely restricted. A substantial share of lifelong residents with deep and continuous roots in the territory of that state are rendered stateless. And all these categories and gradations of marginalization are enforced by legal, political, and security measures imposed by state actors who are accountable to only a portion of the population.

Naming this reality is politically contentious, even as a consensus has formed about the abiding and severe inequalities that define it. A flurry of reports by Israeli and international nongovernmental organizations documenting these inequalities have driven the term "apartheid" from the margins of the Israeli-Palestinian debate to its center. Apartheid refers to the system of racial segregation that South Africa's white minority government used to enshrine white supremacy from 1948 to the early 1990s. It has since been defined under international law and by the International Criminal Court as a legalized scheme of racial segregation and discrimination and deemed a crime against humanity. Major human rights organizations, including Human Rights Watch and Amnesty International, have applied the term to Israel. So have many academics: according to a March 2022 poll of Middle East–focused scholars who are members of three large academic associations, 60 percent of respondents described the situation in Israel and the Palestinian territories as a "one-state reality with inequality akin to apartheid."

The term may not be a perfect fit. Israel's system of structural discrimination is more severe than those of even the most illiberal states. But it is based not on race, as apartheid was defined in South Africa and is defined under international law, but on ethnicity, nationality, and religion. Perhaps this distinction matters to those who wish to take legal action against Israel. It is less important politically, however, and is virtually meaningless when it comes to analysis. What matters politically is that a once taboo term has increasingly become a mainstream, common-sense understanding of reality. Analytically, what matters is that the apartheid label accurately describes the facts on the ground and offers the beginnings of a road map to change them. Apartheid is not a magic word that alters reality when invoked. But its entry into the political mainstream reveals a broad recognition that Israeli rule is designed to maintain Jewish supremacy throughout all the territory the state controls. Israel's system may not technically be apartheid, but it rhymes.

RUDE AWAKENING

It is primarily Israelis and Palestinians who must grapple with the one-state reality. But that reality will also complicate Israel's relationship with the rest of the world. For half a century, the peace process allowed Western democracies to overlook Israel's occupation in favor of an aspirational future in which the occupation would come to a mutually negotiated end. Israeli democracy (however flawed) and the nominal distinction between Israel and the occupied Palestinian territories also helped outsiders avert their gaze. All these diversions are gone. The one-state reality has long been embedded in Israeli law, politics, and society, even if it is only now being broadly acknowledged. No ready alternatives exist, and it has been decades since there was any meaningful political process to create one.

Perhaps the recognition of these facts will not change much. Many enduring global problems are never resolved. We live in a populist world, where democracy and human rights are under threat. Israeli leaders point to the Abraham Accords, which established Israel's relations with Bahrain, Morocco, Sudan, and the United Arab Emirates (UAE), to argue that normalization with Arab states never required resolving the Palestinian issue. For their part, Western leaders may simply continue to pretend that Israel shares their liberal democratic values while many pro-Israel groups in the United States double down on their support. Liberal Jewish Americans may struggle to defend an Israel that has many characteristics of apartheid, but their protests will have little practical effect.

Yet there are reasons to believe that the transition from an aspirational two-state world to a real one-state world could be rocky. The mainstreaming of the apartheid analogy and the rise of the Boycott, Divestment, and Sanctions movement—and the intense backlash against both—suggest that the political terrain has shifted. Israel may enjoy more physical security and regional diplomatic recognition than ever before, with few international or local constraints on its activities in the West Bank. But control requires more than brute strength. It also requires some semblance of legitimacy, with the status quo sustained by its taken-for-granted nature, its naturalization as common sense, and the impossibility of even contemplating justifiable resistance. Israel still has the material power to win the battles it picks. But as those battles proliferate, each victory further erodes its fighting position. Those wanting to defend the one-state reality are defending colonialist principles in a postcolonial world.

Many lifelong residents of Israel have been rendered stateless.

The struggle to define and shape the terms of this one-state reality may take new forms. In the past, dramatic interstate wars created openings for negotiations and high-stakes diplomacy. But in the future, U.S. policymakers are not likely to confront conventional conflicts such as those that broke out between Israel and Arab states in 1967 and 1973. Instead, they will face something closer to the first and second Intifada—sudden outbursts of violence and mass popular contestation such as those that occurred in May 2021. At that time, clashes in Jerusalem sparked a wider conflagration involving rocket fire between Israel and Hamas, demonstrations and violence in the West Bank, and ugly incidents where Israelis of Jewish and Palestinian ancestry (and the Israeli police) behaved as if ethnicity trumped citizenship. Daily acts of violence and sporadic bouts of popular upheaval—perhaps even a full third Intifada—seem inevitable.

Policymakers in the United States and elsewhere who have long talked about the need to preserve a two-state solution are increasingly being forced to react to crises for which they are unprepared. The problems engendered by the one-state reality have already sparked new solidarity movements, boycotts, and societal conflicts. Nongovernmental organizations, political movements supporting various Israeli and Palestinian causes, and transnational advocacy groups are seeking to alter global norms and sway individuals, societies, and governments with new and old media campaigns. Increasingly, they aim to label or boycott goods produced in places controlled by the Israeli government (or outlaw such boycotts) and invoke civil rights laws to mobilize their supporters and find alternatives to the feckless diplomatic efforts of government leaders.

But all these movements and campaigns seek to mobilize constituencies that are deeply divided. The Palestinians are divided between those who bear Israeli citizenship and those who have other forms of residency, as well as among those who live in East Jerusalem, the West Bank, and Gaza. They are divided between those living in the one-state reality and those living in the diaspora. They are divided between the Fatah political faction that holds sway in the West Bank and the Hamas organization that controls Gaza. They are also increasingly split along generational lines. Younger Palestinians feel less attached to the movements that channeled the political commitments and energies of their parents and grandparents and are more likely to gravitate to new groups and adopt new tactics of resistance.

Israeli Jews are similarly divided about the nature of the state, the role of religion in politics, and a host of other matters, including the rights of gays, lesbians, and other sexual minorities. Liberal Israeli Jews have organized massive protests against the Netanyahu government's assault on democracy and the judiciary, but they have mobilized around the Palestinian issue far less, showing how internal disagreements have edged aside questions about a peace process that no longer exists.

The result is that leaders on both sides do not lead. There are politicians in all camps who want to keep a lid on the conflict, generally not in service of any strategy for resolution but out of a sense of inefficacy and inertia. Other politicians want the opposite: to shake things up and move in a sharply different direction, as U.S. President Donald Trump did with his "deal of the century," promising an end to the conflict in a matter that virtually erased Palestinian rights and national aspirations. Jews pushing formal annexation of the occupied territories and Palestinians advocating for new modes of resistance to Israeli rule also hope to upend the status quo. But all such efforts founder on the firmly established structures of power and interests.

Under these conditions, any diplomacy undertaken in the name of resolving the conflict in a just manner will likely fail because it misreads both the possible alternatives to the current impasse and the will among all parties to achieve them. Policymakers wishing to construct better choices will have to pay attention to the ways in which the one-state system operates and evolves. They will need to understand how its various inhabitants imagine their homeland, how rights are enforced or violated, and how demographics are slowly but portentously changing.

GHOSTS OF THE ARAB SPRING

Acknowledgment of the one-state reality has important—and contradictory—implications for the Arab world. The argument for the two-state solution has long assumed the importance of the Palestinian cause to Arab publics, if not to their governments. The 2002 Saudi peace initiative, which offered normalization of relations between Israel and all Arab states in exchange for complete Israeli withdrawal from the occupied territories, established a baseline: peace with the Arab world would require a resolution of the Palestinian issue.

The Abraham Accords, brokered by the Trump administration and enthusiastically sustained by the Biden administration, explicitly targeted that assumption by accelerating political normalization and security cooperation between Israel and several Arab states without requiring progress on the Palestinian issue. This decoupling of Arab normalization from the Palestinian issue went a long way toward entrenching the one-state reality.

Thus far, the Abraham Accords have proved durable, surviving the formation of Netanyahu's government with its extremist ministers. The normalization of relations between Israel and the UAE, at least, will likely outlast the next round of Israeli-Palestinian violence and even overt Israeli moves toward annexation. But since the accords were signed, no additional Arab countries have sought to normalize relations with Israel, and Saudi Arabia has continued to hedge its bets by holding off on establishing formal ties with Israel.

Arab normalization is likely to remain tethered to the Palestinian issue indefinitely outside of the Gulf countries. It is all too easy to imagine a scenario in which Israel moves to confiscate more property in Jerusalem, provokes widespread Palestinian protests, and then responds to this unrest with even greater violence and faster dispossession—eventually triggering the final collapse of the Palestinian Authority. Such an escalation could easily spark large-scale protests across the Arab world, where long-simmering economic hardship and political repression have created a tinderbox. There is also the even graver threat that Israel will expel Palestinians from the West Bank or even Jerusalem—a possibility, sometimes euphemistically called a "transfer," that polls suggest many Israeli Jews would support. And that is to say nothing of how Hamas or Iran might exploit such conditions.

Arab rulers might not care about the Palestinians, but their people do—and those rulers care about nothing more than keeping their thrones. Fully abandoning the Palestinians after more than half a century of at least rhetorical support would be risky. Arab leaders do not fear losing elections, but they remember the Arab uprisings of 2011 all too well, and they worry about anything that invites mass popular mobilizations that could rapidly mutate into protests against their regimes.

EXIT, VOICE, OR LOYALTY?

Acknowledging the one-state reality could also polarize the American conversation about Israel and the Palestinians. Evangelicals and many others on the political right might embrace this reality as the realization of what they consider legitimate Israeli aspirations. Many Americans who are left of center may finally recognize that Israel has fallen from the ranks of liberal democracies and may abandon the fanciful promise of two states for the goal of a single state that grants equal rights to all its residents.

The United States bears considerable responsibility for entrenching the one-state reality, and it continues to play a powerful role in framing and shaping the Israeli-Palestinian issue. Israeli settlement construction in the West Bank would not have survived and accelerated, and occupation would not have endured, without U.S. efforts to shield Israel from repercussions at the United Nations and other international organizations. Without American technology and arms, Israel would probably not have been able to sustain its military edge in the region, which also enabled it to solidify its position in the occupied territories. And without major U.S. diplomatic efforts and resources, Israel could not have concluded peace agreements with Arab states, from Camp David to the Abraham Accords.

Yet the American conversation about Israel and the Palestinians has willfully neglected the ways in which Washington has abetted the occupation. U.S. support for the peace process has been couched both in terms of Israel's security and in terms of the idea that only a two-state solution could preserve Israel as both Jewish and democratic. These two goals have always been in tension, but a one-state reality makes them irreconcilable.

Although the Israeli-Palestinian issue has never been high on the American public's list of priorities, U.S. attitudes have shifted notably: support for a two-state solution has declined, and support for a single state that ensures equal citizenship has risen over the past few years. Polls show that most American voters would support a democratic Israel over a Jewish one, if forced to choose. Views on Israel have also become far more partisan, with Republicans, especially evangelicals, growing more supportive of Israeli policies and the overwhelming majority of Democrats preferring an evenhanded U.S. policy. Young Democrats now express more support for the Palestinians than for Israel. One reason for this shift, especially among young Democrats, is that the Israeli-Palestinian issue is increasingly viewed as an issue of social justice rather than strategic interest or biblical prophecy. This has been particularly true in the era of Black Lives Matter.

The one-state reality has especially roiled the politics of Jewish Americans. From the earliest years of Zionism, most Jewish American supporters of Israel held as sacrosanct the aspiration for Israel to be simultaneously Jewish and liberal. Netanyahu's latest government might be the breaking point for this group. It is difficult to square a commitment to liberalism with support for a single state that offers the benefits of democracy to Jews (and now seems to tread on some of those) but explicitly withholds them from the majority of its non-Jewish inhabitants.

Most Jewish Americans see basic liberal principles such as freedom of opinion and expression, the rule of law, and democracy not only as Jewish values but also as bulwarks against discrimination that ensure their acceptance and even survival in the United States. Yet Israel's commitment to liberalism has always been shaky. As a Jewish state, it fosters a form of ethnic nationalism rather than a civic one, and its Orthodox Jewish citizens play an outsize role in determining how Judaism shapes Israeli life.

In 1970, the political economist Albert Hirschman wrote that members of organizations in crisis or decline have three options: "exit, voice, and loyalty." Jewish Americans have those same options today. One camp, which arguably dominates major Jewish institutions in the United States, exhibits loyalty enabled by denial of the one-state reality. Voice is the increasingly dominant choice of Jewish Americans who were previously in the peace camp. Once focused on achieving a two-state solution, these Americans now direct their activism toward defending Palestinian rights, safeguarding the shrinking space for Israeli civil society, and resisting the dangers posed by Netanyahu's right-wing government. Finally, there are the Jewish Americans who have chosen exit, or indifference. They simply do not think much about Israel. That might be because they do not have a strong Jewish identity or because they see Israel as misaligned with or even opposed to their values. There is some evidence that the more Israel lurches to the right, the larger this group becomes, especially among young Jewish Americans.

REALITY CHECK

So far, the Biden administration has sought to sustain the status quo while urging Israel to avoid major provocations. In response to continued settlement construction in the West Bank and other Israeli violations of international law, the United States has issued empty statements calling on Israel to avoid actions that undermine a two-state solution. But this approach misdiagnoses the problem and only makes it worse: Netanyahu's far-right government is a symptom, not a cause, of the one-state reality, and coddling it in an attempt to coax it toward moderation will only embolden its extremist leaders by showing that they pay no price for their actions.

The United States could instead meet a radicalized reality with a radical response. For starters, Washington should banish the terms "two-state solution" and "peace process" from its vocabulary. U.S. calls for Israelis and Palestinians to return to the negotiating table rely on magical thinking. Changing the way the United States talks about the Israeli-Palestinian issue will change nothing on the ground, but it will strip away a facade that has allowed U.S. policymakers to avoid confronting reality. Washington must look at

Israel as it is and not as it has been assumed to be—and act accordingly. Israel no longer even pretends to maintain liberal aspirations. The United States does not have "shared values" and should not have "unbreakable bonds" with a state that discriminates against or abuses millions of its residents based on their ethnicity and religion.

A better U.S. policy would advocate for equality, citizenship, and human rights for all Jews and Palestinians living within the single state dominated by Israel. Theoretically, such a policy would not prevent a two-state solution from being resurrected in the unlikely event that the parties moved in that direction in the distant future. But starting from a one-state reality that is morally reprehensible and strategically costly would demand an immediate focus on equal human and civil rights. A serious rejection of today's unjust reality by the United States and the rest of the international community might also push the parties themselves to seriously consider alternative futures. The United States should demand equality now, even if the ultimate political arrangement will be up to the Palestinians and the Israelis to determine.

To that end, Washington should begin conditioning military and economic aid to Israel on clear and specific measures to terminate Israel's military rule over the Palestinians. Avoiding such conditionality has made Washington deeply complicit in the one-state reality. Should Israel persist on its current path, the United States should consider sharply reducing aid and other privileges, perhaps even imposing smart, targeted sanctions on Israel and Israeli leaders in response to clearly transgressive actions. Israel can decide for itself what it wants to do, but the United States and other democracies can make sure it knows the costs of maintaining and even intensifying a deeply illiberal, discriminatory order.

The clearest global vision articulated by the Biden administration has been its full-throated defense of international laws and norms in response to Russia's invasion of Ukraine. Even if one ignores the one-state reality, the same norms and values would surely be at stake in Israel and Palestine, as is widely understood across the global South. When Israel violates international laws and liberal norms, the United States should denounce Israel for those violations as it would any other state. Washington needs to stop shielding Israel in international organizations when it faces valid allegations of transgressions against international law. And it needs to refrain from vetoing UN Security Council resolutions that aim to hold Israel accountable, stop resisting Palestinian efforts to seek redress in international courts, and rally other countries to demand an end to the siege of Gaza—another supposedly temporary measure that has become a cruel and an institutionalized reality.

But the one-state reality demands more. Looked at through that prism, Israel resembles an apartheid state. Instead of exempting Israel from the strong norm against apartheid, enshrined in international law, Washington must reckon with the reality it helped create and begin viewing that reality, talking about it, and interacting with it honestly. The United States should stand up for international, Israeli, and Palestinian nongovernmental organizations, human rights organizations, and individual activists who have been demonized for courageously calling out structural injustice. Washington must protect Israeli civil society organizations that are the country's last refuge of liberal values and Palestinian ones whose efforts will be critical to avoiding bloody conflict in the months to come. The United States should also oppose Israeli arrests of Palestinian leaders who offer a nonviolent vision of popular resistance. And it should not seek to stop or punish those who choose to peacefully boycott Israel because of its abusive policies.

The United States bears considerable responsibility for the one-state reality.

Although Washington cannot prevent normalization of relations between Israel and its Arab neighbors, the United States should not lead such efforts. Nobody should be fooled by the mirage of the Abraham Accords thriving while the Palestinian issue festers. Decoupling such normalization agreements from Israel's treatment of Palestinians has only empowered the Israeli far right and cemented Jewish supremacy within the state.

These U.S. policy changes would not immediately bear fruit. The political backlash would be fierce, even though Americans—especially Democrats—have grown far more critical of Israel than have the politicians they elect. But in the long run, these changes offer the best hope for moving toward a more peaceful and just outcome in Israel and Palestine. By finally confronting the one-state reality and taking a principled stand, the United States would stop being part of the problem and start being part of the solution.

Iraq and the Pathologies of Primacy

The Flawed Logic That Produced the War Is Alive and Well

STEPHEN WERTHEIM

Twenty years ago, the United States invaded Iraq. It spent a decade breaking the country and then trying to put it back together again. It spent another decade trying to forget. "We have met our responsibility," U.S. President Barack Obama told the nation in 2010 while declaring a short-lived end to the U.S. combat mission in Iraq. "Now, it is time to turn the page."

For Obama, moving on meant taking the fight to al Qaeda and the Taliban in Afghanistan through a surge of U.S. troops. Obama's critics, for their part, soon found another reason to tell Americans to "get over Iraq": the debacle was, in their view, making the president and the public too reticent to use military force, this time to sort out Syria's civil war, which erupted in 2011. Obama refrained from striking Damascus, but he ended up deploying troops to Iraq and

STEPHEN WERTHEIM is a Senior Fellow in the American Statecraft Program at the Carnegie Endowment for International Peace and Visiting Lecturer at Yale Law School and Catholic University. He is the author of *Tomorrow, the World: The Birth of U.S. Global Supremacy*.

Syria in 2014 to fight the Islamic State (also known as ISIS), which emerged out of the maelstrom of the United States' original invasion.

By 2021, it was President Joe Biden's turn to urge the country to move on from post-9/11 debacles. "I stand here today, for the first time in 20 years, with the United States not at war," he declared in September. Biden had just withdrawn U.S. forces from Afghanistan. The United States nevertheless continued to conduct counterterrorism operations in multiple countries, including Iraq, where 2,500 ground troops remained. "We've turned the page," Biden said.

Have we? Over two decades, Americans have stubbornly refused to move on from Iraq. That is partly because the U.S. military is still fighting there and many other places besides. More profoundly, the country cannot "turn the page" without reading and comprehending it—without truly reckoning with the causes of the war. It may be painful to revisit what drove American leaders, on a bipartisan basis, to want to invade a country that had not attacked the United States and had no plans to do so, facts widely appreciated at the time. Yet without looking back, the country will not move forward with confidence and unity.

To be sure, Washington has absorbed several hard-earned lessons from the conflict. American policymakers, politicians, and experts now generally reject wars to change regimes or rebuild nations. In weighing the use of force, they have rediscovered the virtue of prudence. And they now appreciate that democracy is rarely imposed at gunpoint and takes hard work to establish and preserve, even in deep-rooted democracies such as the United States.

These are necessary lessons, but they do not suffice. They reduce the Iraq war to a policy error, which could be corrected while the United States goes on pursuing the hegemonic world role it assigned itself when the Cold War ended. In fact, the decision to invade Iraq stemmed from the pursuit of global primacy. Primacy directs the United States to fund a massive military and scatter it across the globe for an essentially preventive purpose: to dissuade other countries from rising and challenging American dominance. Promising to keep costs low, primacy assumes that U.S. hegemony will not engender resistance—and strikes hard to snuff out any that appears. It sees global dominance almost as an end in itself, disregarding the abundant strategic alternatives that wide oceans, friendly neighbors, and nuclear deterrents afford the United States.

The invasion of Iraq emerged from this logic. After the 9/11 attacks, the architects of the invasion sought to shore up U.S. military preeminence in the Middle East and beyond. By acting boldly, by targeting a galling adversary not involved in 9/11, the United States would demonstrate the futility of resisting American power.

As "shock and awe" gave way to chaos, insurgency, destruction, and death, the war should have discredited the primacist project that spawned it. Instead, the quest for primacy endures. U.S. power is meeting mounting resistance across the globe, and Washington wishes to counter almost all of it, everywhere, still conflating U.S. power projection with American interests, still trying to overmatch rivals and avoid curbing U.S. ambitions. The results were damaging enough during the United States' unipolar moment. Against major powers armed with nuclear weapons, they may be much worse.

BULLY ON THE BLOCK

The ideological foundations for the Iraq war took shape well before American tanks rolled into Baghdad in 2003. Just over a decade earlier, three of the men who would become the most influential officials in the George W. Bush administration—Dick Cheney, Colin Powell, and Paul Wolfowitz—were working in the Pentagon to devise a new concept to guide U.S. strategy in the post–Cold War world. Even though the Soviet Union had collapsed, they wanted the United States to keep projecting superior military power across the globe. In 1992, Powell, then chairman of the Joint Chiefs of Staff, put the objective plainly. The United States must possess "sufficient power" to "deter any challenger from ever dreaming of challenging us on the world stage," he told Congress. "I want to be the bully on the block."

So did Cheney, serving at the time as President George H. W. Bush's secretary of defense. He assigned his deputy, Wolfowitz, to supervise the drafting of the Defense Planning Guidance, a comprehensive framework for U.S. security policy written in 1992. In 46 pages, Wolfowitz and his colleagues explained how to sustain U.S. global dominance in the absence of formidable rivals. The key, they reasoned, was to think and act preventively. Lacking challengers to balance against, the United States should keep new ones from emerging. It must work to dissuade "potential competitors from even aspiring to a larger regional or global role." To this end, the United States would maintain a massive military, sized to dwarf all others and capable of fighting two large wars at once. It would retain alliances and garrison troops in every region of the world that Washington considered to be strategically significant. It would, in short, replace balances of power with an American preponderance of power.

In this vision of American hegemony, the United States would be benevolent. It would internalize the core interests of allies and act to benefit much of the world. In formulating its own foreign policy, the Pentagon planners recommended, the United States should "account sufficiently for the interests of the advanced industrial nations to discourage them from challenging our leadership or seeking to overturn the established political and economic order." U.S. primacy would thereby suppress the security role of U.S. allies as well as adversaries. Every nation, save one, would have nothing to gain and much to lose by building military power of its own. In this way, the United States could stay on top for good, delivering global security at reasonable cost.

The Iraq war seems to have vanished from collective memory altogether.

There were two principal problems with this theory, and they surfaced as soon as Wolfowitz's draft leaked to reporters that March. The first flaw was that the United States' bid for hegemony might induce others to push back. Rather than submit to perpetual peace on Washington's terms, other countries could develop capabilities to counter U.S. might. With Russia reeling after the Soviet Union's collapse and China still poor, the United States would not face determined opposition for years to come. But the more the sole superpower expanded its defense commitments and military reach, the more it might encounter and even stimulate resistance. In time, the United States could find itself overstretched and risking wars detached from U.S. interests, except for those interests circularly created by seeking globe-spanning dominance in the first place. Cheney's Pentagon wanted American primacy to make resistance futile. What if resistance made American primacy futile instead?

It was also unclear whether the American people would be willing to bear the costs of global dominance, especially if those costs were to rise. The Pentagon's document sparked an immediate backlash. Conservative commentator Pat Buchanan, amid his insurgent presidential campaign, denounced the plan as a "formula for endless American intervention." The bald ambition for primacy likewise repelled leading

Democrats, who favored a peace dividend for Americans and collective security for the world. Biden, a U.S. senator at the time, scoffed: "The Pentagon vision reverts to an old notion of the United States as the world's policeman—a notion that, not incidentally, will preserve a large defense budget." The Cold War consensus in favor of containing Soviet communism had been forged in response to an existing great-power threat. To police the post–Cold War world, which featured sundry challenges but no major enemy, was a new and untested proposition that more than a few Americans thought dubious.

The rest of the 1990s constituted the heyday of American unipolarity, yet signs of international opposition and domestic apathy abounded. China and Russia worked to resolve their bilateral disputes and began to assemble what became the Shanghai Cooperation Organization. Together, they touted "the multipolarization of the world." In a 1997 letter to the UN Security Council, Beijing and Moscow declared, "No country should seek hegemony, engage in power politics, or monopolize international affairs." Even some American allies voiced similar concerns. Two years later, French Foreign Minister Hubert Vedrine dubbed the United States a "hyperpower" and called for "real multilateralism against unilateralism, for balanced multipolarism against unipolarism."

Most nettlesome at the time were the so-called rogue states of Iran, Libya, North Korea, and especially Iraq. After expelling Iraqi forces from Kuwait in 1991, the U.S. military did not try to depose Iraqi dictator Saddam Hussein, but U.S. officials hoped Saddam would fall and encouraged popular uprisings by the country's Shiite majority in the south and its Kurdish minority in the north. When Saddam held on by suppressing these uprisings and killing thousands of Iraqis, the United States did not walk away. For the rest of the decade, it contained Iraq through no-fly zones, routine bombings, weapons inspections, and economic sanctions. For this purpose, among others, the United States indefinitely stationed tens of thousands of troops in the Persian Gulf, including in Saudi Arabia, for the first time in history.

President Bill Clinton embraced his predecessor's goal of hegemony in the Middle East and pursued the "dual containment" of Iran and Iraq. Yet this was not enough to satisfy right-wing primacists. In 1997, intellectuals William Kristol and Robert Kagan formed the Project for the New American Century, a think tank devoted to a foreign policy of "military strength and moral clarity." For them, Saddam's Iraq

A lonely road: a U.S. soldier in Baghdad, April 2003

GORAN TOMASEVIC / REUTERS

represented unfinished business. The dictator was "almost certain" to acquire deliverable weapons of mass destruction—WMD—and use them to challenge U.S. forces and partners in the region, according to the group's 1998 open letter, signed by Donald Rumsfeld, Wolfowitz, and a handful of other soon-to-be officials in the George W. Bush administration. The United States, they argued, must seek regime change in Iraq—a goal enshrined as U.S. policy by the Iraq Liberation Act later that year. The resolution passed the House overwhelmingly, 360 to 38, and the Senate unanimously. The rise of this "regime change consensus," as historian Joseph Stieb writes, did not make a full-scale invasion a serious possibility before 9/11. But it delegitimized the alternative policy of leaving Saddam in power while keeping him contained. Washington had set its desired end: ousting Saddam.

The means were another matter. After winning the Gulf War and helping to reunify Germany within NATO, President George H. W. Bush had been booted from office in 1992. The voters preferred a Vietnam War draft evader promising to "focus like a laser beam on the economy." Clinton, for his part, had taken pains to minimize U.S. casualties even as he used military force frequently and enlarged American alliances. The death of 18 U.S. Rangers in Mogadishu in 1993 caused him to withdraw from Somalia completely and brought the term "mission creep" into the American lexicon. Clinton's most daring intervention, intended to stop ethnic cleansing in Kosovo, relied on airpower alone. NATO planes flew high enough to remove any risk to pilots, even though doing so made targeting less accurate.

Madeleine Albright, Clinton's secretary of state, is remembered for proclaiming the United States to be "the indispensable nation." Often forgotten is that she did so at a televised town hall in 1998 in Columbus, Ohio, during which her defenses of American policy in Iraq were met with hostile questions and occasionally drowned out by hecklers. The first post–Cold War decade showed that such opposition would not swell into a determined political force as long as the United States could exercise global hegemony on the cheap. If the costs went up, however, who could say? How could an "indifferent America," as Kristol and Kagan lamented in these pages, be made to "embrace the possibility of national greatness, and restore a sense of the heroic"?

Even inside the Beltway, the depth of support for a muscular U.S. foreign policy was questionable. As the Clinton administration came to a close, Wolfowitz justifiably bragged that the ideas in his Defense Planning Guidance, much maligned on its introduction years earlier, had become conventional wisdom in both political parties. Writing in *The National Interest* in 2000, he nevertheless admitted: "In reality today's consensus is facile and complacent." As Wolfowitz bemoaned, the country displayed a "lack of concern about the possibility of another major war, let alone agreement about how to prevent one." Most of Washington was now singing from the same hymn book, but in Wolfowitz's eyes, there were alarmingly few true believers.

DEMONSTRATING DOMINANCE

That started to change on September 11, 2001. The 9/11 attacks supplied a sense of existential threat that gave purpose to American power after a decadelong search. But the attacks could have been interpreted very differently: as a horrific case of blowback and a portent of resistance to U.S. hegemony. In the days and weeks following 9/11, more than a few Americans entertained this possibility as they tried to understand why 19 terrorists would give their lives to kill people halfway across the globe. The writer Susan Sontag suggested the attacks were "undertaken as a consequence of specific American alliances and actions." Osama bin Laden, after all, had declared war on the United States years before, citing three main grievances: the

U.S. troop presence in Saudi Arabia, American coercion of Iraq, and U.S. support for Israel. In *The New York Times*, the journalist Mark Danner pointed out: "The American troops and warships in the Gulf, the unpopularity of our presence there, the fragility of the regimes we support—these facts are not secrets but among Americans they are not widely known."

After 9/11, those facts might have become more widely known, especially if the United States had stayed focused on the specific enemy that attacked it: al Qaeda. Americans might have concluded that the way to make themselves safe from terrorists in the Middle East was ultimately to stop occupying the region and killing people there. They might have asked, once the United States retaliated for 9/11, whether the quest for global dominance was diminishing their own security.

The Iraq War was not just a policy error.

For President George W. Bush and his foreign policy principals, it was crucial that the country come to a different conclusion: the problem was not too much American power but too little. The attackers, they assured Americans, were motivated by pure evil and not at all by anything the United States might have done. "Americans are asking, why do they hate us?" Bush said in an address to the nation nine days after 9/11. His answer: "They hate our freedoms."

Just as important, "they" were not only the jihadists of al Qaeda. To focus solely on the group that had attacked New York and Washington would miss the larger stakes, namely the struggle to sustain U.S. global hegemony against all manner of opposition. As Wolfowitz, now deputy secretary of defense, told Congress on October 4, 2001, "Osama bin Laden, Saddam Hussein, Kim Jong Il and other such tyrants all want to see America out of critical regions of the world." The 9/11 attacks were just an instance of resistance, which had to be confronted as a whole. "That is why our challenge today is greater than winning the war against terrorism," Wolfowitz continued. "Today's terrorist threat is a precursor of even greater threats to come."

Viewed in this light, the 9/11 attacks presented the Bush administration with an opportunity. By mounting a spectacular response, the United States could nip gathering international resistance in the bud. It could dissuade a wide variety of potential adversaries from "even aspiring" to a larger role, as the 1992 Defense Planning Guidance had urged.

This time, moreover, the nation's leaders could galvanize public support. At last, the American people would positively embrace, not just passively accept, the once abstract primacist mission.

For such purposes, not even a "global war on terror" would suffice. The United States must "go massive," Rumsfeld told an aide four hours after the Twin Towers fell. According to the aide's notes of the conversation, Rumsfeld said, "Sweep it all up. Things related and not." That meant hitting "S.H. @ same time—Not only UBL" (referring to Saddam and bin Laden). U.S. intelligence promptly identified al Qaeda as the perpetrator of the hijackings, yet Rumsfeld, along with Wolfowitz and other officials, began advocating an attack on Iraq. The idea struck the National Security Council's counterterrorism coordinator, Richard Clarke, as nonsensical. "Having been attacked by al Qaeda, for us now to go bombing Iraq in response would be like our invading Mexico after the Japanese attacked us at Pearl Harbor," Clarke later recalled saying on September 12. As the country embarked on an uncertain war in Afghanistan against a shadowy enemy that might well strike again, it was remarkable for senior officials to contemplate invading Iraq, too, let alone to devote 130,000 soldiers to the task within 18 months.

The Bush administration advanced several rationales for attacking Iraq, but at the center were allegations (some but not all of which were backed by U.S. intelligence) that Saddam was stockpiling chemical and biological weapons and seeking to develop nuclear weapons. The United States might not have invaded if officials had known that Saddam's weapons program was a mirage, a bluff intended to bolster the dictator's power and ward off enemies such as Iran. It is nonetheless difficult to know how much explanatory weight to give to the fear that Saddam might one day pass WMD to terrorists, who could then employ them on the U.S. homeland—a nightmare scenario conjured by many advocates of the war. The prospect was always entirely speculative, although policymakers did not want to suffer another "failure of imagination" after failing to anticipate how commercial airliners could be hijacked and turned into missiles.

But whereas Saddam might never use WMD against the United States proper, it was more certain that his presumed weapons would pose an obstacle to American designs in the Middle East. "A likelier problem was that they would affect our willingness to defend U.S. interests," Douglas Feith, who served as undersecretary of defense during the run-up to the war, subsequently wrote. Revealingly, Feith dismissed as "beside the point" the possibility that Saddam had no intention of attacking the United States. "Saddam might even prefer to leave us alone," he acknowledged. "The issue was whether Iraq's WMD capabilities would compel us to leave him alone—free to attack Americans and our friends and interests." That is, a well-armed Saddam would impede U.S. hegemony in the Middle East. Taking him out would make American dominance more secure, whether or not it was the best way to protect the United States itself.

Retrospective accounts, including a recent book by historian Melvyn Leffler, fixate too narrowly on the issue of WMD, a far from sufficient cause of the invasion. Even if Bush administration officials had not misrepresented some of the intelligence concerning Iraq's programs, the desire to disarm Saddam would not account for key aspects of the march to war. Fear of Saddam's arsenal is an inadequate explanation for why the Bush administration moved so rapidly after 9/11 to attack Iraq, which was not thought to be on the cusp of acquiring a major new type of weapon. Nor can it account for why the Bush administration pulled UN weapons inspectors out of Iraq in March 2003, by which time the UN team had conducted more than 550 inspections without notice, believed it was making progress, and wanted to continue. If disarming Saddam had been the paramount motivation, the Bush administration could have allowed the inspections to continue and potentially avoided war. To the contrary, some advocates of an invasion, such as Cheney, had never wanted to give weapons inspections a chance.

The rush to war is better explained by a desire to shore up U.S. primacy soon after the United States was beset by a devastating attack. "The demonstration effect" was how Cheney's deputy national security adviser at the time, Aaron Friedberg, later characterized the thinking. The administration aimed "not just to be a tough guy but to reestablish deterrence," he told the journalist Barton Gellman. "We have been hit very hard, and we needed to make clear the costs to those who might have been supporting or harboring those who were contemplating the acts." It was imperative to do something big, to restore a general sense of fear without which U.S. global hegemony could provoke endless antagonism. "If the war does not significantly change the world's political map, the U.S. will not achieve its aim," Rumsfeld wrote Bush on September 30.

Occupied: arresting a man near Baquba, Iraq, October 2005

JORGE SILVA / REUTERS

The United States should seek, among other things, "new regimes in Afghanistan and another key State (or two)."

From this standpoint, it scarcely mattered whether Iraq was connected to the 9/11 attacks, what the precise status of its weapons program was, or whether the U.S. government could align on a plan to govern Iraq before dismantling its regime. What mattered was the "order of magnitude of the necessary change," in Rumsfeld's phrasing. What mattered, as political scientist Ahsan Butt argues, was that the United States would destroy an adversary and send a message: don't underestimate our power or our willingness to use it.

The war's architects doubtless believed they were protecting U.S. national security. Yet what they were directly attempting to achieve was something distinct: fortifying the United States' preeminent power position through a preventive war. Although they assumed that such preeminence was necessary for American security, the very argument for the Iraq war should have suggested otherwise. Ousting Saddam required the United States to pay upfront costs in lives and treasure in return for highly speculative benefits. (If the costs appeared minimal at the outset, that was only because the war's cheerleaders discounted the possibility that U.S. forces would be treated as invaders and occupiers. "We will, in fact, be greeted as liberators," Cheney promised in March 2003.) The potential benefits of removing Saddam would accrue to Israel, Saudi Arabia, and other U.S. security partners in the region. The United States would benefit only insofar as maintaining U.S. hegemony in the Middle East was worthwhile. But could the United States better obtain security for itself by reducing its involvement in the region? The question went unexamined as the pursuit of primacy ironically deflected from its deadly costs by generating new and deadlier missions.

DOMESTIC BLOWBACK

Over the next decade, Americans would hear no shortage of reasons for why the war in Iraq went wrong: the Bush administration failed to plan for postwar reconstruction. It let the Iraqi state collapse into civil war. Democracy is rarely imposed at the point of a gun. Nation building does not work.

Those insights are all true and meaningful. They are also inadequate. A parade of small lessons allowed larger ones to go unlearned—and allowed the war's supporters to avoid scrutiny of their main misconceptions. A year into the war, Kristol and Kagan conceded that Bush had "not always made the right decisions on how to proceed" in reconstructing Iraq while urging U.S. forces to remain "as long as needed." In an influential 2005 book on the war, the writer George Packer blasted the Bush team for "criminal negligence." The problem with the invasion, in his view, lay less in its conception than in its execution. "The Iraq war was always winnable; it still is," he concluded. "For this very reason, the recklessness of its authors is all the harder to forgive."

Small wonder that the targets of Packer's critique adopted a similar stance, the better to redeem the decision for war and salvage the ongoing campaign to fight insurgents and terrorists and establish a viable Iraqi state. In 2006, Bush and Secretary of State Condoleezza Rice admitted to errors in "tactics"—"thousands of them, I'm sure," Rice added unhelpfully. They nonetheless cast the invasion as strategically sound.

By then, the American public was turning against the war and Washington's excuses. Over the next decade, voters delivered three electoral surprises that revealed the depth of their discontent. Invading Iraq was supposed to demonstrate American power and Washington's will to shape the world, unconstrained by internal doubt or external norms. When political elites proceeded to treat the war as a tactical mistake, born of incorrect intelligence or insufficient planning, they did not eliminate the sense of existential purpose with which they initially invested the invasion. Instead, they tried to paper over the war's deeper meaning, only to be hit by blowback at home, as well as abroad.

The first surprise came in the congressional election of 2006. Bush's White House expected to wield the war to the Republican Party's advantage, accusing Democrats of "retreat and defeatism," in Cheney's words. By Election Day, it was the GOP that had retreated from the debate. Led by Nancy Pelosi, who decried the invasion as a "grotesque mistake," Democrats won the House of Representatives after 12 years of Republican rule. A majority of voters viewed the Iraq war as the single most important issue of the election and expected Democrats to reduce or terminate U.S. military involvement in the country.

The "next Iraq" could well take the form of a great-power war.

Bush, however, ordered a "surge" of troops into Iraq as a last-ditch effort to stabilize the country. The next election, in 2008, produced an even bigger surprise: the victory of Obama, young, Black, and liberal, over the more senior senators Hillary Clinton and John McCain. Both Clinton and McCain had voted to authorize the Iraq war. Obama stood out for opposing it in October 2002 as "dumb" and "rash." His stance on Iraq constituted perhaps his chief advantage in the primary campaign. "I don't want to just end the war," he declared. "I want to end the mindset that got us into war in the first place." Obama seemed to offer a clean break not only from the Bush administration but also from a "foreign policy elite that largely boarded the bandwagon for war," as he put it on the campaign trail.

The clean break turned out to be a false one. In office, Obama treated the "mindset" behind the war mostly as a psychological deficiency. Whereas Bush had acted impulsively, Obama would think carefully. He would calculate consequences before opening fire. Obama withdrew U.S. forces from Iraq in 2011, but he kept the war in Afghanistan going and ended up sending troops back to Iraq in 2014. Meanwhile, he maintained the security partnerships he inherited and enlarged and routinized a program of terrorist killing by drones and special forces. Obama found himself bogged down in the Middle East, perhaps against his better judgment, for much the same reason that his predecessor had launched the war in Iraq: the United States sought to remain the dominant power in the region and, as Obama repeated, the "indispensable nation" globally.

In the next presidential election, Washington presumed that George W. Bush's younger brother Jeb would be the Republican frontrunner. The former Florida governor became a political casualty of his brother's war. At first, asked if he would have invaded Iraq even "knowing what we know now," he said yes. Then he attempted to skirt follow-up questions. Finally, he decided he would not have invaded after all. It fell to Donald Trump to capitalize on the public's untended outrage. The demagogue delivered the third shock to the political establishment when, in 2016, he blasted the war as possibly the "worst decision" in American history. Trump was lying when he claimed to have opposed the invasion all along, but at least he recognized in hindsight that the war was a disaster. It was proof enough for some voters to trust him as commander in chief and ignore the chorus of elites that deemed him unfit to lead.

UNFINISHED BUSINESS

Today, political leaders once again seek to turn the page. Perhaps the appearance of forbidding adversaries will allow them to succeed where prior efforts failed. In the face of China's rise and Russia's aggression, the United States has acquired renewed purpose for its global power. Never mind that balancing behavior by major powers was exactly what U.S. global primacy was supposed to avert: now that its theory of the case has come up short, Washington wants to look forward, not backward. Sometimes the Iraq war seems to have vanished from collective memory altogether. Biden recently referred to Russia's war against Ukraine as the only large-scale invasion the world has witnessed in eight decades. "The idea that over 100,000 forces would invade another country—since World War II, nothing like that has happened," Biden proclaimed in February. He spoke these words within a month of the 20th anniversary of the U.S. invasion of Iraq, a war that then Senator Biden voted to authorize.

Attempting to forget is the only way to guarantee failing to learn. If the United States applies to peer competitors the same will to dominate that brought it into Iraq, a far weaker country, the consequences will be severe. The "next Iraq" could well take the form of a great-power war. Few Americans would seek such a conflict, but neither did many advocate for a direct invasion of Iraq before 9/11 or anticipate the scale and duration of Operation Iraqi Freedom before it commenced. The pathologies of primacy made war appear necessary and worth the price, and those pathologies continue to put the United States on a collision course with other countries. First, Washington conflates U.S. interests with its far-flung military positions and alliance commitments, almost excluding in advance the possibility that offloading some responsibilities could increase American security and enhance American strategy. Second, Washington systematically discounts how its power threatens others, who then act accordingly. Together, these errors force U.S. foreign policy to fight the tendency of power to balance power, just when an overstretched United States needs to harness that tendency.

Since February 2022, the United States has rightly helped Ukraine defend itself against Russia's brutal invasion. Yet it has evaded serious consideration of U.S. policy mistakes that set the stage for this conflict and potentially more to come. By enlarging NATO through an open-ended, open-door process, the United States extended its dominance of European security affairs while hoping that Russia would not turn hostile. That hope was naive from the start. The creation of a dividing line within Europe, creeping ever closer to Moscow, rendered especially vulnerable whichever countries NATO would not admit.

NATO expansion therefore came at the expense of Ukraine—and the United States. By entrenching its dominance of European defense, the United States gave its allies ample reason to outsource their security to Washington. As a result, it now falls principally on the United States to orchestrate international aid for Ukraine and to put its soldiers and cities on the line if Russia were to attack NATO countries in the future. The only escape from this self-imposed trap is to break with the logic of primacy and gradually but decisively turn leadership of European defense over to the Europeans, who can mobilize ample resources to deter Russia and defend their territory.

As it runs greater risks in Europe, Washington is also barreling toward confrontation with Beijing. An emerging bipartisan consensus seeks to get ever tougher on the world's number two power. Yet what the United States wants its relationship with China to consist of in the coming decades remains ill defined and superficially considered. A hostile direction, without a desired destination, makes for unwise policy. Although passions are less intense and the public less engaged, the environment in Washington increasingly resembles the lead-up to March 2003, when politicians and officials, eager to take on an adversary, neglected to assess the potential trajectories of a post-Saddam Iraq and underestimated the agency of others in determining the outcome.

If the United States and China are serious about avoiding a cold war, or a world-rending shooting war, both sides will have to work to establish terms of coexistence. Yet those terms are getting more elusive by the day. Amid the torrent of objections to Chinese practices, it often seems that the United States opposes China's rise altogether. After the Trump administration identified China as a threat, Biden has taken potentially fateful measures, eroding the "one China" policy that has allowed Washington and Beijing to agree to disagree over Taiwan and imposing broad restrictions on China's access to technology, including advanced semiconductors. How China will react is not yet known, but its capability to harm the United States is substantial. In defending its preeminent power position—which ought to be a means to an end—the United States is assuming enormous risks without appreciating how intensified rivalry could make Americans poorer and less safe.

Better options are available: the United States should disentangle itself from the Middle East, shift defense burdens to European allies, and seek competitive coexistence with China. If it sometimes sounds as though policymakers are doing just that, the facts say otherwise. For all the talk of strategic discipline, about as many U.S. troops are stationed in the Middle East today, around 50,000, as there were at the end of the Obama administration. Washington is still in thrall to primacy and caught in a doom loop, lurching from self-inflicted problems to even bigger self-inflicted problems, holding up the latter while covering up the former. In this sense, the Iraq war remains unfinished business for the United States.

Kagame's Revenge

Why Rwanda's Leader Is Sowing Chaos in Congo

MICHELA WRONG

The speech was vintage Paul Kagame. Addressing a group of foreign ambassadors in Kigali in February 2023, the Rwandan president complained bitterly of being hounded about his country's involvement in the neighboring Democratic Republic of the Congo, where he stands accused of backing a rebel group that is rapidly gobbling up land and whose members are mostly ethnic Tutsis, like Kagame.

Instead of acknowledging Rwanda's support for the M23 Movement—named after a March 23, 2009, peace accord its fighters say the Congolese government violated—Kagame reminded his audience about another rebel group operating in eastern Congo, this one led by those responsible for Rwanda's 1994 genocide. The Democratic Forces for the Liberation of Rwanda, known by the French acronym FDLR, was founded more than two decades ago by extremist ethnic Hutu soldiers and militia members who fled to Congo after massacring hundreds of thousands of Tutsis.

MICHELA WRONG, a former Africa correspondent for the *Financial Times*, is the author of *Do Not Disturb: The Story of a Political Murder and an African Regime Gone Bad.*

According to Kagame, the group still poses an existential threat to Rwanda. "It's about our lives," he said of the dangers of the FDLR. "It's about our story. It's about our history. It's about our identity. It's about our existence."

The FDLR has long been a scapegoat for Rwanda, blamed whenever Rwandan interference in Congo draws criticism. Kagame both denies backing the M23 and routinely implies that the Hutu extremist group has forced his hand—rhetoric that silences unhappy allies and reminds Rwandans what they owe him for defeating the country's genocidal government three decades ago. He has been playing the FDLR card incessantly of late, prompting Rwandan officials, civil society organizations, and survivors' groups in the diaspora to pick up the refrain that a second genocide is imminent, this time targeting not only Tutsis living inside Rwanda but also those living across the border in Congo.

Aside from Kagame loyalists, however, almost no one buys this tired line. Rwanda's unacknowledged exploits in Congo have long since ceased to be about self-defense or even revenge. They are intended, instead, to assert hegemonic dominance over Rwanda's neighbors and guarantee access to the natural resources of a vast region that has been only fitfully governed since President Mobutu Sese Seko fled into exile in 1997.

This is not the first time Rwanda has used its M23 proxies to plunge eastern Congo into chaos. In 2012, the group swept across the province of North Kivu and briefly took control of the region's lakeside capital, Goma. The United States and other Western countries responded by slashing aid to Kigali and threatening to sanction Rwandan officials for aiding and abetting war crimes. This unified international response forced Rwanda to withdraw its support for the rebels, paving the way for their swift defeat.

Now the M23 is back, but Western countries have failed to penalize Kagame for his renewed meddling. Over the last decade, Rwanda has made itself indispensable by supplying disciplined peacekeepers to trouble spots across the continent and, increasingly, by offering to house asylum seekers Europe does not want. As a result, the M23 rebellion has been allowed to escalate, drawing Congo's neighbors into the conflict and risking a wider regional conflagration. Not since 2012 has Africa's Great Lakes region been on such a troubling trajectory. But this time, no one is pumping the brakes.

CONGOLESE QUAGMIRE

The M23 movement was established in April 2012 by mutinying Congolese soldiers who accused Congo's government of breaking a promise to integrate them into the national army and failing to protect the country's beleaguered Tutsi community. Since it reemerged in November 2021, the insurgency has displaced between 600,000 and 800,000 Congolese, many of whom are either sleeping on the streets of Goma or gathering in makeshift refugee camps rife with cholera. The United Nations, which always struggles to raise funds for Congo, says feeding, housing, and providing medical care to those uprooted by the fighting will push the humanitarian aid bill for the country to a record $2.25 billion.

The violence these refugees are fleeing has been documented in gut-wrenching detail by human rights groups: gang rapes of women, mass executions of men, and forced recruitment of young boys to serve as porters, guides, and child soldiers. In February, the M23 captured the settlement of Mushaki. Next to fall was the nearby town of Rubaya, where coltan—used in smartphones, laptops, and electric vehicle batteries—is mined, followed by the settlement of Mweso. As of mid-March, the rebels had progressed to the outskirts of Sake, 15 miles northwest of Goma and situated on a main supply route. As the noose around Goma has tightened, the prices of basic foodstuffs have soared.

Congo and Rwanda are on the brink of all-out war.

The spiraling insurgency has brought Congo and Rwanda to the brink of all-out war. Congolese President Félix Tshisekedi, who is campaigning for reelection in December, surprised many observers by sending military jets into Rwandan airspace in January, and he appears to have hired eastern European mercenaries to help his notoriously ill-disciplined army. For his part, Kagame has warned that his troops have deployed "massively" along Rwanda's border with Congo in response to shelling by the FDLR and that he is willing to send them across if necessary. "Both men have painted themselves into a corner with all their public declarations," Alexis Arieff, an Africa policy specialist at the Congressional Research Service, told me. "I'm not sure [they] wanted to find themselves where they are right now."

The conflict is also pulling in a growing number of African states. Kenyan soldiers, part of a multinational force dispatched by the East African Community in response to an appeal for help from Tshisekedi, deployed around Goma late last year. Burundian troops joined the EAC force in March and were attacked almost immediately. South Sudanese and Ugandan soldiers are expected to deploy to eastern Congo as well, and

Angola has said it will send 500 troops to help monitor a cease-fire that has been repeatedly violated. In theory, this international operation is a cheering example of "African solutions to African problems," a favorite mantra of the African Union. But the incoming army commanders are fast encountering the problem that has long hampered the UN peacekeeping mission in Congo, one of the oldest and largest in the world: the furious contempt of the very communities they are meant to protect.

Already, the Kenyans stand accused of doing little more than creating buffer zones that save the M23 from having to fight the Congolese army. The head of Congo's National Assembly, Christophe Mboso, has hinted that these troops could be asked to leave if "within a reasonable time" they fail "to support us against the aggressor." Eastern Congo threatens to become a new quagmire for regional powers.

NOTHING TO SEE HERE

For years, Kagame has denied using Congolese Tutsis as proxy forces. But in December 2022, the UN released a report that finally confirmed the open secret of Rwandan support for the M23. Citing aerial footage along with photographic and video evidence, UN experts described a sophisticated rebel force boasting mortars, machine guns, and long-range firepower thought to be provided by Kigali. Its fighters move in organized columns of 500 militants, sporting helmets, Kevlar jackets, backpacks, and uniforms identical to those used by the Rwandan army. Bintou Keita, the special representative of the UN secretary-general in Congo, told the UN Security Council in June 2022 that the M23 "has behaved more and more like a conventional army rather than an armed group."

Notwithstanding the damning evidence, Kagame maintains a stance of outraged innocence. The M23 is a purely Congolese problem, he insists, and its fighters—who are almost exclusively Tutsis—are driven by the need to protect their community from the xenophobia that has threatened it since long before he was born. What is more, he points out, the Congolese army has repeatedly gone into battle alongside the reviled FDLR.

Such claims neatly reverse cause and effect. Congolese Tutsis are certainly being targeted by members of other ethnic groups in the provinces of North and South Kivu. They have been stoned in the streets, and their homes and businesses have been burned. But such intercommunal attacks, however vicious and unmerited, are not the cause of the M23 rebellion but a response to it: many Congolese of other ethnicities automatically assume local Tutsis support the rebel

group and have therefore lashed out against them. Congolese Tutsis, in other words, are also victims of the M23's new campaign.

Kagame's claims that the FDLR poses a threat to Rwanda are similarly risible. In the 1990s, a predecessor of the group boasted tens of thousands of fighters who held military exercises in the enormous refugee camps established in the Kivus in the wake of the Rwandan genocide. Their leaders, the ousted generals of the assassinated Rwandan president, Juvénal Habyarimana, plotted to reinvade their country. But time has taken its toll. Many militants have returned to Rwanda to be "reeducated" and join the national army; others have come to regard the Masisi region of eastern Congo as home. The FDLR's fighters, who are thought to number between just 500 and 1,000, threaten the local Congolese population far more than they threaten the Rwandan government.

IGNORE ME AT YOUR PERIL

Ever since Mobutu was pushed into exile by a rebel coalition supported by nine African countries, successive presidents of Congo have struggled to keep the giant state in one piece and its neighbors' hands off its eye-watering resources. During the Second Congo War, which raged from 1998 to 2003, Rwanda and Uganda both profited handsomely from the illegal mining of gold, tin, coltan, diamonds, and tungsten that lie just across the border in eastern Congo, more than 1,500 miles and an entire time zone away from the capital of Kinshasa. This blatant asset stripping eventually morphed into lively cross-border smuggling operations, the proceeds of which still flow into Rwandan and Ugandan coffers.

But the lust for minerals does not by itself explain what is happening in North Kivu today. The area now controlled by the M23 contains few important mines, and the fighting has, if anything, disrupted smuggling activities. The real reason that Kagame has resurrected the M23—and risked both his carefully cultivated image as an African statesman and Rwanda's reputation as a business-friendly, development-oriented state—lies in his hunger for recognition as the region's most important player. The French have a word for this: *incontournable*, or "unavoidable." Kagame has long believed in his right to be *incontournable* not only in Rwanda but also in the region, on the continent, and even in the global arena.

The first M23 insurgency, which climaxed with the seizure of Goma in 2012, came to an end only after exasperated Western donors cut aid to Rwanda. Germany, the Netherlands, the United Kingdom, the United States, and the European Union together slashed an estimated $240 million

Resurgence: M23 rebels near Rumangabo military base, Congo, January 2023

in assistance, according to Rwanda's finance minister, causing Rwandan GDP growth to fall from a projected 7.6 percent to 4.6 percent in 2013. Washington also warned Rwandan officials that they could face prosecution in the International Criminal Court. Abandoned by Kigali and under military pressure from a southern African force that had deployed in the Kivus, the M23 disbanded with impressive speed; by November 2013, its fighters had dispersed to refugee camps in Rwanda and Uganda.

For the next eight years, eastern Congo was relatively quiet. After Tshisekedi's contested election in 2019, relations between Congo and Rwanda enjoyed something of a honeymoon, with the leaders of both countries exchanging words of mutual esteem and the Rwandan army conducting anti-FDLR operations in eastern Congo with Tshisekedi's blessing. Kagame even attended the funeral of Tshisekedi's father, Étienne, a veteran politician famous for his long-standing opposition to Mobutu.

But in recent years, the budding friendship has soured. The trigger appears to have been the signature in May 2021 of a surprise deal between Tshisekedi and Ugandan President Yoweri Museveni that authorized Uganda to move heavy mechanized equipment into northeastern Congo to clear swaths of equatorial forest and repair roughly 140 miles of road, an infrastructural upgrade that was expected to boost cross-border

GUERCHOM NDEBO / AFP VIA GETTY IMAGES

trade—both legal and illegal—between the two countries, eliminating the need to move goods through Rwanda. Six months later, Ugandan troops crossed into Congo to neutralize another rebel group known as the Allied Democratic Forces, which was using the region as a base.

The two initiatives appeared to both panic and infuriate Kagame, who viewed them as part of a joint attempt by Tshisekedi and Museveni to sideline him economically and strategically. In April 2022, Congo joined the East African Community, reinforcing the impression that Tshisekedi—who had once seemed anxious to curry favor with Kagame—was now going over Rwanda's head to engage directly with other East African leaders.

By renewing support for the M23, Kagame is reminding the leaders of neighboring countries of his readiness and capacity to destabilize the entire region if any attempt is made to leave him out of the loop. "Ignore me at your peril" is the subtext of the insurgency.

The M23 rebellion has certainly stalled Uganda's plans in eastern Congo. After the M23 seized the Congolese border town of Bunagana last June, the Ugandan authorities were forced to withdraw their road-building equipment and pause plans to upgrade 55 miles of road linking the frontier outpost to Goma. By then, Museveni had approved a fence-mending trip to Kigali by his son, Muhoozi Kainerugaba, a general in Uganda's military, an overture that has eased bilateral tensions but done nothing to halt the burgeoning M23 encroachment.

The insurgency's impact is even more damaging in Congo. With the encouragement of the Congolese army, dozens of ragtag Congolese militias that previously had little in common are putting aside their differences to fight what they see as an invading Rwandan-backed force. And with so many African countries now embroiled in the conflict and so many fighters with guns hoping to benefit, the Balkanization of the Kivus and the destabilization of the broader Great Lakes region have become real possibilities.

DITHERING DONORS

Unlike in 2012, Western countries have refused to take muscular action against Kagame this time around, even though Rwanda is arguably more vulnerable to economic pressure. COVID-19 hit the Rwandan economy hard, and a series of prestige projects—including a new airport planned south of Kigali and the expansion of the national carrier, RwandAir—have bitten deep into the government's finances. And although it claims to be progressing toward middle-income status, Rwanda has actually grown more dependent on foreign aid:

between 1994, when a guilt-ridden international community rushed to rescue the shattered country, and 2021, net aid rose from $1.04 billion to $1.25 billion.

Belgium, France, Germany, Spain, and the United States—as well as the United Nations and the EU—have all called on Rwanda to halt its support for the M23. So far, however, self-interest has stopped many of them from pulling the economic levers that worked in 2012.

France has proved to be an especially important backer. After spending years repairing a relationship soured by French President François Mitterrand's friendship with Habyarimana, Paris has embraced Kagame as its favorite new African strongman and is grateful for the role his forces have played policing the Central African Republic and Mali, both former French colonies. Kagame also deployed Rwandan peacekeepers to Mozambique in 2021, taking on a jihadi insurgency that had forced the closure of a liquified natural gas plant run by the French giant Total. On a trip to Kinshasa in March, French President Emmanuel Macron pledged 34 million euros (about $36 million) in humanitarian aid for eastern Congo but seemed determined to avoid blaming Rwanda for the violence there and stressed that any sanctions would have to wait until peace talks had run their course.

Over the last decade, Rwanda has made itself indispensable to the West.

The United Kingdom, another high-profile ally of Rwanda, is beholden to Kagame for different reasons. Its Conservative Party, which has long promised voters it is getting tough on illegal immigration, signed a deal with Kigali in 2022 to fly asylum seekers to Rwanda for processing. That agreement is being contested in British courts: an appeal of a ruling that deemed the policy legal was to be heard in late April. Not a single migrant has yet been deported to Rwanda, but London has already paid Kigali 140 million pounds (about $169 million) for its cooperation. And in March, British Home Secretary Suella Braverman made a lightning trip to Kigali, where she visited two housing estates earmarked for migrants and told journalists that deportations could start by the summer. "Many people in government hope the asylum project won't happen," one British official told me. "But while it's still in the offing, we are having to pander to Kigali over human rights and issues like [Congo]." Kagame also has a loyal friend in Sunak's minister of state for development and Africa, Andrew Mitchell, who makes no secret of his admiration for the Rwandan leader.

The United States has been more outspoken in its criticism of Rwanda. Its relationship with Kagame had already begun to sour before the latest crisis, in part because of his treatment of the rights activist Paul Rusesabagina, a U.S. resident who was renditioned back to Rwanda in 2020 and sentenced to 25 years in prison. It was Tshisekedi, not Kagame, who was honored with a tête-à-tête with U.S. President Joe Biden at the U.S.-Africa Leaders Summit in Washington in December. But thanks to U.S. pressure, Rusesabagina was released in March, removing a key bone of contention between Washington and Kigali and raising the question of whether the Biden administration will continue to push Kagame to withdraw from Congo.

Underlying much of the West's dithering over Rwanda's destabilization of Congo is the realization that Russia—whose foreign minister, Sergey Lavrov, traveled to Africa twice in the span of ten days in early 2023—is aggressively forging new friendships on the habitually neglected continent. Of the 39 states that either abstained or voted against a UN General Assembly resolution calling on Russia to end its yearlong invasion of Ukraine, 17 were African. Western governments would prefer that African countries threatened by Islamist insurgencies turn to Rwanda and its famously disciplined peacekeepers for help instead of to Russia and its notorious Wagner mercenaries.

Pulled in different directions, Rwanda's traditional partners have been unable to forge a common front. According to diplomats in the Great Lakes region, discussions among Western powers have gone little further than debating "smart sanctions" that might target individual M23 and FDLR commanders but not Rwandan or Congolese officials. Such measures would fall far short of the kind of across-the-board aid cuts that prompted Rwanda to pull the plug on the M23 back in 2012.

HERE TO STAY?

While Western donors waver, suspicions are growing that an emboldened Kagame has new ambitions for his proxy force. Today's M23 is different from the one that occupied much of eastern Congo a little more than a decade ago. "This time around, the group's makeup is much less ethnically diverse," Reagan Miviri, an analyst at the Congolese research institute Ebutuli, told me. "The leadership of the old M23 was Tutsi, but most of the fighters on the ground were actually Hutu. This time almost all of them, whether leaders or fighters, are Tutsi."

Early this year, M23 commanders put out the word to those who fled their homes during the group's rapid advance across North Kivu that they should come back, calling for schools to be reopened and life in the areas they now occupy to return to something approaching normal. "Officially, the line from the M23 is 'We want to negotiate with the government,' but on the ground, they've been telling people, 'You should return, as we are here to stay,'" said Eliora Henzler, the coordinator of the Kivu Security Tracker, which maps violence in the region. "It's still in its early stages, but it looks as though something approaching a parallel administration is being established in parts of Masisi."

Setting up a puppet administration in North Kivu, staffed by Congolese Tutsis but receiving direction from Kigali, would take Kagame into daring new territory. The last time Rwanda attempted such a thing was in 1998, when it, along with Uganda, installed an armed faction known as the Rally for Congolese Democracy (RCD) as a regional administration in Goma.

Those were different times. International sympathy for Kagame and his Rwandan Patriotic Front—seen as having ended the genocide in Rwanda—was running high, Congo was in chaos, and the rest of the world viewed the RCD's establishment as a regrettable but understandable part of the country's general fragmentation. A year later, the RCD split into competing factions. In 2006, it fizzled out entirely after a poor electoral performance.

Now, the sheen is gone from Kagame's regime. His international reputation has been permanently dented by revelations that his forces massacred Hutu civilians before, during, and after the 1994 genocide. According to the UN refugee agency, some 200,000 Hutus remain unaccounted for after Rwandan troops broke up the refugee camps in eastern Congo, chasing their inhabitants through the forests. Reports from the UN and various watchdog groups detailing how Rwanda then used its proxy guerrilla forces to systematically plunder Congo's assets have hardly improved his image. The Congolese gynecologist and human rights activist Denis Mukwege, who won the Nobel Peace Prize in 2018, has made it his mission to highlight Rwanda's toxic role in eastern Congo, and the country's population is angrier at Kigali than ever.

By relentlessly upping the ante, Kagame is making it impossible for either his fellow African heads of state or his Western allies to ignore him. But he is also ensuring that when they reluctantly take action—and take action they eventually must—he will have permanently lost the moral high ground he once claimed, notwithstanding all evidence to the contrary, as the man who ended the bloodletting in Africa's Great Lakes region.

REVIEW ESSAY

The Forty-Year War

How America Lost the Middle East

LISA ANDERSON

Grand Delusion: The Rise and Fall of American Ambition in the Middle East BY STEVEN SIMON. Penguin Random House, 2023, 496 pp.

In March 2023, China's announcement that it had brokered renewed diplomatic relations between Saudi Arabia and Iran threw into sharp relief the United States' rapidly diminishing role in the Middle East. Shortly after President Joe Biden came to office, the United States completed its inept withdrawal from Afghanistan, a country that Washington had spent 20 years trying and failing to bring into the Western fold. Then the president, who as a candidate had cast Saudi Arabia as a "pariah" because of Crown Prince Mohammed bin Salman's alleged involvement in the murder of the regime critic Jamal Khashoggi, soon found the Saudis rebuffing a U.S. request to increase oil production during the war in Ukraine. Meanwhile, U.S. diplomatic efforts to revive the Iran nuclear deal faltered amid a violent wave of repression by the Iranian regime. And the administration looked on helplessly as the most far-right government in Israeli history came to power, threatening the country's claims to democracy, fueling a new wave of violence, and jeopardizing the Washington-backed Abraham Accords.

Observers may be forgiven for wondering whether U.S. influence in the region has declined permanently. Or for that matter, whether the Biden administration even cares, amid the war in Ukraine and the growing U.S. rivalry with Russia and China. Although former Presidents Barack Obama and Donald Trump paid lip service to a "pivot" away from the Middle East, they both engaged in multiple military deployments and

---

LISA ANDERSON is James T. Shotwell Professor of International Relations Emerita at Columbia University and was President of the American University in Cairo from 2011 to 2015.

Illustration by John Lee

large-scale diplomatic initiatives, from promoting democracy during the Arab uprisings to engineering peace deals between Israel and Bahrain, Morocco, Sudan, and the United Arab Emirates. Today, despite the region's far-reaching challenges—including the ravages of civil war in Libya, Syria, and Yemen; economic decay in Egypt, Lebanon, and Tunisia; the growing threats of climate change, inequality, and region-wide instability; and resurgent authoritarianism everywhere—very little of that ambitious U.S. agenda remains.

In *Grand Delusion: The Rise and Fall of American Ambition in the Middle East*, the former National Security Council member and veteran Middle East expert Steven Simon attempts to explain how this collapse happened. Tracing U.S. efforts to shape the region from the Iranian revolution in 1979 to Benjamin Netanyahu's return to power in Israel in December 2022, Simon draws stark lessons: Washington's Middle East strategy has been, as his title suggests, "delusional," fabricated in the continual "superimposition of grand ideas" by policymakers convinced of their own virtuous intentions toward a region about which they knew little and cared less. As he writes, "It is a tale of gross misunderstandings, appalling errors, and death and destruction on an epochal scale." These conclusions are true, although perhaps not quite sufficient. A more urgent question today is how—or even whether—Washington can learn from these catastrophic blunders to craft a more constructive approach in an era of waning U.S. influence.

EIGHT KINDS OF FAILURE

In offering a comprehensive, even magisterial review of U.S. policy in the Middle East over the past half century, *Grand Delusion* aspires to convey "the worldview of the author as witness and as historian." Simon certainly has the credentials to do this, having been directly involved in many of the policies and strategies he writes about here. He worked in the U.S. State Department during the Reagan and first Bush administrations and served in senior National Security Council positions in the Clinton and Obama administrations. Between his stints in government, he has held senior positions at several think tanks and universities and written widely noted books on terrorism and the Middle East.

Yet Simon finds little reason to applaud the policies he helped shape. In fact, he now believes that, during his decades in Washington, U.S. efforts in the Middle East have often been a fool's errand. More often than not, ambitious plans to secure stability, promote democracy, and thwart terrorism resulted instead in strengthening autocracy, aggravating economic misery, and inciting violence. "The delusion," he writes, "was rooted in the conviction that facts don't matter, just intentions; that we create and inhabit our own reality, our capacities are unconfined, and the objects of our policy have no agency." This is strong stuff, but Simon does not flinch. As he observes, the fact that U.S. policymakers, himself included, wanted to make the Middle East a better place while advancing Washington's strategic interests is not "exculpatory" but rather the heart of the problem.

Grand Delusion tells the story of eight successive U.S. presidential administrations, which gives the narrative a chronological clarity even if it obscures broader historical trends. The book begins with President Jimmy Carter's negotiation of the Camp David accords, the historic 1979 peace agreement between Israel and Egypt. According to Simon, U.S. involvement in the Middle East up to that point had been relatively modest. For the most part, Presidents Dwight Eisenhower, John F. Kennedy, and Lyndon Johnson "steered clear" of the region, leaving military intervention to the British. After Camp David, that decisively changed. "It is really after 1979 that we see America militarizing its Middle East policy," he writes.

The consequences of this shift, in Simon's view, can be seen in everything from the Reagan administration's botched intervention in the Lebanese civil war in the early 1980s to Obama's self-described "shit show" in Libya, the disorderly U.S.-led NATO campaign that followed the 2011 uprising against the Libyan dictator Muammar al-Qaddafi. Moving quickly past the Camp David accords, Simon devotes many pages to Carter's hapless Iran policy, which ended with the disastrous effort to rescue American hostages in Tehran. In his estimation, this unforced error contributed to Ronald Reagan's victory in the 1980 presidential contest and dramatically amplified the role of Middle East policy in American electoral politics. In his chapter on Reagan, Simon reviews the president's responses to terrorism, Israel's 1982 invasion of Lebanon, and the Iran-contra scandal, concluding that "there was nothing the administration attempted in the Middle East in its two terms that left the United States better off."

During President George H. W. Bush's momentous single term in office, the United States drove Iraqi forces out of Kuwait and then, at the 1991 Madrid Conference, helped usher in several decades of negotiations between the Israelis, the Palestinians, and, occasionally, other Arab states. Yet in Simon's view, the administration accomplished not much else. Indeed, as he sees it, the victory in the Gulf War and the launch of the Israeli-Palestinian peace process were little more than "twin illusions" that Bush bequeathed to Bill Clinton. Under the Clinton administration, the Oslo accords, a pair of agreements signed in 1993 and 1995, produced the mutual recognition of Israel and the Palestine Liberation Organization. But no real progress was made on constructing a Palestinian state, and Clinton's second-term efforts to secure a genuine peace agreement came to naught. In the end, after several years of hope, Clinton's bequest to President George W. Bush was little better than what he himself had received.

In Simon's telling, the September 11, 2001, attacks by al Qaeda on the United States brought the militarization of U.S. policy in the Middle East to a climax. As astonishing as the assaults themselves were, the failure of the White House to see them coming dumbfounds Simon: "It later seemed incredible that the Bush administration could be so heedless of the intelligence warning of an imminent attack." Moreover, in the aftermath, the Bush team twisted the nature of the jihadist threat, using 9/11 to justify a Captain Ahab–like quest for revenge overseen by neoconservative and hawkish officials recycled from the Reagan and first Bush administrations. Rather than al Qaeda's leader, Osama bin Laden, the principal target soon became Saddam Hussein despite counterterrorism officials' conclusion that the Iraqi dictator had no meaningful links to the terrorist group.

The result was the invasion and occupation of Iraq, in which an even more radically anti-American terrorist group—the Islamic State, also known as ISIS—was incubated. Amid this costly conflict and the parallel one unfolding in Afghanistan, little progress was made in securing U.S. interests or making the Middle East better off. Simon's verdict on these years is devastating. Acting in the belief that the United States was "the greatest power on earth," the Bush administration "lost wars in Iraq and Afghanistan and killed, or caused to die, hundreds of thousands of people."

The Obama administration came into office wanting to quit these troubled waters, only to find itself dragged back in by the rise of ISIS, which foiled the president's efforts to withdraw from Iraq, and by the unexpected Arab uprisings of 2010–11. In the wake of Obama's well-received 2009 speech in Cairo promising a new beginning in U.S. policy in the region, the administration's equivocating responses to the popular revolts against U.S.-allied regimes left democrats and autocrats alike feeling betrayed. For Simon, it is a bitter irony that Obama's single significant strategic accomplishment, the 2015 nuclear deal with Iran, known as the Joint Comprehensive Plan of Action, was almost immediately repudiated by Trump. His administration instead embarked on a vengeful but ineffective pressure campaign against the Islamic Republic while embracing autocratic regimes on which Washington had long if anxiously relied, including President Abdel Fattah el-Sisi's Egypt and, especially, the Saudi government being reshaped by Prince Mohammed. The administration also dropped the pretense of American support for the decades-long Israeli-Palestinian peace process, choosing instead to move the U.S. Embassy to Jerusalem and to engineer the Abraham Accords. That agreement brought together Israel and, eventually, four Arab states—Bahrain, Morocco, Sudan, and the United Arab Emirates—that seemed to share Israel's concerns about Iran, were eager for Israeli business, and no longer even feigned much interest in the fate of the Palestinians.

In taking these steps, Simon argues that Trump's transactional deal-making exacerbated the chaotic nature of U.S. Middle East policy, which had vacillated between pieties about democracy promotion and realist visions of strategic dominance. "On the whole," he tells us, "Trump's Middle East looked worse than Obama's four years earlier." Trump did much to accelerate the erosion of U.S. influence, sharing with Obama what Simon calls "a declining sense of the utility, purpose, and effectiveness of American engagement, and especially of military intervention, in the Middle East." By the time Biden reached office in 2021, U.S. strategy was self-defeating, and neither friends nor foes among the region's leading states had much regard for the United States or its policy.

OUR OWN WORST ENEMIES

Given the extraordinary scale of American involvement in the Middle East over the past four and a half decades, why have U.S. policies been so consistently ham-fisted? Simon offers several answers. First and most colorful is his assessment of the people responsible for creating them. Carter's inner circle was "dysfunctional." The Reagan administration was peopled by "thin-skinned, devious, recalcitrant antagonists" whose vision of an Arab-Israeli peace process was "nearly perfectly silly." George H. W. Bush's team was "blinded" by "the glare of U.S. power and comforts of wishful thinking." Clinton's Middle East advisers were "hobbled by an attraction to faulty doctrines." George W. Bush was "demonstrably narrow-minded, incurious, and impulsive," with a "crude approach to foreign policy dilemmas." Obama's trouble in Libya reflected no malign intent, only "incompetence." And then there was Trump, who assigned the Middle East portfolio to his son-in-law Jared Kushner in pursuit of "self-dealing crony capitalism." After reading this catalog, it is hard to resist the conclusion that U.S. tax dollars have been paying the salaries of an astonishing collection of rascals and reprobates.

Equally important for Simon is a deeply flawed policy process. Rather than common sense or strategic insight, U.S. policymaking in the region has invariably been shaped by "political imperatives, ideological fixations, emotional impulses, and a coordination process that necessitates some sort of interagency consensus on the part of cabinet members whose priorities are often incompatible." Even the most gifted analysts, he suggests, would have trouble getting good ideas implemented. Simon cannot resist (and who can blame him) reminding readers that more than 18 months before the 9/11 attacks, he and the counterterrorism expert Daniel Benjamin published an article in *The New York Times* warning that there would soon be "a mass casualty attack against the United States by Sunni extremists." So much for operational understanding and early warning.

Yet there are other explanations for the United States' Middle East failures that Simon neglects. By organizing *Grand Delusion* around successive administrations, he is compelled to foreground the political cycles that shape short-term policy choices rather than focus on broader national inclinations and global developments. As the Cold War ended, American triumphalism inhibited the sort of soul-searching in Washington that might have produced more serious deliberation about the consequences of U.S. policies and what, exactly, U.S. interests in the Middle East should be. For example, Simon points out that when Washington began its plunge into the region in the 1970s, "the vulnerability of Saudi Arabia and Israel appeared striking." But by the beginning of the twenty-first century, under the tutelage and extravagant backing of the United States, both countries had grown into regional powerhouses that were increasingly ready to challenge Washington when their interests diverged. Although such nurturing of vulnerable countries into powerful players (and frequent irritants) counts as success according to Simon, he also asks, "At what cost?" That is a crucial consideration: the United States and the region have both paid a high price for U.S. patronage of Israel and Saudi Arabia. But this largely unquestioning support also raises the question of whether the security of Israel and assured access to Gulf oil—which were hardly adequate measures of U.S. interests in the Middle East 50 years ago—should continue to shape Washington's policies toward the region today.

Simon's emphasis on bilateral relations with allies and adversaries is also revealing for what it leaves out. In an era in which digital innovation has transformed media, expanded supply chains, enriched the finance industry, reshaped military technology, revolutionized espionage and autocracy, and generated growing inequality, the role and interests of the world's most powerful country have necessarily changed as well. Yet he does not discuss the kinds of social, economic, and technological forces—from Internet penetration and literacy rates to population growth and youth unemployment—that have long shaped daily lives in the Middle East. The omission of these issues seems hard to justify, particularly since many of the drivers of change have been technologies developed in and associated with the United States.

Simon complains that intelligence analysts are good at exposing weaknesses in policy proposals "but never offer any ideas about how to make them better." *Grand Delusion* suffers from some of the same limitations. Would smarter, more honest, clear-eyed policymakers, unencumbered by hubris or bureaucratic pettiness, make better policy? Although Simon discusses roads not taken that might have led to better outcomes at specific points in his story, tactical agility is not strategic insight, and he does not put forward a vision of a more effective U.S. strategy toward the region.

LISTEN OR LOSE

Washington has long defined the Middle East in the negative, by what should be prevented rather than what should be promoted. Thus did policymakers jockey to contain Soviet influence during the Cold War and to maneuver Iraq and Iran into blocking each other in Clinton's post–Cold War "dual containment" strategy. Successive administrations have devoted enormous resources to deterring rogue states, foiling terrorists, preventing nuclear proliferation, searching for weapons of mass destruction, controlling refugee flows, and otherwise searching out and averting myriad perceived dangers in the region. But prevention does not amount to engagement, however expensive and time-consuming it has been. Sporadic efforts to involve the region's people have faltered in the face of electoral victories and negotiations that produced leaders who did not reflect U.S. policy preferences. These sometimes unsettling reflections of local political aspirations—such as the election of Hamas in Gaza in 2007 or of a Muslim Brotherhood president in Egypt in 2012 or, for that matter, a right-wing Israeli government in 2022—quickly became yet further rationales for policies of prevention and containment.

What, apart from Biden's tired gestures toward the now hollow rhetoric of "cooperation, stability, security, and prosperity," does the United States want to promote in the Middle East? George W. Bush went to war in Iraq to advance "liberty"; Obama intervened in Libya to secure "human rights." Trump simply wanted to midwife a few lucrative deals in a region he called "one big, fat quagmire." At this point, merely lowering the volume of declarations from Washington would be a welcome change. Indeed, it might prompt U.S. policymakers to listen to voices in the region, particularly if American diplomats are pushed out of their fortified embassies to walk among the people to whose governments they are accredited. Behind the megaprojects touted by those governments and the glittering trade fairs showcasing the latest and most expensive new technologies in weapons and cybersecurity, they might notice the vibrant tech-startup scene that is struggling to emerge in Egypt's informal economy and use U.S. influence to urge reform of the regulatory environment for small business. They might read the public opinion polls in Libya that blame the continuing violence on foreign interference and advise Washington to enforce the country's universally flouted arms embargo. They might see the deteriorating utilities infrastructure in Lebanon and push for international efforts to rebuild the electric grid. They might resist the temptation to see everything through the lens of security threats, devoting their energy to sniffing out any country's pursuit of technologies that might conceivably be "dual use"—turned into weapons—and working to frustrate them. There is enough frustration in the Middle East.

Until the United States defines its interests in the region, it will remain in a limbo of disillusioned involvement, reduced to trying—and increasingly failing, as China's recent diplomatic triumph suggests—to thwart others. Even as Washington shows a growing reluctance to engage, it will remain unable to disengage. Simply "taking out" local military leaders in occasional military strikes is guaranteed only to produce more disaffected and embittered people who see no alternative to violence to make themselves heard. From that perspective, perhaps Simon's final assessment, offered in a spirit of resignation, is actually an occasion for hope: "Whatever the future holds for the United States in the Middle East, it will scarcely resemble either the past or the present."

REVIEW ESSAY

Keeping the World at Bay

Does Globalism Subvert Democracy—or Strengthen It?

MARK MAZOWER

Against the World: Anti-Globalism and Mass Politics Between the World Wars BY TARA ZAHRA. Norton, 2023, 400 pp.

The end of the Cold War was the beginning of globalization—or, at least, that is when people began to talk about it. The term itself entered mainstream discourse in 1983, with an article in the *Harvard Business Review* by the economist Theodore Levitt. The article lauded the global expansion of markets for manufacturers as the start of a process that would inexorably make the world a better place by breaking down "the walls of economic insularity, nationalism, and chauvinism." A decade later, talk of globalization was ubiquitous. By then, capitalism had triumphed over communism, and one form of capitalism—dedicated to dismantling economic and labor regulations, barriers to trade, and exchange controls—had supplanted the more managed, state-run version of the immediate postwar decades.

Globalization was more than a mere term, of course. Over the last three decades, the world has radically changed and become far more connected by revolutionary technologies, supply chains, and delivery systems. Trade in goods has soared as a proportion of world GDP; cross-border financial flows have grown faster still. Geopolitical shifts in economic power have seen the rise of a prosperous middle class across much of what is commonly referred to as "the global South," or the bulk of African, Asian, and Central and South American countries. As producers opted for cheaper labor overseas, especially in China, Central America, and Southeast Asia, organized labor in the former manufacturing heartlands of the developed world was decimated. Interdependence and hyperconnectivity also sped up the

MARK MAZOWER is Ira D. Wallach Professor of History at Columbia University and the author of *Governing the World: The History of an Idea*.

transmission of global afflictions, from the series of sovereign debt crises that ran across South America, eastern Europe, and East Asia in the 1990s to the COVID-19 pandemic.

For a long time, this extraordinary shift in the way the world works lacked any serious historical contextualization. Economists had long ago lost their predecessors' interest in history and instead turned toward mathematics. Historians, for their part, were becoming ever less numerate, and by the time of the 2007–8 financial crisis, they had relinquished almost any interest in macroeconomic change. In fact, it is only in the last decade that scholars have seriously begun to think historically about globalization.

Against the World, a new book by the historian Tara Zahra, makes a thought-provoking contribution to this literature. Zahra delves into the tumultuous years between World War I and World War II to argue that it was resistance to globalism and globalization that ended up weakening Europe's then fragile democracies. Zahra writes that after World War I, free trade and internationalist politics came under fire, leading to stronger tariff barriers and immigration controls and eventually contributing to the continent's slide into dictatorship. Echoes of that time seem to ring loudly today.

As angst about globalization fuels antidemocratic politics in the United States, Europe, and elsewhere, Zahra suggests parallels between the rise of authoritarianism then and its resurgence now. Her book, she writes, "with its emphasis on the popular politics that animated anti-globalism, is no less a history of the present." Yet such an analogy insists a little too much. Globalization's cheerleaders claim that free trade and economic liberalization pave the way for the spread of democracy. History suggests a more ambiguous relationship and shows that democracy can be undone by both nationalist and global forces.

THE LENS OF THE PRESENT

Starting in 1913 in Budapest and ending in New York at the World's Fair in 1939, *Against the World* ranges broadly across Europe and the Atlantic. Zahra takes readers through events as disparate as the American pacifist movement and central European famines during World War I before delving into incipient fascism and the rise of the Bolsheviks after the war, the growth of immigration restrictions, and the rise of Nazism. Unlike most conventional treatments of these years, the book features as its protagonists not only statesmen and diplomats but also labor activists, farmers, and writers. Familiar figures such as the British economist John Maynard Keynes, the Austrian writer Stefan Zweig, the American industrialist Henry Ford, and the Indian anticolonial leader Mahatma Gandhi sit alongside relative unknowns, such as the anti-Semitic Italian American immigration lawyer Gino Speranza, author of the xenophobic and racist screed *Race or Nation: A Conflict of Divided Loyalties*. More salubrious characters include the Czech entrepreneur Tomas Bata, "the King of Shoes," who piloted his own three-motor airplane more than 20,000 miles across the Middle East and Asia in pursuit of new markets. In discussing the Hungarian Jewish activist Rosika Schwimmer, Zahra

Partners in crime: Adolf Hitler and Benito Mussolini in Venice, June 1934

ULLSTEIN BILD / GETTY IMAGES

introduces readers to the world of peace conferences and a moment when the collapse of the great central European empires yielded the dream of a world united under a single government.

If Zahra's prose is readable, her approach is often strikingly anecdotal. As in the case of Schwimmer, individuals and places stand in for larger themes. Zahra relies on such pen-portraits to make a few key points. The relative openness of borders before World War I fostered political activism and economic entrepreneurship. The closing of borders during the war, along with the British continental blockade, led to malnutrition, pandemics, and an enduring anxiety throughout the interwar years about ensuring the security of the national food supply. Fascism's breeding ground lay in the poverty and instability caused by the collapse of political order in central Europe, in particular, as well as in the dislocation caused by the international economic crisis of the early 1930s. What unites Zahra's large and diverse cast of characters is their role in the grand drama of the struggle between those who stood for some kind of internationalism and their more nationalist and nativist opponents.

Much of this history will be familiar to students of fascism, a subject that already boasts a vast literature. Indeed, it would scarcely be an exaggeration to say that the professional study of twentieth-century European history grew from an interest in fascism's origins and why fascism succeeded in some places and failed in others. Zahra's contribution seems to have been motivated by the resurgence of right-wing authoritarian politics in the present. "I began this book in 2016," she notes. "Donald Trump had been elected president.... There was a refugee crisis, and populist, right-wing parties were winning elections across

Europe with anti-migrant platforms." Trump's presidency revived interest in fascism past and present in the United States. His rise, fueled by various populist and nationalist grievances, also suggested for the first time that analyzing the crisis of democracy required paying attention to opponents of globalization. This modern context explains the novel frame with which Zahra approaches some old questions about the upheavals of the interwar years. "The past is supposed to help us better understand the present," she writes. "But in this case, I have been more surprised by the ways in which the present has altered the way I see the past."

Seeing the past through the present can be fraught. If globalization is a term devised in the late twentieth century, can it be used meaningfully to describe events in the interwar years? Zahra is much too good a historian not to consider the risks of anachronism. She tackles the problem head-on and insists that globalization was, in its fundamentals, a long-term process that stretched back at least into the nineteenth century.

Although the term was not used in its current sense until the 1980s, that does not mean that globalization as a phenomenon could not have existed before then. In some respects, it clearly did. Trade, for instance, expanded rapidly across the world at various points in the nineteenth century. According to one recent study, the openness of the world economy (measured in terms of exports as a proportion of GDP) grew between 1830 and 1870 at a rate that would not be matched again until the late twentieth century. The rise of New York as one of the world's great metropoles was as sudden as the growth of Mexico City or Jakarta over the past half century. Zahra finds early opponents of globalization in people who disliked free trade and unfettered immigration, worried about fragile, far-flung supply chains across oceans and fretted when domestic workers lost out to cheaper labor abroad. The Italian dictator Benito Mussolini, she writes, was "both radically nationalist and anti-global"; anti-Semitic violence in central Europe was "a violent manifestation of anti-globalism," and "Jews were targeted as symbols of international finance, unchecked migration, cosmopolitanism, and national disloyalty." In these and other ways, the concerns of "anti-globalizers" a century ago sound familiar today.

THE MURK OF THE PAST

On the other hand, the growth patterns of recent decades are unprecedented and without plausible parallel. Between 1980 and 2008, Europe's export-to-GDP ratio grew from 24.3 to 41.1 percent, and the worldwide figure from 20.4 to 31 percent. Border-crossing financial markets, institutions, and elites rapidly gained enormous control over national economies. In short, the degree of openness in the world economy around the year 2000 was far greater than in any other period in history.

Not only was the world economy opening up after 1980 in a way that had no historical precedent, but it was doing so in a more permanent way. World trade at the bottom of the interwar slump was down a third from its 1929 height; the slump after 2009 was not nearly so pronounced or so lengthy. In other words, the interwar years in Europe—the core of

Zahra's book—were roiled by a crisis of a severity that has not been matched since. Any attempts to mine the past for lessons should take this stark truth into account.

In Zahra's story, the term globalization serves as a synonym for a number of quite different things, including the ability to travel without a passport, a smoothly functioning international monetary system based on the gold standard, and international conferences of pacifists from around the world. Insofar as a global order existed before World War I, it was an imperial one run by bourgeois and aristocratic elites. Zahra acknowledges at the start that those she calls globalizers tended to be white and well-off, and she accepts that figures such as Keynes and Zweig were exponents of a kind of liberalism that emerged out of a world of empires and could only with difficulty adapt to the era of decolonization that followed World War II.

Yet perhaps because Zahra's wonderful early work often focused on the Austro-Hungarian Empire, her intellectual roots in the study of the Habsburg world, and perhaps a certain attachment to its values, go deep. Time and again, readers of *Against the World* will feel beneath the historian's warnings the tug of a kind of Zweigian nostalgia for what was lost with the end of Habsburg rule. It is helpful to be reminded that the inhabitants of the Adriatic port of Fiume, now Rijeka in Croatia, felt worse off when the empire collapsed because they faced commercial calamity and that it was for this reason that many of them sympathized with the swashbuckling protofascist Gabriele D'Annunzio when he seized control of the town for Italy in 1919. But it does not add much to shoehorn these developments, as Zahra does, into some struggle between those for and against globalization. D'Annunzio wanted a larger Italy to compete in a world of empires: did that make him a globalizer or an antiglobalizer? The answer is surely neither. After the fascists took charge of Italy in 1922, they started out committed to the gold standard and free trade and then reversed course. Italian fascism and globalism were not inherently opposed until the Great Depression forced the issue.

THE INESCAPABLE NATION-STATE

One comes away from Zahra's book feeling that, on the whole, nationalism is a bad thing and that fascist politics were what you might well end up with if you turned your back on free trade, unrestricted migration, and the gold standard—in short, what she presents as the interwar version of globalism. Zahra thus offers a message rather like that of globalization's proponents today. In so doing, she portrays interwar politics in ways that obscure some of the real challenges of those times.

The question of how to deal with the spread of nationalism after World War I was unquestionably at the top of the international agenda a century ago. The nation-state's march of triumph had begun in the mid-nineteenth century and continued with new vigor at the Paris Peace Conference in 1919, when the victorious Allies presided over the dismembering of the Habsburg and Ottoman empires, creating the modern map of eastern Europe and the Middle East. The process resumed again after World War II with decolonization in what was left of the European empires. Borders proliferated and made international economic life harder.

No real alternatives stood in the way of the spread of the nation-state. Empires could not simply be restored: one cannot find a plausible politics in Zweig's nostalgia for the helpless cosmopolitanism of Habsburg life. Yet preserving prosperity in a world of nation-states was complicated by radical changes in every domain of life. For one thing, world wars had increased rates of political participation and taken governance out of the hands of older elites. At the same time, the collapse of the nineteenth-century gold standard meant that the international monetary system required concerted management for the first time. In the 1920s, the Bank of England, the U.S. Treasury, and the Financial Committee of the League of Nations decided to resurrect a version of the gold standard. What they produced was political crisis: the gold standard presupposed a degree of fiscal discipline that strained the newly democratic politics of many countries beyond what they could bear. Organized labor resisted the downward pressure placed on wages by the effort to remain on the gold standard; downward pressure on commodity prices produced turmoil internationally. The effort to return to old-style globalization slammed into the mass politics of the interwar years with catastrophic results.

In such circumstances, opposition to globalization was rational. It made sense for many national governments in the early 1930s to abandon the gold standard, opt for autarky, support or nationalize industry that sought to replace imports, and subsidize domestic grain production. Such moves did not inevitably lead to fascism: the outcome in many countries was quite different. Indeed, from the 1930s to the 1960s, the thrust of development economics across much of the global South was premised on this model: the promotion of national prosperity by state-led industrialization drives that identified infant industries and facilitated urbanization.

If a return to empire offered no clear ideological alternative to interwar nationalism, that left only one other option: Bolshevism. It is curious—but oddly characteristic of a lot of contemporary U.S. historical scholarship—that communism's global impact hardly registers in Zahra's book. And yet it was the manifest failures of early twentieth-century capitalism to improve living standards for the masses that more than any other single factor helped give Bolshevism worldwide appeal. Apart from an allusion to the possibility of revolution in central Europe in 1919, Zahra largely ignores the Soviet experiment. Is this because Lenin's desire to export world revolution failed or because the universal ambitions of communism complicate even further the book's binary framework of globalizers and antiglobalizers? The commitment to build socialism in one country never led the Kremlin to abandon its longer-term desire to see communism triumph worldwide. Theirs was surely a form of global politics, utterly distinct from any other.

THE RIGHT LESSON?

Against the World is at its best in recalling the unexpected ways in which the collapse of the imperial world of nineteenth-century trade and bourgeois hegemony played out in the era of mass politics. It sketches a convincing and fresh picture of the torment World War I brought to eastern Europe and of the plight of Europe's Jews, in particular. Zahra also draws out the new forms of mass mobilization that flourished between the wars and the new actors who emerged onto the political scene.

Her attempt to draw parallels with today's anxieties about globalization, however, leads away from the real lessons to be learned from the collapse of European democracy in the interwar years and its subsequent postwar revival. Nationalism not only framed democracy's demise in the 1930s; it also framed democracy's recovery after 1945. Democracy was not restored in western Europe because of globalization. That restoration came about because of how national governments stewarded their economies, producing steady economic growth and decades of low unemployment. Indeed, after 1950, national economies opened up only slowly to one another: regional integration took decades.

The real lesson drawn at the time from the tumultuous interwar years was that laissez-faire economics could be fatal and that politicians had to understand the need for strategic national leadership. Today, thanks in no small measure to decades of globalization, politicians have abandoned this understanding of their responsibility and have ceded their power to central banks, constitutional courts, and the private sector. The last thing societies need at the moment is to be told that democracy, now or in the past, depends on globalization.

REVIEW ESSAY

Is India's Rise Inevitable?

The Roots of New Delhi's Dysfunction

MILAN VAISHNAV

India Is Broken: A People Betrayed, Independence to Today
BY ASHOKA MODY. Stanford University Press, 528 pp.

Of the many tropes that have cluttered foreign policy analysis in recent decades, few are as widespread or as enduring as the inevitability of India's rise. Built on a foundation of liberal democracy, fueled by a population of more than a billion people occupying a vast territory, and enabled by the United States' desire to find a counterbalance to an expansionist China, India has been inching toward the geopolitical spotlight. Now, a confluence of recent events has convinced some observers—and arguably India's own leadership—that its moment has finally arrived.

According to the International Monetary Fund (IMF), India is set to be the world's fastest-growing economy in 2023. Its GDP is expected to expand by 6.1 percent, well above the emerging market average of four percent and five times the pace of the industrialized world's average of 1.2 percent. Amid China's protracted slowdown, COVID-19 missteps, and rising labor costs, global firms interested in relocating their manufacturing facilities, including Apple and Foxconn, are considering expanding operations in India. Any day now, India's growing population—last pegged at 1.41 billion—will surpass that of China. India's relative youth (about 40 percent of the country is under the age of 25) is seen as valuable, not just because of the potential boost it provides to economic productivity but also because of what it signals about India's latent consumer base in the coming decades. Armed with smartphones, connected to digital payment systems, and culturally predisposed to global brands such as Coke and Netflix, India's young consumers occupy

MILAN VAISHNAV is a Senior Fellow and Director of the South Asia Program at the Carnegie Endowment for International Peace.

pride of place in the growth forecasts of many Fortune 500 companies.

Historically, India's fractious politics have limited the country's ability to expand infrastructure, reform tax laws and financial regulations, and improve basic welfare services, but that may be changing. The Bharatiya Janata Party, led by Prime Minister Narendra Modi, has won consecutive parliamentary majorities, in 2014 and 2019. The party's success, coupled with the decline of its rival Congress Party, has all but assured governmental stability for the foreseeable future. Weaker Indian governments in the past often had to balance the competing agendas of factions in ruling coalitions and onerous horse-trading that resulted in inaction and sclerosis. The BJP will almost certainly maintain power in the 2024 general elections; the only question worth debating is the size of its majority. Its strong hold over Parliament gives the party the political heft required to push through long-pending economic reforms.

Even India's refusal to unequivocally condemn Russia's invasion of Ukraine has not damaged the country's international standing. To the contrary, Western interlocutors are convinced that the combination of Russia's Ukraine quagmire and China's flagrant aggression on the Sino-Indian border makes the time ripe to wean India off its addiction to Russian arms and consolidate its anti-China posture. This year, India will simultaneously hold the presidencies of the G-20 and the Shanghai Cooperation Organization, a Eurasian political and security group historically dominated by China and Russia—a symbolic victory for its efforts to be seen as a leading, rather than a balancing, power on the global stage.

On closer inspection, the narrative hyping India's inexorable rise appears less assured. Reckoning with India's contradictions is an exercise in cognitive dissonance. Economically, it is a mixed bag. On the one hand, India is on track to become the world's third-largest economy by the decade's end. On the other, India's services-heavy development model is hamstrung by weak job growth, premature deindustrialization, and a vast informal sector. Politically, meanwhile, India is touted as a shining democratic beacon in the Asia Pacific. But it is also one of the world's most disappointing illiberal backsliders, with growing religious majoritarianism, weakening separation of powers, and a muzzled media. Few democracies can rival the array of affirmative action measures that India's constitution affords historically disadvantaged minorities or match the diversity of its top leadership. Yet Muslims in Indian cities are increasingly ghettoized, women make up a minuscule share of the workforce, and manual scavenging—in which workers remove human excrement by hand—is a legally prohibited, yet widely observed, form of blue-collar employment.

Among this tangle of conflicting narratives is a new book by the economist Ashoka Mody that is well positioned to become an exemplar for the glass-half-empty view of India. *India Is Broken* methodically demolishes the bumper-sticker version of India's story that CEOs and politicians conjure at glitzy international conferences such as the World Economic Forum in Davos. It takes readers on a tour of India's dark underbelly, where corruption has triumphed over compassion, and democracy exists in theory but rarely in practice. Many recent critiques of India's trajectory focus on Hindu nationalism and the rise of the BJP. But Mody goes further by connecting the failures of successive Indian governments—alternately led by the Congress, the BJP, and smaller regional parties—since independence, showing the deep roots of India's troubles.

NOT ALL THAT GLITTERS

Mody, an Indian-born economic historian at Princeton, spent decades at the World Bank and the IMF troubleshooting international economic crises. On the day Mody took U.S. citizenship, Mody's father said his son would "always be an Indian at heart." It is that intimate connection to his homeland that propels Mody's sense of outrage; he approaches his topic armed not with a scalpel intended to contour the conventional understanding of India but with a sledgehammer meant to smash it to bits.

Mody's thesis is alluringly simple: after 75 years of independence, India's democracy and economy are fundamentally broken. India may boast competitive elections—with more than 600 political parties, high voter turnouts, and the regular alternation of power—but Mody dismisses such mechanics of democracy as deficient indicators of democratic health. Instead, he notes that "weakened norms and accountability have made the rules and institutions of democracy a plaything of the privileged and powerful." Today, criminal behavior and self-dealing have almost become prerequisites for political success. Four out of ten elected members of Parliament face pending criminal cases at the time of their election; eight out of ten are *crorepatis*, a term loosely translated to mean "millionaires"; and nearly all see prolific campaign spending as a worthwhile down payment on massive future returns.

When it comes to the vaunted Indian economy, Mody avoids economists' traditional obsession with GDP and focuses instead on the availability of jobs and the level of human development. On this score, he argues that India has consistently failed to generate enough jobs to keep up with labor demand or to deliver quality public goods, such as health and education, that can equip its citizens with basic life skills. India's employment struggles, Mody posits, are as old as the republic. He puts the country's jobs shortfall in 1955 at around 25 million; in 2019, he writes, it was at least 80 million and was likely much higher after the COVID-19 pandemic. Despite tangible gains on poverty, India has not achieved commensurate progress on key standard of living metrics. Malnutrition remains stubbornly high even in better-off regions of the country: in the economically dynamic southern state of Tamil Nadu, 30 percent of young people are malnourished—ten percentage points higher than the number in Vietnam, despite similar levels of per capita income.

In his lament for India's broken economy and democracy, Mody spares no one blame. He acknowledges that India's inaugural prime minister, Jawaharlal Nehru, was a "beloved leader" who "did not seek personal gain or prestige," but he eviscerates Nehru for putting "all

Making do: students at an outdoor lesson, New Delhi, November 2022

ADNAN ABIDI / REUTERS

his chips on heavy industrialization, a strategy that fared poorly in employing the large numbers who wanted jobs." Nehru's daughter and eventual political successor, Indira Gandhi, "established herself as a cynical, slogan-peddling politician intent on holding onto power." Lacking any coherent economic or political ideology, "she saw preservation of her power as her main goal." Modi, India's current prime minister, may be a darling of the international community, but he is a "folk hero" for Hindutva—the BJP's guiding ideology of Hindu nationalism—whose economic credentials were built not on promoting entrepreneurship but on "subsidizing favored industrialists." Mody's glum assessment leads him to see parallels between India today and "the Hindu-Muslim divide and egregious economic inequalities" of the torturous years leading up to the bloody partition of the subcontinent in 1947. If this is India's moment in the spotlight, it could be for all the wrong reasons.

When taking aim at India's flawed development model, there are plenty of targets to choose from. Federalism, weak state capacity, and the interventions of accountability institutions in New Delhi, including the Central Vigilance Commission (an anticorruption agency) and the Comptroller and Auditor General (which scrutinizes government expenditure), have all thrown sand in the gears of India's growth. Mody places the blame elsewhere, arguing that India's underperformance is about ideas, not interests or institutions. His indictment of the Indian political elite's intellectual bankruptcy is premised on two charges: Indian leaders have never committed to a market-based economy or maintained a core conviction about the need to provide citizens with basic public goods.

DOOMED FROM THE START

In Mody's account, Nehru's flawed economic beliefs were the original sin that set India on a trajectory of jobless growth. Critics have long castigated Nehru for unabashedly propagating Fabian socialism, an ideology that marries a suspicion of markets with an embrace of state-led heavy industry. Nehru hoped this economic model would catalyze investment and self-sufficient growth in a newly decolonized India. Mody departs from this received wisdom, arguing that "whether [Nehru] was inspired by Fabian socialism, Soviet ideology, or his own professed commitment to equality and fairness, he practiced none of them." In fact, Nehru was a disciple of the "big push" industrialization strategy popularized by the economist Paul Rosenstein-Rodan and modernization theorists such as Walt Rostow. As Nehru put it, he believed Indian industry would be "self-feeding, self-propelling, self-developing."

Mody writes that by stubbornly committing to such a development model, Nehru missed a golden opportunity to mimic Japan's success under the Meiji restoration, which was premised on a mutually reinforcing cycle of high-quality education, investments in agricultural productivity and domestic manufacturing, and the aggressive pursuit of exporting to foreign markets. Nehru, he writes, was too mesmerized by his effort to build massive steel plants, power stations, and dams—what the prime minister famously called the "temples of modern India"—to get his hands dirty negotiating the complex bureaucratic politics of funding and sustaining primary education.

The oligopolistic industrial structure, import controls, and onerous business licensing regime that Nehru built proved too politically tempting for his daughter, Indira Gandhi, to do away with. Under her reign, this "license raj" flourished, private entrepreneurship was stifled, and public goods were an afterthought. When asked about India's developmental infirmities, Gandhi replied with a famous quip: "I don't know how important literacy is. What has it done for the West?"

Only the prospect of sovereign bankruptcy in 1991 pushed India to open its economy and embrace significant liberalizing reforms, a transformational event whose importance Mody surprisingly downplays. In Mody's telling, liberalization involved only the most grudging steps toward promoting a market economy, resulting in "the narrowest and most cynical economic growth strategy." As for the historic reductions in poverty that India's post-1991 growth surge helped bring about, Mody argues that lifting millions of citizens just above a meager poverty line of $1.90 a day is simply "wishing away the country's poverty."

Three decades after India's economic opening, Mody sees no signs of an ideological commitment to markets or the fundamentals of human development. The "Gujarat model"—which entails the aggressive use of tax, land, and loan incentives to attract large corporate investment—that Modi (and the media) touted as he catapulted from provincial politician to the highest elected office in the land is "marauding development on steroids." Even the record investments Modi's government has made in the public distribution of private goods, such as toilets, gas cylinders, and electricity connections, have done little to impress the author; for him, they are symbolic amenities that help win elections rather than sustainable fixes to India's human development travails.

ANGER MANAGEMENT

Mody's critique of Indian democracy is harder to pin down. But his basic argument seems to be that charismatic Indian politicians have papered over India's twin crises of lack of jobs and poor human development with a mix of populism, clientelism, and identity politics. Nehru may have worked tirelessly to foster a democratic ethos in newly independent India, but his economic failures triggered widespread anxiety and social protest. As long as Nehru was in power, Indian institutions held firm. But under a populist such as Indira Gandhi, economic and political turmoil were used as a pretext to undermine democratic institutions. In 1975, Gandhi ushered in a nearly two-year period of emergency rule in which elections were put on ice and basic civil liberties suspended. Gandhi's role in India's democratic decay was pivotal, in Mody's view, because she willfully eroded democratic norms. "For when norms break," Mody writes, "democracy goes into a 'death spiral.'"

Although India's descent into overt autocratic rule would prove short-lived, corruption and institutional subversion became the new normal. Economic anxiety provided plentiful oxygen for toxic identity politics, especially along religious lines. According to Mody, India's "angry young men" have taken on many forms—from proponents of the chauvinist politics of the nativist Shiv Sena party to the mobs that in 1992 razed the Babri Masjid, a centuries-old mosque that Hindu nationalists claimed sat on sacred grounds, to the foot soldiers of the Hindutva movement, who have set their sights on fighting imaginary demons such as "love jihad," a conspiracy theory claiming that Muslim men are seducing Hindu women to convert them to Islam. In this regard, Mody offers little sympathy for India's secular politicians, whose commitment to liberal ideals was, in his view, skin-deep and who pandered to religious interests in the name of political expediency.

How might India escape from this path? Mody is silent on detailed policy prescriptions, instead advocating for broad reform principles. India must deepen democracy by promoting greater decentralization to municipal and village governments, where local citizens can more easily hold their leaders accountable. In addition, he calls for harnessing the power of civil society to build "civic communities" that can foster norms of equality, tolerance, and shared progress. Here, he finds inspiration in the work of the Harvard political scientist Robert Putnam who emphasizes the democratic role of civic associations, nonprofits, professional organizations, and mutual aid societies. Techno-evangelists tout the ability of big data, artificial intelligence, and smartphones to improve welfare delivery, but Mody is not entirely sold. Technology can help, but it is no substitute for fiscal resources, social action, and human capital.

DOING ITS BEST

Mody is a gifted writer, and *India Is Broken* is the rare book that distills India's complex political economy into digestible bites. But that is also the book's great weakness. Mody's account is powered by simple binaries that do not always stand up to scrutiny.

Mody makes it clear that India's populace would have been better served had its leaders pursued the export-led, labor-intensive manufacturing model popularized by India's East Asian neighbors. But there is one key difference: the successful East Asian "tigers" were all autocracies when they embarked on their new model, which allowed them to repress labor, enact sweeping land reform, and keep civil society in check. If anything, India's growth as a democracy looks even more impressive in hindsight; as the economists Rohit Lamba and Arvind Subramanian have pointed out, since 1950, India has been the only continuous democracy (other than perhaps Botswana) to maintain an average GDP growth rate between three and 4.5 percent for nearly four decades (which India has done since its growth takeoff in 1980).

Mody's critique of India's woeful human development record is more compelling, but here, too, his anger is misplaced. Under the Indian constitution, important public services such as law and order, public health, sanitation, and water are all the responsibilities of India's state governments, not central authorities. New Delhi provides broad policy guidance and financial resources, but states are ultimately responsible for implementation. It is an open secret that most Indian states are hardly paragons of virtue; they are hotbeds of illiberalism, parochialism, and patronage politics. If anything, what is happening today at the national level is the scaling up of a model that was first perfected in India's state capitals.

Furthermore, Mody's dismissal of India's developmental gains in the three decades since liberalization comes across as churlish. Decades ago, demographers sounded the alarm about India's impending "population bomb." Yet fertility has declined dramatically and has now dipped just below replacement levels, an unsung success in family planning. Women are seriously underrepresented in the labor force—an unsightly blight on India's economic model—but they now turn out to vote in larger numbers than men in most state-level elections, and India's long-standing male-heavy sex ratio has finally begun to rebalance. Mody may criticize the current government's gambit to ramp up the distribution of private welfare amenities as a cynical vote-catching ploy, but research from peer countries finds that access to clean cooking fuel, electricity connections, and piped water can greatly improve job prospects, health standards, and gender norms inside the household. Surely, these basic amenities are requisites for building a country's industrial base.

These shortcomings aside, *India Is Broken* is a useful corrective to the glib, one-sided conversation about India often encountered in think tanks and corporate boardrooms. In laying bare the inherent frailties of the Indian model, Mody also sends a message to Western policymakers who have made big bets on India's ability to be an economic, political, and strategic bulwark against China and other authoritarian states. India may be touted as the "next big thing," but as with any marketing campaign, one would be well advised to read the fine print.

Recent Books

Political and Legal

G. JOHN IKENBERRY

The Project-State and Its Rivals: A New History of the Twentieth and Twenty-first Centuries
BY CHARLES S. MAIER. Harvard University Press, 2023, 528 pp.

The history of the twentieth century is frequently rendered as an epic struggle between liberal democracy and its autocratic challengers, culminating in the fall of the Berlin Wall and the triumph of capitalism and democracy. Maier offers an alternative account of the last century, looking at how a wide range of actors tried to harness industrial modernity in the pursuit of power and material interests. He focuses on the rise of "project-states," activist governments of every political persuasion that sought to transform their societies and energize their citizens rather than merely govern. U.S. President Franklin Roosevelt steered his version of a project-state and so, too, did Adolf Hitler and Joseph Stalin. In Maier's view, the interplay of these actors, along with the forces of global capitalism and attempts to construct transnational rules and institutions, shaped the twentieth century. The 1970s loom larger in this telling than the end of the Cold War because it was then that Western project-states began to take a neoliberal turn, ceding more ground to the market. Seen through this lens, the moral arc of the twentieth century vanishes: instead, Maier weaves a narrative about the explosive interplay of economic privilege and political grievance.

Empires of Eurasia: How Imperial Legacies Shape International Security
BY JEFFREY MANKOFF. Yale University Press, 2022, 384 pp.

Mankoff argues that a new "age of empire" is emerging in the heartland of Eurasia. Each of the region's major powers—China, Iran, Russia, and Turkey—is pursuing a "new imperial geopolitics" and intervening in the affairs of smaller neighboring states. In Syria and Ukraine, Russia's neoimperial turn has taken the form of direct military intervention and the de facto redrawing of borders. China's agenda in the region has relied on cultivating economic ties and building on ethnic and linguistic links. Old imperial traditions, according to Mankoff, stand behind this new Eurasian geopolitics. All four states are successors to empires that collapsed in the early twentieth century. Modern setbacks have encouraged their leaders to turn to their imperial pasts for inspiration, symbolism, and legitimacy. Russian President Vladimir Putin and Turkish President Recep Tayyip Erdogan are particularly eager to portray themselves as heirs to hallowed imperial traditions. Mankoff argues the imperial past does not merely inflect modern rhetoric; in a more profound sense, these countries, by dint of their imperial pasts, are not (and are not likely to become) nation-states content to inhabit sharply defined territories. When it comes to international relations, the past is never really past.

Algorithms for the People: Democracy in the Age of AI
BY JOSH SIMONS. Princeton University Press, 2023, 320 pp.

In this important book, Simons provides one of the best accounts of how advances in artificial intelligence challenge democracy and what societies can do about it. Machine learning is as profound as it is simple: a collection of techniques and methods for discovering patterns in data to make predictions. As Simons shows, in the right hands, it can be a powerful tool for governments to allocate resources and corporations to reach consumers. But the technology can also reduce the roles of human judgment, empathy, and creativity. Companies, courts, and welfare agencies, as Simons demonstrates, can use machine learning in ways that reinforce societal inequality. But even the most elaborate systems of machine learning do not eliminate the space for human judgment and moral choice; after all, people make decisions about the design of the models and the criteria for selecting data and patterns. The book's message is that the artificial intelligence revolution is ultimately a political phenomenon, and its benefits and dangers will be determined by society's willingness to regulate its use.

Legitimacy Politics: Elite Communication and Public Opinion in Global Governance
BY LISA DELLMUTH AND JONAS TALLBERG. Cambridge University Press, 2023, 250 pp.

For decades, political elites have championed international organizations as vital tools to manage an increasingly interdependent world. Yet today, institutions such as the International Criminal Court, the United Nations, the World Health Organization, and the World Trade Organization are increasingly under vociferous attack on many fronts. This impressive study disentangles the complex ways in which political elites shape public perceptions of the virtues and pitfalls of such global institutions. Public interest in the activities of an international organization determines whether government leaders will support its work, which in turn influences how effective it can be on the global stage. At the same time, elites shape how the public perceives such organizations. Citizens of democratic countries tend to know very little about the goals and activities of international institutions. Sifting through opinion data and survey experiments, the authors do not find a long-term decline in public support for them. In politically polarized countries such as the United States, citizens tend to take their cues from political party elites, who offer sharply divergent narratives about international organizations. Citizens are more likely to support them when they are seen as transparent, efficient, impartial, and oriented toward problem solving.

Economic, Social, and Environmental

BARRY EICHENGREEN

The Great Polarization: How Ideas, Power, and Policies Drive Inequality
EDITED BY RUDIGER L. VON ARNIM AND JOSEPH E. STIGLITZ.
Columbia University Press, 2022, 400 pp.

This volume of essays focuses on the rise of inequality in advanced economies, a phenomenon typically attributed to two forces: technical change that has favored well-educated, highly skilled workers and globalization that has thrown less skilled workers into competition with those in the developing world. Although they do not dismiss these ideas, von Arnim and Stiglitz observe that inequality outcomes vary enormously across countries similarly exposed to technical change and globalization. Rising inequality has been more pronounced in the English-speaking world than in other advanced economies. Those differences arise from the economic, political, and social policies that have accompanied technical change and globalization. The contributors discuss tax-and-transfer policies as well as those dealing with education, competition, intellectual property, labor organization, and collective bargaining. Throughout, they emphasize how the interests of economic and political elites often lie behind policy choices. Such arguments are not new, but they are made here with singular clarity and accompanied by extensive documentation, mainly (although not exclusively) relating to the United States. Contributors are less convincing in specifying how governments might pursue alternative approaches in the present political climate. It is easier to imagine inequality-reducing policies than it is to determine how they might be implemented.

Fiscal Policy Under Low Interest Rates
BY OLIVIER BLANCHARD.
MIT Press, 2023, 176 pp.

Public debts soared in the wake of the global financial crisis of 2008–9 and then again after the beginning of the COVID-19 pandemic. Many observers worry that these debts will threaten financial stability and jeopardize the prospects for economic growth, as well as limit the ability of governments to pursue social programs and use fiscal policy to restrain a cycle of booms and busts. Blanchard provides a cool-headed and refreshingly nontechnical discussion of these issues. As he shows, although debt as a share of GDP has risen sharply in recent decades, interest payments on that debt (again as a share of GDP) remain little changed, for the most part, since real interest rates (market rates adjusted for inflation) have been trending downward. The big question is whether this trend will continue or might reverse, which would have alarming consequences for the sustainability of public finances. The author is relatively sanguine on the matter. Real interest rates depend on the balance of saving and investment, and many of the factors that determine global savings, such as demography, will continue to evolve in the same direction as before and favor low real interest rates. He cautions governments to nevertheless prepare for the worst. His analysis may not carry over to emerging markets, however, where real interest rates are higher than those in wealthy countries.

Securing the Private Sector: Protecting U.S. Industry in Pursuit of National Security
BY DARREN E. TROMBLAY.
Lynne Rienner, 2021, 293 pp.

The Biden administration's decision to ban exports to China of advanced semiconductor design and manufacturing equipment underlines the problem of how governments should manage and protect advanced technologies. Tromblay argues that companies may not always appreciate the national security implications of their operations, leaving them vulnerable to disruption by malevolent actors who target their critical infrastructure. Government regulation can hurt companies by prohibiting exports to foreign markets and forcing firms to invest in hardening their defenses. At the same time, government agencies struggle to protect the private sector from threats. In the U.S. case, the federal government delegates to one agency, the FBI, too much responsibility for protecting cutting-edge intellectual property. When it comes to cybersecurity, on the other hand, it assigns the same function to multiple agencies, leading to confusion and inefficiency. Tromblay does not always provide definitive resolutions to these problems or clearly distinguish instances when government interventions are justified from when they are not. But his book remains valuable as an analytical and erudite approach to a set of controversial questions.

An Exchange Rate History of the United Kingdom: 1945–1992
BY ALAIN NAEF. Cambridge University Press, 2022, 266 pp.

Naef's financial history of the United Kingdom focuses on the management of the pound sterling exchange rate since World War II. He uses data on market operations from the Bank of England's archives to document the bank's efforts to defend and stabilize the rate during currency crises in 1949, 1967, and 1976. A fourth, culminating crisis took place in 1992, when the Bank of England expended three billion pounds in a futile attempt to defend the currency against speculators. Having failed, the bank was then forced to cobble together a new framework for monetary policy; it quickly settled on the policy known as inflation targeting (setting a numerical target for inflation and adjusting policy in order to hit it). For the better part of three decades, this approach proved remarkably successful at delivering price—if not also financial—stability. Since 1992, the central bank has engaged in few interventions in the foreign exchange market, instead allowing the British currency to fluctuate with market conditions. Naef concludes that this is for the best: such interventions are unlikely to work in a world of immensely large and liquid global financial markets. Only credible, substantive monetary policy measures, such as changes in interest rates, are effective in this environment.

Military, Scientific, and Technological

LAWRENCE D. FREEDMAN

The Wandering Army: The Campaigns That Transformed the British Way of War
BY HUW J. DAVIES. Yale University Press, 2022, 384 pp.

In this fascinating and richly drawn account of British warfare from the War of the Austrian Succession in the 1740s to the Crimean War just over a century later, Davies shows how armies can learn from grueling experience. The book opens with the British defeat at the hands of the French at the Battle of Fontenoy in 1745, which was followed a decade later by another French triumph over the British, this time with the help of Native Americans at the Monongahela River in Pennsylvania. These losses encouraged a "military enlightenment" among British leaders, with a greater appreciation of the value of irregulars and light infantry, the dangers of getting lured into frontal attacks, and the advantages of meticulous planning. The new approach was successful for the British in fighting the Seven Years' War in Canada but not in fighting the American War of Independence, during which the British lacked troops and suffered from overstretched supply lines. The lessons continued to be learned, however, as the army "wandered" through India and Europe as well as North America, culminating in the Duke of Wellington's successful campaigns in the Napoleonic Wars. The system then atrophied, with the army knocked out of its complacency once again by setbacks experienced during the Crimean War.

Triumph Regained: The Vietnam War, 1965–1968
BY MARK MOYAR. Encounter Books, 2022, 732 pp.

This is the second book in a trilogy in which Moyar seeks to revise the understanding of the Vietnam War from one that the United States was bound to lose to one that it might have won. The first in the series, *Triumph Forsaken* (2006), took the story up to the start of the large-scale U.S. military commitment in 1965, faulting the administration of U.S. President John F. Kennedy for the assassination of South Vietnamese President Ngo Dinh Diem during a military coup in 1963. In this second volume, Moyar describes the recovery from these errors. He produces a valuable history of the fighting, with good use of both Vietnamese and American sources. Moyar is not the first scholar to note the contrast between the actual state of the war and how it was perceived domestically or to blame the American media and liberal opinion makers for casting a winnable war as doomed. But a long war that involved the continued loss of American life on behalf of a corrupt and incompetent client state was always going to be hard to sustain.

Managing the Military: The Joint Chiefs of Staff and Civil-Military Relations
BY SHARON K. WEINER. Columbia University Press, 2022, 256 pp.

Recent years have seen an intense debate in the United States about the condition of civil-military relations and, in particular, about whether the military has come to exert too much sway. At the heart of this debate is the role of the chairman of the Joint Chiefs of Staff, a figure granted more power by the Goldwater-Nichols Act of 1986. In her illuminating contribution, Weiner considers not just how chairmen have influenced operational decisions but also how they have shaped the size and structure of the defense budget. Weiner looks at three instances when there was pressure to reduce expenditures: after the end of the Cold War during Colin Powell's tenure as chairman; between 2001 and 2006, when Defense Secretary Donald Rumsfeld attempted to use technology to streamline the military; and when President Barack Obama renewed demands for cuts. She identifies three key factors that determined the chairman's influence: the relative assertiveness of the chairman, the general state of relations between the executive and the legislature, and the degree of support given the chairman by the other service chiefs.

The Pentagon, Climate Change, and War: Charting the Rise and Fall of U.S. Military Emissions
BY NETA C. CRAWFORD. MIT Press, 2022, 392 pp.

Scholars tend to present the link between climate change and war in terms of how extreme weather, deforestation, and rising sea levels can create conditions conducive to conflict. In this thoroughly researched and original analysis, Crawford turns this notion around, pointing out how armies have contributed to global greenhouse gas emissions. The imperatives of modern warfare, with the vast production of armaments and heavy vehicles and with forces constantly on the move and aircraft in the air, demanded the enormous consumption of petroleum products. Ensuring fuel supplies was an operational objective in war that shaped U.S. foreign policy, notably in the Middle East, after 1945. So important were fossil fuels that despite being the largest emitter in the federal government, the Pentagon lobbied to be exempted from the 1997 Kyoto Protocol because of the impact of its strictures on military operations. In recent years, the military, more sensitive to the vulnerability of its bases to extreme heat and flooding, has become greener, although Crawford argues that it could still do much more.

Hinge Points: An Inside Look at North Korea's Nuclear Program
BY SIEGFRIED S. HECKER WITH ELLIOT A. SERBIN. Stanford University Press, 2023, 410 pp.

As the former head of Los Alamos National Laboratory, Hecker had unique opportunities to visit North Korean nuclear facilities between 2004 and 2010 and played a role in the negotiations intended to stop North Korea from becoming a credible nuclear power. Here, he describes the failure of that diplomatic effort. Hawks in the George W. Bush administration did not trust the secretive dictatorship and undermined the 1994 Agreed Framework deal that was meant to freeze the North Korean nuclear program. In 2006, Pyongyang announced that it had successfully tested a nuclear bomb. In 2009, under President Barack Obama, Washington tried diplomacy again to persuade Pyongyang to denuclearize. But Obama paid far more attention to Iran's nuclear program. President Donald Trump tried to bond with North Korean leader Kim Jong Un (Trump claimed the two "fell in love"), but they failed to reach any substantive agreement after National Security Adviser John Bolton persuaded the president to demand more than Kim could offer and then walk away from further negotiations. The cumulative effect of neglect and several poorly judged initiatives is that North Korea has acquired thermonuclear weapons and long-range missiles earlier than might otherwise have been the case.

The United States

JESSICA T. MATHEWS

The Point of No Return: American Democracy at the Crossroads
BY THOMAS BYRNE EDSALL. Princeton University Press, 2023, 448 pp.

For more than a decade, Edsall's weekly columns in *The New York Times* have traced the evolution of U.S. politics, culture, demography, and large-scale social and economic change. The columns are packed with data, summaries of recent social science research, and the analysis of a large stable of academic and think-tank experts. Although he writes in a restrained, almost scholarly voice, the columns Edsall chose for this collection—covering the five years from just after the 2016 election through 2021—paint an unmistakably grim picture captured in the book's title. The Republican Party has become an "antidemocratic party" with elected officials at both the state and federal levels engaged in a "calculated effort to subvert" free and fair elections. This leaves the Democrats "obliged by default" to defend democracy. But for a variety of institutional, political, and constitutional reasons that Edsall illuminates, they are ill positioned to do so. Both parties have changed greatly in recent years. The share of Democratic voters who are rich, highly educated, and white has doubled in the last 20 years. The richest counties in the country are now blue rather than red. The Republican Party, on the other hand, has become as much the party of the working class in its voter support (although not in policy) as Democrats have traditionally been. Edsall believes that policies promoted by the Democrats' progressive wing undermine the party's appeal to minorities and working- and middle-class whites, threatening devastating election results.

Uncertain Ground: Citizenship in an Age of Endless, Invisible War
BY PHIL KLAY. Penguin Press, 2022, 272 pp.

Klay enlisted in the U.S. Marines in the years after the 9/11 attacks. He served as an officer for four years, including one spent in Iraq during the 2007 surge in Anbar Province. As a public affairs officer, he did not directly participate in combat, but he was immersed in the pervasive violence that surrounded him. His short-story collection *Redeployment*, based on that experience, won the 2014 National Book Award for fiction. His gifts as a writer are equally evident in this collection of nonfiction pieces. Klay is sensitive to the irreducible gap between the fewer than one percent of Americans who served in Afghanistan and Iraq and the 99 percent who did not. Most Americans knew little and cared even less about what was happening in their name in these wars. But the book's most powerful passages are introspective and philosophical. They deal with Klay's personal experiences of war, positive and negative, and the shock of returning to civilian life. He wrestles with the moral risks of soldiering and how serving affected his religious faith. He appreciated the clarity of purpose offered by war and the support of his fellow marines. But at the same time, he found himself unable to understand the point of their sacrifice as they fought to control Fallujah, an Iraqi city U.S. forces had already "won" twice before. He was left to contemplate the profound difference between the capacity to use force and the power to achieve desired ends.

On Dangerous Ground: America's Century in the South China Sea
BY GREGORY B. POLING. Oxford University Press, 2022, 336 pp.

This authoritative, timely volume traces the detailed history of U.S. engagement in the most contested and likely most dangerous body of water in the world, the South China Sea. Brunei, China, Indonesia, Malaysia, the Philippines, Taiwan, and Vietnam all make overlapping claims to hundreds of islands, rocks, and reefs in this sea. Beijing has seized, built, and expanded military facilities on many of these disputed sites. In addition to these minuscule but strategic bits of land, the sea's littoral countries also vie for sovereignty and economic rights over contested waters. Fishing fleets, oil and gas developers, and naval vessels regularly harass one another. Washington maintains numerous alliances in the region; most important is its Mutual Defense Treaty with the Philippines, which it must honor not least because of the signal that failing to do so would send to every current and potential U.S. alliance partner in the region and beyond. Poling writes with great clarity, finishing with an excellent chapter defining an urgent U.S. political and economic policy for the region grounded in the deployment of American hard power while recognizing that there are no military solutions to the problems of the South China Sea. Important U.S. policy steps taken since the book went to press, especially in the tightening of military relations between the United States and the Philippines, closely follow his recommendations.

On Shedding an Obsolete Past: Bidding Farewell to the American Century
BY ANDREW BACEVICH. Haymarket Books, 2022, 368 pp.

Bacevich followed an over 20-year career as a U.S. Army officer with another as a professor, a prolific author, and a leading critic of an overly militarized, overly interventionist American foreign policy. His great literary skill and willingness to write what others are reluctant to say in public have made him one of the country's most notable advocates of a foreign policy of restraint. He argues that the United States left World War II not only with a determination to push back communism but, more important, with the goal of preserving "ideological, economic, political and military primacy" globally—the disease of American exceptionalism. This imperative produced what he calls the "very long war," stretching from Vietnam to Afghanistan and encompassing nearly 50 years. Allotting the conflicts in this span to separate wars—namely, the Cold War and the global war on terror—leads to the error of missing their intimate connection. American misadventures during those two long wars and "serial misuse of military power" in many places—he lists in chronological order Panama, Iraq (three times), Somalia (twice), Haiti, Bosnia, Kosovo, Serbia, Afghanistan (twice), Sudan, the Philippines, Libya, various West African countries, and Syria—not only cost lives and vast sums of money but also contributed to the domestic disorders that plague the United States today.

Western Europe

ANDREW MORAVCSIK

Iron and Blood: A Military History of the German-Speaking Peoples Since 1500
BY PETER H. WILSON. Harvard University Press, 2023, 976 pp.

This astonishingly ambitious and detailed 900-page study of militaries in Austria, Germany, and Switzerland is not for the faint of heart. Yet Wilson's masterful history is a must-read for at least two types of readers. One type is the reader who is professionally or personally interested in military history. Wilson belongs to a new generation of historians for whom military history is far more than a chronicle of commanders, campaigns, and decisive battles. He offers an absorbing overview of how slowly changing societal forces—such as fiscal systems, scientific and technological capabilities, ideological and cultural beliefs, and the social background of soldiers—have transformed the use of military force across modern times. The other type of reader is interested in what caused the great wars that defined European history over this period. The received wisdom is that Germany, flanked by potential enemies and imbued with a Prussian "iron and blood" tradition of militarism, developed a uniquely aggressive culture that provoked not just the two world wars but most other major European conflicts since 1750. Wilson believes this view is at best simplistic, perhaps even wrong. Historically, Germany was both more decentralized and more peaceful than aggressive imperial neighbors such as France, Spain, and the United Kingdom. Only the dominance of Prussia, a foreign power to much of Germany, and severe strategic errors by its leadership led to the two world wars that earned it a reputation for belligerence.

The Socialist Patriot: George Orwell and War
BY PETER STANSKY. Stanford University Press, 2023, 150 pp.

Many on the political left have long struggled to support any war, no matter how just—as some still do with regard to the one in Ukraine today. The evolution of the English writer George Orwell's thinking about war is instructive. In this slim and readable volume, Stansky considers how four wars transformed Orwell's worldview. Still at Eton and too young to fight in World War I, Orwell penned vulgar poems suffused with the jingoism for which his elite school was famous. Twenty years later, he became a resolved antifascist and anticommunist after witnessing how Moscow-backed radicals betrayed the socialists in the Spanish Civil War. Yet he had also come to believe that capitalism was almost as bad as communism and hardly worth defending, and so he espoused pacifism. He then reversed himself after the Soviet Union and Nazi Germany agreed to the Molotov-Ribbentrop Pact in 1939, which paved the way for World War II. Orwell supported the war effort as a British patriot, standing firm with fellow democracies. The Cold War solidified his anticommunism, as expressed in his novels *Animal Farm* and *1984*. Only democracy, he came to believe in his final years, could enable the emergence of his preferred democratic socialism—although he doubted that such politics could ever hold sway in North America.

Keeping Friends Closer: Why the EU Should Address New Geoeconomic Realities and Get Its Neighbors Back in the Fold
BY VASILY ASTROV, RICHARD GRIEVESON, CHRISTIAN HANELT, VERONIKA JANYROVA, BRANIMIR JOVANOVIC, ARTEM KOCHNEV, MIRIAM KOSMEHL, ISILDA MARA, MARKUS OVERDIEK, THIESS PETERSEN, OLGA PINDYUK, OLIVER REITER, NINA VUJANOVIC, AND STEFANI WEISS. Vienna Institute for International Economic Studies and the Bertelsmann Stiftung, 2023, 104 pp.

The European Union is a significant military and cultural power, but its most important sources of global influence are economic. This uniquely detailed and data-rich study systematically reviews the extraordinary extent to which Europe's neighbors in the former Soviet Union, the Mediterranean, and parts of Africa depend on the continent for export markets for goods and services, foreign direct investment, foreign aid, technological and knowledge exchanges, infrastructure connectivity, and labor mobility—far more than they rely on China, Russia, or the United States. Issue by issue and country by country, the team of researchers behind this study suggests ways Europe can optimize and defend its preeminence. Perhaps a second study will extend the analysis, examining when and how the EU can best deploy such influence in the form of sanctions, grants of aid and market access, and technical assistance. This is an indispensable source for anyone interested in the workings of international influence in the twenty-first century.

Retracing the Iron Curtain: A 3,000-Mile Journey Through the End and Afterlife of the Cold War
BY TIMOTHY PHILLIPS.
The Experiment, 2023, 480 pp.

This book traces the author's trip in 2019 along the entire length of what used to be the Iron Curtain, from the small Norwegian port of Grense Jakobselv on the Barents Sea to Sadarak, an Azerbaijani town on the easternmost point on the old Soviet-Turkish border. As he proceeds by public transport, bicycle, car, and even on foot for over 900 miles, he sprinkles his travelogue with anecdotes from the Cold War. Yet the author struggles to do more than skim the surface: a few pages treat East German culture, for instance, a few more the 1968 Soviet invasion of Czechoslovakia, and a couple of others espionage in Vienna. And he fails to capture the surreal nature of the barrier that separated East and West decades ago or its equally surreal absence today. (For example, most of the wall that one can visit around Berlin is just a museum-like replica.) Yet the book does illustrate the ironies and paradoxes of what remains today. Russian border guards are friendlier and more lax than Western guards. Some people in the borderlands still harbor grievances about centuries-old wrongs. Others maintain strong sentimental attachments to communism, and some border cities still resemble twentieth-century communist towns more than they do twenty-first-century capitalist ones farther west.

Spain: The Trials and Triumphs of a Modern European Country
BY MICHAEL REID. Yale University Press, 2023, 336 pp.

In the quarter century after the 1975 death of Francisco Franco, the longtime dictator of Spain, the country has engineered a transition to democracy, modernized its economy, suppressed Basque separatist terrorism, and entered both the EU and NATO. This book is a solid general-interest introduction to twenty-first-century Spanish politics. The author, the *Economist*'s man in Madrid, asks why Spain's trajectory seems to have reversed: since 2000, it has been buffeted by economic stagnation, the rise of the far right, and political tumult in

Catalonia. Yet his answers are unsatisfying. In keeping with his work as a journalist, the book reads like a series of extended magazine articles. Driven by anecdotes and quotes, it is leavened with potted histories of topics such as Spanish nation building and Franco's rule. Little evidence backs up his central claim: that Spain suffers from the problems typical of middle-income countries such as Brazil, Poland, and South Korea. These maladies include real estate bubbles, escalating debts, income inequality, and corruption, which in turn have fostered political disillusionment, extremist politics, minority governments, and regional separatism. The book's conclusion—that if something is not done, citizens may lose patience—leaves the reader entirely in the dark about what, if anything, could address these problems.

Western Hemisphere

RICHARD FEINBERG

Cuban Privilege: The Making of Immigrant Inequality in America
BY SUSAN EVA ECKSTEIN.
Cambridge University Press, 2022, 300 pp.

In this exhaustive, authoritative study, Eckstein details U.S. immigration policies that have privileged Cubans, especially in contrast to policies that have excluded Haitians. After the 1959 socialist revolution in Cuba, migrants from the island gained ready access to lawful permanent residency in the United States and, eventually, to citizenship—and with it, the right to vote. Cuban migrants have received multiple resettlement entitlements, including cash transfers, workplace training, and access to health care—advantages that help explain their relative success once in the United States. As Eckstein documents, these exceptional benefits were repeatedly renewed and expanded by a succession of U.S. presidents and Congresses. Initially, the Kennedy administration imagined that an exodus of middle-class Cuban professionals might destabilize the government of Cuban President Fidel Castro; in fact, the mass migration removed potential sources of dissent from the island. Over time, increasingly prosperous Cuban Americans lobbied to perpetuate their community's privileges; Florida politics, rather than national security, became the main driver of U.S. policies toward Cuba. Eckstein also records the influence of Castro on migration flows, notably during the Mariel boatlift of 1980 and the rafter crisis of 1994, when the Cuban leader suddenly relaxed exit restrictions. Through their determination, ordinary Cubans seeking to reach American shores also shaped the course of history.

Cooperating With the Colossus: A Social and Political History of U.S. Military Bases in World War II Latin America
BY REBECCA HERMAN. Oxford University Press, 2022, 320 pp.

Burrowing deep into the national archives in Brazil, Cuba, and Panama, Herman has produced a splendid, well-balanced history of an extraordinary but seldom studied period in inter-American relations. She pushes back against the still prevalent academic caricature of the United States as an all-powerful imperial actor, aligning herself instead with a younger generation of scholars that has emphasized Latin American agency and the ability of Latin Americans to astutely bargain with Washington. To protect its southern flank during World War II, the United States moved swiftly to build over 200 defense installations and airfields in Latin America, in seeming contradiction to President Franklin Roosevelt's earlier Good Neighbor policy of withdrawing U.S. occupation forces. Herman deftly demonstrates how onsite U.S. commanders and diplomats cooperated with local authorities to find informal, flexible solutions to potentially tricky issues, such as the correct legal jurisdiction over U.S. soldiers, the employment rights of local workers on U.S. bases, and the health regulation of sex workers. These fixes met U.S. military needs and avoided offending the nationalist sensibilities of the host countries. Such pragmatic accords successfully managed the inherent tensions between international security cooperation and national sovereignty, enabling a brilliant if brief chapter of solidarity in the Western Hemisphere.

Code Name Blue Wren: The True Story of America's Most Dangerous Female Spy—and the Sister She Betrayed
BY JIM POPKIN. Hanover Square Press, 2023, 352 pp.

After nearly 17 years at the Defense Intelligence Agency, Ana Montes was arrested by U.S. authorities in 2001 on charges of spying for Cuba. The self-confessed traitor, who was recently released, served 21 years in a high-security federal prison. Unable to reach the imprisoned, unrepentant spy, Popkin relied on interviews with Montes's family and friends and on government psychological assessments to anatomize "the cocktail of resentment, narcissism, and insecurity" that explains Montes's high-risk decision to supply her Cuban handlers with inside information, acts of betrayal for which she received no monetary compensation. Yet in *Code Name Blue Wren* (the label given by U.S. officials to Montes's case), Popkin dismisses Montes's avowed reason for spying—her deeply felt opposition to U.S. policies in Central America and Cuba—but fails to offer a compelling portrait of a complex personality. Popkin echoes counterintelligence hawks in sensationalizing the damage Montes caused. For one thing, the pervasive Cuban security apparatus likely already knew the identities of U.S. intelligence agents operating on the island. Popkin also does not present credible evidence that Montes, as some of his sources allege, significantly distorted the intelligence community's characteristically tough-minded assessments of Cuba.

Autocracy Rising: How Venezuela Transitioned to Authoritarianism
BY JAVIER CORRALES. Brookings Institution Press, 2023, 256 pp.

A worthy sequel to Corrales's earlier classic *Dragon in the Tropics: Venezuela and the Legacy of Hugo Chávez* (2011), *Autocracy Rising* rigorously examines the paradox of the perseverance of the Venezuelan dictator Nicolás Maduro in the midst of economic collapse and severe international sanctions. Corrales offers three compelling explanations for Maduro's survival: asymmetric party system fragmentation, wherein the strength of the ruling party (rooted in deep networks of clientelism and cronyism) eclipses a fragmented opposition; institutional destruction and colonization, with the state exercising tremendous control over the electoral authorities, the coercive apparatus, and the courts (what Corrales labels "autocratic legalism"); and, most originally, institutional innovation ("functional fusion") in which institutions begin to multitask. The military acquires business functions, a constituent assembly becomes a legislature, local political councils become food distribution networks, and criminal syndicates acquire some of the functions of the state. In addition, Corrales provides valuable comparative case studies: Nicaragua offers a similar story of ascendant authoritarianism, but Colombia and Ecuador suggest that liberal democracy can fight back. Somewhat surprisingly, Corrales concludes that Maduro's rule remains tenuous, well short of true autocratic consolidation.

Eastern Europe and Former Soviet Republics

MARIA LIPMAN

Overreach: The Inside Story of Putin's War Against Ukraine
BY OWEN MATTHEWS. Mudlark, 2023, 432 pp.

For most Russians, as well as for Russian President Vladimir Putin, whom Matthews calls a "Russian everyman," the years that followed the collapse of the Soviet Union were a time of deep humiliation at the hands of the West. Putin sought to restore Russia as a global power, and in a series of military campaigns in Chechnya, Georgia, and Syria, demonstrated the country's new military might. Ukraine's supposed "betrayal" of Russia and the dreaded prospect of its joining NATO, Matthews emphasizes, lay at the heart of the "aggrieved patriotism" that drove Putin to plunge from a sophisticated if unscrupulous foreign policy to a reckless and devastating war that has effectively erased two decades of Russia's development. Putin's perception of a weak and divided West, along with Europe's dependence on Russian gas, inspired Putin's bid to create a Greater Russia by force. Drawing on his reporting from Russia and Ukraine during the first six months of the war, Matthews reveals how this sense of destiny proved misguided as the invasion of Ukraine foundered.

The book's shrewd analysis, insightful observations, and clear and succinct style are somewhat tainted by a number of factual inaccuracies.

Everyday War: The Conflict Over Donbas, Ukraine.
BY GRETA LYNN UEHLING. Cornell University Press, 2023, 210 pp.

Between 2015 and 2017, Uehling, an anthropologist, traveled across Ukraine to interview residents of its easternmost regions displaced by the military conflict in the Donbas that followed the 2014 Maidan revolution. Many of these people felt threatened by the new pro-Western leadership in Kyiv but were forced to flee to Ukraine's government-controlled territories. Uehling's main focus was the effect of the conflict on interpersonal relations. Family ties, friendships, and marriages were often broken when friends or loved ones found themselves on opposite political sides. Uehling describes a set of practices she calls "everyday peace": the ways in which people avoided contentious topics in conversation, kept away entirely from friends with opposing views, or attributed the political discord to their opponents' "zombification." The book's other focus is on how people engage in caring for others in the midst of their own disrupted lives. In one striking story, volunteer body collectors took terrible risks to travel to the separatist-controlled zone and back to bring home the remains of Ukrainian soldiers. They secretly combined this moral duty with smuggling insulin in unused body bags to diabetic children in an orphanage forsaken by separatist leaders.

Soviet Samizdat: Imagining a New Society
BY ANN KOMAROMI. Northern Illinois University Press, 2022, 318 pp.

News From Moscow: Soviet Journalism and the Limits of Postwar Reform
BY SIMON HUXTABLE. Oxford University Press, 2022, 272 pp.

Two new books explore the role of official and unofficial publications in the culture of the Soviet Union after the death of Stalin. Komaromi's extensive academic study is devoted to samizdat, or the production and circulation of informal, uncensored, "self-published" texts in the post-Stalin Soviet Union. Samizdat did not emerge as a reaction to oppression, as Komaromi points out. Rather, the partial liberalization of speech under the Soviet leader Nikita Khrushchev in the mid-1950s inspired small groups of individuals to push the boundaries and produce periodicals on a broad variety of topics usually suppressed, banned, or dismissed by the communist authorities. Based on a vast selection of samizdat periodicals (a list takes up around 30 pages), Komaromi portrays a diverse unofficial public sphere that included rights activists; nationalist, religious, and gender-based groups; literary and artistic communities; and fans of rock music and "bard" music (akin to folk), among others. These periodicals were mostly typewritten, five or six carbon copies at a time, but Komaromi also cites the amazing example of a group of unregistered Baptists who built their own printing presses out of "washing machine wringer rollers, bicycle pedals and chains, and other assorted materials" that could be disassembled at short notice to avoid detection by the authorities.

Based on a vast body of academic literature and archival materials, Huxtable traces the evolution of the youth newspaper *Komsomolskaya Pravda*, the third-largest Soviet daily, to illustrate Soviet social dynamics during the two decades that followed Stalin's death in 1953. He studies editorial meetings in which *KP* journalists debated the paper's mission and searched for innovations, one of the most striking being the launch of a short-lived in-house polling organization after about two decades when the science and practice of sociology were banned under Stalin. The early post-Stalin period was inspired by the new Soviet leadership's efforts to reestablish true Leninist principles after decades of terror, to reignite enthusiasm for building communism, and to make Soviet socialism more humane. Nevertheless, the earnest pursuit of honesty coexisted with censorship and efforts to veil the memory of the dark past. Attempts to overcome "formalism" and "didacticism" were constrained by mandatory adherence to Marxist dogma. And although journalists may have seen themselves as agents of social change, they remained servants of the Communist Party. In later years, and especially after the Soviet invasion of Czechoslovakia in 1968, enthusiasm for revival had vanished, consumerism superseded loftier pursuits, and the party tightened its constraints over journalists.

The Moralist International: Russia in the Global Culture Wars
BY KRISTINA STOECKL AND DMITRY UZLANER. Fordham University Press, 2022, 208 pp.

In their short but in-depth book, Stoeckl and Uzlaner offer an interpretation of Russia's powerful shift toward moral conservatism and "traditional values" under President Vladimir Putin. The authors dispute the broadly accepted view that ascribes this turn exclusively to the historical belief in Russia's "special path," the Russian Orthodox faith, or an enduring national identity. Instead, they demonstrate the importance of transnational influences in Russia's embrace of conservatism and explore Russia's place in the global culture wars. The Russian Orthodox Church had no position on social issues under communism, and in the early post-Soviet period, it had little to say about the challenges of social modernity related to abortion, gender, or changing views of the family. It accepted instruction from Western teachers, including the Christian right in the United States. Ironically, as Russia moved toward vehement anti-Westernism, the Russian Orthodox Church and Russian government officials continued to welcome contacts with conservative U.S. organizations. Gradually, Russia grew from student to seasoned practitioner in the global culture wars and claimed the mantle of "the last protector of traditional Christian values." In the past decade, Putin has personally supplanted the church as the chief paragon of orthodox moral values, making his traditionalism a pivotal part of his domestic and foreign political agendas.

Asia and Pacific

ANDREW J. NATHAN

Deadly Decision in Beijing: Succession Politics, Protest Repression, and the 1989 Tiananmen Massacre
BY YANG SU. Cambridge University Press, 2023, 330 pp.

Su rejects the conventional view—based partly on *The Tiananmen Papers*, a 2001 compilation of secret Chinese official documents that I co-edited—that the Chinese leader Deng Xiaoping ordered a brutal military attack on pro-democracy demonstrators in Beijing in 1989 to suppress what he saw as an existential threat to the ruling party. Instead, the author constructs a lively narrative of elite maneuvering in which Deng first prolonged the crisis and then used excessive force against the protesters in order to purge the liberal faction led by the Communist Party's general secretary, Zhao Ziyang. The murders of students and the imprisoning of workers were incidental to this political gambit. After the crisis, Deng sidelined the conservatives, led by Premier Li Peng, who wanted to maintain a command economy. By the time he died in 1997, Deng had set China on the course where it remains today, with a closed political system and a relatively open economy.

Patrol and Persuade: A Follow-Up Investigation to 110 Overseas
BY SAFEGUARD DEFENDERS. Safeguard Defenders, 2022, 33 pp.

In this report, the nongovernmental organization Safeguard Defenders reveals the existence of 102 "overseas police service stations" that Chinese authorities have installed in 53 countries without the permission of the host governments. The Chinese media boast that agents in these stations have "persuaded" hundreds of thousands of criminal suspects to return home voluntarily to face justice. But Safeguard Defenders labels the work of these agents "transnational repression" because they use threats against family members back home and other coercive tactics to force their targets abroad, often people accused of corruption, to surrender. Other reports on the Safeguard Defenders website discuss the "Fox Hunt" and "Sky Net" programs through which Chinese agents have repatriated fugitives and their assets; Beijing's use of Interpol "red notices" to hunt down China's critics; and abusive practices in China used to target dissidents, including house arrest, enforced disappearances, detention in psychiatric prisons, show trials, and televised forced confessions.

Hostile Forces: How the Chinese Communist Party Resists International Pressure on Human Rights
BY JAMIE J. GRUFFYDD-JONES. Oxford University Press, 2022, 272 pp.

The Chinese government does not always prevent foreign criticisms of its human rights record from reaching its citizens.

If the critique comes from a "hostile foreign power," such as the United States, and seems to threaten a core interest, such as control of Tibet, or to impugn the Chinese system as a whole, official media are happy to spread the story to show how unjustly foreigners are treating China. In so doing, Gruffydd-Jones's careful research demonstrates, Beijing manages to dampen public demands for human rights reforms. Authorities are more alarmed by criticisms that focus on individual cases, come from sources not locked in a geopolitical competition with China, or place blame on particular leaders rather than for the system writ large; they censor such critiques. The same logic works in other authoritarian regimes as well. This dynamic poses a dilemma for U.S. diplomats and nongovernmental organizations: the more strongly they call out human rights violations, the less effective they are in generating internal pressure for change.

Unity Through Division: Political Islam, Representation, and Democracy in Indonesia
BY DIEGO FOSSATI. Cambridge University Press, 2022, 250 pp.

Fossati designed a series of surveys to find out why the rise of political Islam after Indonesia's democratic transition in 1998 has not destabilized the country's politics. Patronage relations play a big role in elections, as do economic issues, but he finds that religious affiliations are a major determinant of how people vote. Indonesians who believe that Islam should enjoy a privileged status in state policy form a majority of the electorate, and they vote at high rates. The government has not—so far—met most of their demands. Yet these voters report high levels of satisfaction with the way democracy works in their country. It is true that Indonesian politics are increasingly polarized. But so far, the belief among Islamist voters that the political system is listening to them has helped stabilize Indonesia.

Chasing Freedom: The Philippines' Long Journey to Democratic Ambivalence
BY ADELE WEBB. Liverpool University Press, 2021, 240 pp.

The middle classes are supposed to drive democratic reform, but in the Philippines, those citizens have often supported authoritarians, such as Ferdinand Marcos and Rodrigo Duterte. Webb finds the roots of this ambivalence not in an immature political culture, for which Filipinos are often blamed and blame themselves, but in the legacies of colonization by the United States. From 1898 to 1946, Washington imposed a set of U.S.-style democratic institutions while rejecting Filipino demands for independence (often on racist grounds). The United States continued to dominate the archipelago country after its independence in 1946. As a result, educated Filipinos often chose to support populist nationalists, such as Marcos and Duterte, who claimed to stand up to U.S. interference and to fight crime and corruption. But at other times, the middle class has risen up against such leaders, as it did against Marcos in the 1980s when political rights and civil liberties seemed under assault.

Plato Goes to China: The Greek Classics and Chinese Nationalism
BY SHADI BARTSCH. Princeton University Press, 2023, 304 pp.

Chinese public intellectuals see the Greek classics as a key to understanding the differences between China and the West. Bartsch, a classicist, undertook the considerable challenge of learning Chinese to find out what the Chinese saw in the ancient texts. In an agile and often witty critique, she shows that Chinese thinkers in the more liberal 1980s borrowed Aristotle's emphasis on the active citizen and the value of reason to explain why Western societies were successful, implying that China should reform accordingly. By contrast, in the 1990s and after, conservative nationalists cited the theories of Plato's *Republic* to show that China was right to cultivate meritocracy and social harmony and that the West had lost its way in selfish individualism. The often esoteric readings of Western texts by Chinese intellectuals invite Bartsch's own esoteric interpretations of their texts: if China is indeed superior, readers may wonder, why do their intellectuals feel compelled to borrow the authority of Western classics to prove it? Perhaps a barb against the regime is hidden in Chinese praise of Plato's "noble lie," the idea that the elite can propagate a myth to maintain social cohesion. Bartsch shows one thing for sure: ideologies shape the way people read texts.

Middle East

LISA ANDERSON

A Vanishing West in the Middle East: The Recent History of U.S.-Europe Cooperation in the Region
BY CHARLES THÉPAUT. Bloomsbury Academic Press, 2022, 272 pp.

Thépaut, a French diplomat, carefully catalogs decades of foolishness and failure in this revealing chronicle of U.S.-European efforts at cooperation in the Middle East since the end of the Cold War. As a friendly but dispassionate observer, he begins with an analysis of the dysfunctions of U.S. policymaking. American officials rarely consult with allies as much as they should because they have to spend so much time managing interagency coordination: once the National Security Council, the State and Defense Departments, and Congress agree on a course of action, policymakers do not have much room to adjust based on the views or preferences of other actors. Europeans are hardly better: the EU's policies rarely represent the consensus view of its members, and individual countries routinely work at cross-purposes, pursuing their own goals even when they undermine their putative partners. Thépaut argues that whatever the appeal of Western values and intentions, the inept execution of Western policies has left Middle Eastern countries searching for new supporters and advisers in an increasingly complex and competitive international system.

This Arab Life: A Generation's Journey Into Silence
BY AMAL GHANDOUR. Bold Story Press, 2022, 168 pp.

A mix of memoir and commentary, this slim volume offers an unusually candid glimpse into the rueful bewilderment of Arab elites who have been unable to provide for their children what they had hoped. Born in Lebanon in the early 1960s, raised in privilege there and in Jordan, and educated in the United States, Ghandour expected to live the fruitful, fulfilling life her devoted parents wanted for her. With the uprisings of the past decade as backdrop, she muses about her generation's ignorance of, complicity in, and ultimately defeat by political repression and economic corruption. In effect, she invites readers to eavesdrop on conversations that echoed across the Middle East over countless family dinners. The 2010–11 rebellions began with the hope that young people would accomplish what their parents had failed to achieve. But that expectation turned to shame and rage at the impotence of liberal elites, the failures of the intelligentsia, and the temptations of emigrating to the Gulf, where "stability, order, and good pay is freedom enough for an exhausted youth." In taking readers into her confidence, Ghandour reveals the pain of a generation thwarted by avarice and autocracy.

Yemen in the Shadow of Transition: Pursuing Justice Amid War
BY STACEY PHILBRICK YADAV. Oxford University Press, 2023, 288 pp.

Drawing on nearly two decades of research in Yemen, Philbrick Yadav traces the causes and consequences of the uprising of 2011, with an emphasis on the preoccupation of Yemeni activists, community organizers, educators, and civil society leaders with questions of justice. She crafts an unusually fine grained and often quite inspiring view of the varied communities and advocates who have pursued issues of transitional justice during the past decades of conflict over unification, regime change, and civil war in Yemen. She unearths the vibrant debates that have taken place beneath the drama of high politics, carnage, and destruction, offering remarkably perceptive critiques of international peace-building and humanitarian aid efforts, which have neglected local priorities and failed to address questions of justice. In a revealing insight into the relationship between scholarship and policy, Philbrick Yadav reports that her Yemeni colleagues understand research itself as a form of working toward justice, giving voice to the unheard and documenting the overlooked.

Staple Security: Bread and Wheat in Egypt
BY JESSICA BARNES. Duke University Press, 2022, 320 pp.

Egypt is the world's largest importer of wheat, yet imports represent less than half the wheat consumed in the country annually. In colloquial Egyptian Arabic, the word for bread is *aish*, which also means "life." Egyptians eat bread with every meal, and the government heavily subsidizes the popular *aish baladi* ("local bread," roughly); for the 70 percent of the Egyptians who have ration cards, ten loaves cost less than a dime. Ever since bread riots nearly upended reform plans in 1977, successive governments have carefully guarded the subsidy programs. But as Barnes notes, most of the wheat grown in Egypt never reaches the market at all, constituting instead a part of the mix of subsistence crops planted annually by farmers for their own households. The government is the sole legal buyer of domestic wheat, supplementing it with imports managed by the Ministry of Supply, which then distributes the grain to mills that provide flour to millions of private bakeries. The continuing reliance of Egyptian farmers on subsistence agriculture is quite striking in a country that has long produced cotton and other agricultural goods for global markets; the government's overriding preoccupation with ensuring stability ensures that market forces do not alter that calculus.

Africa

NICOLAS VAN DE WALLE

The Plot to Save South Africa: The Week Mandela Averted Civil War and Forged a New Nation
BY JUSTICE MALALA. Simon & Schuster, 2023, 352 pp.

The assassination in 1993 of Chris Hani, a charismatic and popular young African National Congress leader, threw South Africa's transition out of apartheid into a deep crisis. Radicals on both sides demanded that Nelson Mandela, the ANC head, and President Frederik Willem de Klerk not make any further concessions in negotiations. In this trenchant narrative of the days that followed the murder, Malala masterfully weaves the different threads of the story. The white supremacists who killed Hani hoped the murder would spark a wave of vengeful violence by Blacks that would convince the white minority it had no future in a majority-ruled country. The ploy failed. The ANC stirred popular protests but managed to limit the violence that ensued from them. It simultaneously worked to relaunch negotiations with the government. Malala's account portrays de Klerk as a leader with limited vision and suggests that a crisis was averted thanks only to Mandela's political skills and the ingenuity and pragmatism of the two leaders in charge of negotiations, the ANC's Cyril Ramaphosa (South Africa's current president) and the government minister Roelf Meyer. A speech that

Mandela delivered in the wake of the assassination, in which he appealed for calm and inclusion, established him firmly as the country's moral leader. A year later, national elections would make him president.

Pastoral Power, Clerical State: Pentecostalism, Gender, and Sexuality in Nigeria
BY EBENEZER OBADARE.
Notre Dame Press, 2022, 222 pp.

Pentecostalism is the fastest-growing religion not only in Nigeria but also across much of Africa. In his second book focused on the rising popularity of the faith, Obadare argues that Pentecostal preachers have become figures of national authority and prestige, exercising more influence over Nigerian society and politics. He argues that the decline of Nigeria's universities and intellectuals, as a result of economic crises in the 1980s and 1990s, led to a transfer of prestige in the public sphere from scholars to pastors: a system of authority based on reason has transformed into one based on revelation. The most significant Pentecostal pastors are skillful political and religious entrepreneurs, developing new spiritual narratives to attract and influence parishioners and turning their churches into the engines of substantial revenue-yielding empires. The pastors' prominence and wealth allow them to play an increasingly important role in national politics as power brokers.

China's Rise in the Global South: The Middle East, Africa, and Beijing's Alternative World Order
BY DAWN C. MURPHY. Stanford University Press, 2022, 408 pp.

Murphy assesses the aims and ambitions of Chinese policy in Africa and the Middle East based on a sweeping review of China's diplomatic, military, trade, aid, and investment activities over the last 30 years. She argues that China's actions should be understood as evidence of its desire to develop an alternative world order that will allow China to interact with these two regions on its own terms. This imperative necessarily entails ratcheting up competition with the existing Western-dominated regional order. Still, Murphy insists, the demands of this competition will not drive China to pursue any territorial ambitions in these regions, nor will it prevent China from cooperating with the United States in certain areas. Murphy's discussion of how China uses the regular regional forums it organizes is excellent, as is her analysis of the relationships China has forged in military cooperation, foreign aid, and trade. Her book suffers, however, from neglecting to consider how growing sovereign debt issues in countries in both regions will affect their relations with China.

Ugandan Agency Within China-Africa Relations: President Museveni and China's Foreign Policy in East Africa
BY BARNEY WALSH. Bloomsbury Academic Press, 2022, 232 pp.

Much of the recent literature on Chinese-African relations focuses on Chinese initiatives and policies but affords little agency to African actors, who are typically portrayed as passive, albeit willing, partners. Walsh's well-argued book does the opposite. It considers how Uganda's government under President Yoweri Museveni has proactively used its relationship with China to strengthen its hold on domestic power and project influence throughout east Africa. In particular, Walsh notes that Museveni has skillfully turned Chinese investments in infrastructure into a means of placing Uganda at the center of the regional integration efforts of the East African Community, an intergovernmental organization. Beijing's policies in Africa are often improvised and not based on an overarching strategy, allowing Museveni to shrewdly manipulate the direction of Chinese efforts and investment to the benefit of Ugandan security. For instance, Museveni managed to piggyback on a joint Chinese-Kenyan project to build an oil pipeline to the Indian Ocean from South Sudan. The pipeline originally did not involve Uganda, but Museveni adroitly negotiated with his EAC partners to link it to Uganda's oil resources.

Violence in Rural South Africa, 1880–1963
BY SEAN REDDING. University of Wisconsin Press, 2023, 216 pp.

High levels of violence appear to have plagued rural South Africa in the late nineteenth century and the first half of the twentieth century. The apartheid state understood this violence disdainfully as the result of the cultural proclivities of traditional African society. In this fascinating study, Redding uses court archives of legal proceedings to argue that, in fact, much of the violence of that era stemmed from African responses to the disruptions caused by the emerging apartheid state. She documents well how African powerlessness led to violent incidents over matters such as marriage and land rights. More interestingly, Redding suggests that over time, Africans found ways to explain this violence to the state so they could better navigate the logic of the apartheid judicial system. For instance, violence perpetrated by women appears in court records in the form of accusations of witchcraft, when that violence was much more likely the result of women struggling to cope with the harsh social realities imposed by white minority rule.

Letters to the Editor

Riyadh's Way

To the Editor:

F. Gregory Gause III ("The Kingdom and the Power," January/February 2023) accurately analyzes the shifting power relations between the United States and Saudi Arabia, reflected in Riyadh's flaunting of its expanded ties with China while snubbing U.S. pleas for increased oil output and support for the Ukraine war. But Gause glosses over the true costs of the United States' unprecedented coddling of the Saudi regime, including enabling its catastrophic war in Yemen with billions of dollars in U.S. weapons and military support, which needlessly cost over 500,000 Yemeni lives and destabilized the Gulf region. Gause also fails to question the primary driver of bipartisan efforts to woo Saudi Arabia—to persuade the Saudis to sign the Abraham Accords—even though the price that the Saudi regime now demands from the United States is a dangerous and an ill-conceived security guarantee that risks dragging Washington further into a sociopathic leader's reckless forays in the region. Sadly, U.S. policies on Saudi Arabia and throughout the Middle East have been corrupted by lobbying from foreign governments and the defense industry. A revolving door has allowed hundreds of military and civilian officials to trade up for lucrative jobs in the Gulf, including in the Kingdom, tainting the integrity of their decision-making in office. The question is not whether the United States should cooperate with the Kingdom, as Gause puts it, but to what extent Washington should arm and protect a vicious and wealthy government that shares neither the values nor the interests of the United States.

SARAH LEAH WHITSON

Whitson is the executive director of DAWN, Democracy for the Arab World Now.

Gause replies:

The implication in Sarah Leah Whitson's letter is that Saudi Arabia is uniquely evil among the countries of the Middle East with which the United States does business. The assertion that Saudi Arabia does not share interests with the United States is refuted by the policies of administrations, Republican and Democratic, over the past nine decades. Readers of this magazine can assess for themselves the contention that Riyadh is singularly immoral in a region that includes the Assad regime, the Islamic Republic of Iran, the military government of Egypt, the nascent dictatorship of Tunisia, the continuing Israeli occupation of Palestinian territories, and the various militias that contend for power throughout.

Open Office

To the Editor:
Amy Zegart ("Open Secrets," January/February 2023) makes a compelling argument for greater investment in open-source intelligence. She observes that as long as it "remains embedded in secret agencies that value clandestine information above all, it will languish." The solution, she argues, is to create a new agency dedicated to this form of intelligence. But her eagerness to bypass existing agencies carries significant risks.

Zegart proposes that a new agency could hire experts without security clearances. But doing so would make it easier for hostile foreign intelligence services to plant spies. Although uncleared employees might not have direct contact with classified information, they would require access to sensitive information technology systems—access that would give them insight into U.S. intelligence.

The real problem with open-source intelligence is its vulnerability to manipulation. Disinformation is rife in the era of great-power competition. The new agency's uncleared cadre would not be able to use other agencies' classified insights to validate or refute material, including potential deep fakes. Intelligence collection works best when agencies are integrated. Employees without security clearances would be unable to collaborate with their counterparts in the CIA, the NSA, and other agencies.

Zegart is right that the U.S. government must do more with open-source intelligence. But siloing such information in its own agency is not the answer. Rather, established U.S. intelligence agencies should better integrate information from open sources into their insights from clandestine ones.

DOUGLAS LONDON
London served in the CIA's Clandestine Service for more than 34 years, including three assignments as a chief of station.

Zegart replies:
Douglas London raises important risks of open-source intelligence and the potential pitfalls of a new agency. But these are challenges to be managed, not justifications for continuing down the current failing path. Integrating open-source intelligence doesn't work well today. It won't work tomorrow without a new agency to drive it. The idea that only classified information can validate or refute open-source material is outdated; nongovernmental open-source analysts are already countering deception with unclassified sources. And although managing counterintelligence risk is essential, so, too, is hiring more technical talent much faster, which an open-source agency can do. London's approach of doing more with the current system is no solution. Gone are the days when integrating open-source information meant sprinkling news stories in intelligence reports. Insights from data now freely available are transformational. Without a new agency, the U.S. government will face the perils of the open-source revolution without harnessing its benefits. The biggest risk of all is changing nothing.

Foreign Affairs (ISSN 00157120), May/June 2023, Volume 102, Number 3. Published six times annually (January, March, May, July, September, November) at 58 East 68th Street, New York, NY 10065. Print subscriptions: U.S., $54.95; Canada, $66.95; other countries via air, $89.95 per year. Canadian Publication Mail–Mail # 1572121. Periodicals postage paid in New York, NY, and at additional mailing offices. POSTMASTER: Send address changes to *Foreign Affairs*, P.O. Box 324, Congers, NY 10920. From time to time, we permit certain carefully screened companies to send our subscribers information about products or services that we believe will be of interest. If you prefer not to receive such information, please contact us at the Congers, NY, address indicated above.

July 1943

"The Realities in Africa"

W. E. B. DU BOIS

In 1943, W. E. B. Du Bois, a leading scholar and civil rights activist, examined how capitalism and race relations were influencing World War II. The ongoing conflict was a competition for colonies, he argued, and the postwar fate of Africa was an afterthought for the belligerents. His allegations echo today, when many in Africa think China, Russia, and the United States still view the continent as an arena for competition rather than important in its own right.

The World War of 1914–1918 was caused in part by the German demand for a larger share in the domination over labor and in the exploitation of raw materials in Asia and Africa. An important aspect of the World War of 1939 is the competition for the profit of Asiatic labor and materials—competition in part between European countries, in part between those countries and Japan. Submerged labor is revolting in the East Indies, Burma and India itself. It would be a grave mistake to think that Africans are not asking the same questions that Asiatics are: "Is it a white man's war?"

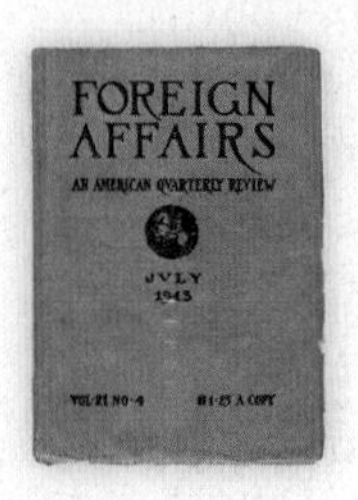

The social development of Africa for the welfare of the Africans, with educated Africans in charge of the program, would certainly interfere with the private profits of foreign investment and would ultimately change the entire relationship of Africa to the modern world. Is the development of Africa for the welfare of Africans the aim? Or is the aim a world dominated by Anglo-Saxons, or at least by the stock of white Europe? If the aim is to keep Africa in subjection just as long as possible, will this not plant the seeds of future hatreds and more war?

One would think that Africa, so important in world trade and world industrial organization and containing at least 125,000,000 people, would be carefully considered today in any plan for postwar reconstruction. This does not seem to be the case. When we examine the plans which have been published we find either no mention of Africa or only vague references.